RESERVATION REELISM

MICHELLE H. RAHEJA

Reservation

UNIVERSITY OF NEBRASKA PRESS   LINCOLN AND LONDON

Reelism

Redfacing, Visual Sovereignty, and
Representations of Native Americans in Film

A version of chapter 5 first appeared as "Reading
Nanook's Smile" in *American Quarterly* 59.4
(2007): 1159–85. Reprinted with permission by
The Johns Hopkins University Press. Copyright
© 2007 American Studies Association. A version
of the epilogue first appeared online at *In Media
Res* at http://mediacommons.futureofthebook.org.
In Media Res is a MediaCommons project.

Library of Congress Cataloging-in-Publication Data
Raheja, Michelle H.
Reservation reelism: redfacing, visual
sovereignty, and representations of Native
Americans in film / Michelle H. Raheja. p. cm.
Includes bibliographical references and index.
ISBN 978-0-8032-1126-1 (cloth: alk. paper)
ISBN 978-0-8032-4597-6 (paper: alk. paper)
1. Indians in motion pictures. 2. Indigenous
peoples in motion pictures. 3. Indians in the
motion picture industry—United States.
4. Stereotypes (Social psychology) in motion
pictures. 5. Motion pictures—United
States—History—20th century. I. Title.
PN1995.9.I48R34 2010
302.23089—dc22 2010026528

Set in New Caledonia by Kim Essman.
Designed by Nathan Putens.

Contents

List of Illustrations *vi*

Preface *ix*

Acknowledgments *xv*

1 Toward a Genealogy of Indigenous Film
   Theory: Reading Hollywood Indians *1*

2 Ideologies of (In)Visibility: Redfacing,
   Gender, and Moving Images *46*

3 Tears and Trash: Economies of
   Redfacing and the Ghostly Indian *102*

4 Prophesizing on the Virtual Reservation:
   Imprint and *It Starts with a Whisper* *145*

5 Visual Sovereignty, Indigenous
   Revisions of Ethnography, and
   Atanarjuat (The Fast Runner) *190*

6 Epilogue *221*

   Notes *241*

   Bibliography *291*

   Index *319*

Illustrations

1 Lizzie Pablo, a Nez Perce actor, during an audition for *Northwest Passage* 14

2 Director Edwin Carewe consults with actors Lupe Velez and John Boles 23

3 James Young Deer and Princess Red Wing in *Young Deer's Return* (1910) 24

4 Nipo T. Strongheart 26

5 Jay Silverheels as Tonto in *The Lone Ranger* (1949) 27

6 Joseph "Suni" Vance Chorre 28

7 Richard Davis Thunderbird 33

8 Luther Standing Bear in regalia 38

9 *Nova Reperta (New Inventions of Modern Times)/America* 48

10 Minnie Ha Ha and Mabel Normand from *The Mack Sennett Weekly* (1917) 55

11 Mildred Nelson, Molly Spotted Elk's younger sister 57

12 Minnie (Minnie Ha Ha) tries on a hat in *Mickey* (1918) 81

13 Chauncey Yellow Robe delivering his prologue in *The Silent Enemy* (1930) 89

14 Neewa (Molly Spotted Elk) flees from a bear attack before being rescued in *The Silent Enemy* (1930) 92

15 Michelle Olson as Molly Spotted Elk in *April in Paris* 97

16 Michelle Olson as Molly Spotted Elk in *Evening in Paris* 98

17 Iron Eyes Cody from the Keep America Beautiful public service announcement *103*

18 Iron Eyes Cody as he appeared in 1984 *112*

19 Characters from James Luna's *Petroglyphs in Motion* (2001) *154*

20 Tonantzin Carmelo as Shayla Stonefeather in *Imprint* (2007) *163*

21 Dave Bald Eagle plays a medicine man in *Imprint* (2007) *165*

22 Concluding scene from *Imprint* (2007) *169*

23 Shanna (Elizabeth Burning) in *It Starts with a Whisper* (1993) *174*

24 Shanna meets Elijah Harper in *It Starts with a Whisper* (1993) *177*

25 Image from Shelley Niro's *Tree* (2006) *182*

26 Nanook (Allakariallak) at the trading
    post in *Nanook of the North* (1922) *192*

27 Panikpak (Madeline Ivalu) and
    Qulitalik Pauloosie (Qulitalik) drive
    evil away from the community at the
    close of *Atanarjuat* (2001) *215*

28 Cast and crew wave from boat while
    credits roll in *Atanarjuat* (2001) *219*

29 Kelley Davis and Andrew Loeffler protest
    school ban on Thanksgiving costumes *228*

30 Image from *Indigenous
    Holocaust* (2008) *239*

Preface

Reel and Real Worlds

Stemming from a long tradition of staged performances such as the Wild West shows that were themselves informed by American literature's obsession with Native American plots and subplots, film and visual culture have provided the primary representational field on which Native American images have been displayed to dominant culture audiences in the twentieth and twenty-first centuries.[1] But these representations have also been key to formulating Indigenous people's own self images. Spokane and Coeur d'Alene writer and filmmaker Sherman Alexie recalls watching western films on television as a child: "I hated Tonto then and I hate him now. However, despite my hatred of Tonto, I loved movies about Indians, loved them beyond all reasoning and saw no fault in any of them."[2] For many Native people, it has been possible to despise the numerous abject, stereotypical characters Native Americans were forced to play and deeply enjoy and relate to other images that resonate in some way with lived experiences of tribal peoples or undermine stereotypes in a visual field that otherwise erased Indigenous history.

The often excluded or undervalued stories and acts of "survivance" of Native American spectators, filmmakers, and actors, and the memories of their descendants have inspired me to imagine the early half of the twentieth century as an era of heartache and happiness, poverty and prosperity, loss, revitalization, and creation of traditions.[3] Because most twentieth-century cinematic images of Indigenous peoples often either reflected important pressures that Native communities were facing or completely elided Native concerns in ways that demonstrate deep-seated cultural anxieties, film scholarship provides a useful framework of analysis for considering how Native Americans have responded to change and persisted in keeping and improvising traditions from the silent film era to the present. Analyzing cinematic images of Native Americans produced by both Indigenous and non-Indigenous artists of the early film period is also vital to understanding how contemporary Native American filmmakers and visual artists engage and critique this field of discourse.

Paul Chaat Smith has argued, "The movies loom so large for Indians because they have defined our self-image as well as told the entire planet how we live, look, scream, and kill."⁴ The plotlines of most westerns feature Native Americans living outside of their historical, geographical, and cultural context, situated in the past with no viable future. Native Americans are often hypervisible in North American films, especially in films produced during the first half of the twentieth century; at the same time they are rendered invisible through plotlines that reinforce the trope of Indigenous people as vanishing or inconsequential, they receive few speaking parts, and they are often uncredited.

Certainly one of the more insidious effects of Hollywood's racial optics regime was that, despite intentional and unintentional inaccuracies, the films served as pedagogy and knowledge production for spectators. These films have been highly influential in shaping perceptions of Native Americans as, for example, a dying race that is prone to alcoholism and is inherently unable and unwilling to adapt to change. Even in films that express admiration for Native Americans, such as Cecil B. DeMille's *The Squaw Man* (1914) or Delmer Daves's *Broken Arrow* (1950), seemingly respectful and balanced representations are often rooted in uncritical, problematic racial ideologies that reflect unexamined notions of Native American culture on the part of the director and on the part of North American society as a whole.

As Alexie's discussion of the figure of Tonto suggests, narrative film has provided a space in which to critique the often fantastic and surreal images of Native Americans. But these cinematic and televisual experiences also enable Indigenous spectators to engage critically with the artifacts of imagined cultural knowledge produced by the films and their long political, narrative, and historical context, stretching from at least 1492 to the present, particularly as film viewers intuited that those images were the partial products of Native actors. These reactions to films are complicated because Native American spectators neither wholly identified with the representations onscreen nor did they entirely reject them. This viewing practice is similar to what Rey Chow calls "ethnic spectatorship," a critical examination of the often intractable and egregious stereotypical spectacles of racialized popular images.[5] Ethnic spectatorship, according to Chow, also involves a politics of identification that radically re-reads the viewing practices of ethnic and racialized spectators as a "suturing" exercise predicated on a sophisticated understanding of what Teresa de Lauretis terms narrative "illusion" rather than one that creates a split or duped self.[6] Narrative film provided a space in which to critique the often fantastic and surreal popular culture images of Native Americans. For spectators like Alexie, films with Native American plots and subplots capture the imagination by signifying at least some sort of *presence*, however vexed, in a representational field defined primarily by *absence*.

This book is my attempt to see an alternate vision of Native American representation and spectatorship as products of a complicated and sometimes discomfiting history with a vibrant, equally complex future rather than only as abject repositories of the victimized. In it, I retrieve and decipher Native American representations in mainstream feature-length films and examine how these images have been reanimated and subjected to scrutiny by contemporary Indigenous narrative and experimental filmmakers. I suggest an Indigenous film theory that focuses on what I call "redfacing," the process and politics of playing Indian; the "virtual reservation," the imagined and imaginative sites produced by the cinema; and "visual sovereignty," a concept specific to visual culture and aesthetics, but rooted in thinking about sovereignty in other contexts. The book begins with an analysis of early feature-length films with Native American plots and then engages these images of Indigenous peoples in conversation with more recent visual culture production by Native American artists. I argue that early Hollywood cinema had more Native American "presences" than subsequent eras in the history of the studio system. It is these presences that allow Native American actors and representations to enter the public memory and take on their own social life, even if in sometimes racist and stereotyped fashion. As such, the representations from early Hollywood are now the basis, sustained over generations, for contemporary Native American narrative cinema, characterized by Indigenous-centered aesthetics and grassroots filmmaking.

The violence of invisibility has plagued Native American communities primarily through its contradictions. Native Americans remain hypervisible in commercial fields such as advertising and consumerism, but virtually invisible when it comes to most everything else of substance.[7] One of the consequences of this contradiction is that Native Americans stand at the center of the dominant culture's self-definition because Euro-American identity submerged and formed upon the textual and visual culture register of the Indigenous "Other."[8] This Manichean binary required the rendering of Native Americans as invisible through the rhetoric of the vanishing Indian.[9] Euro-Americans, therefore, desired a highly controlled, mass-mediated, and virtual Native presence at the same time that Indigenous peoples were deemed threatening, excessive, savage, and less-than-human. "We are shape-shifters in the national consciousness," Smith writes, "accidental survivors, unwanted reminders of disagreeable events."[10]

Historically, it has perhaps been better to be represented in some way, however problematic and contradictory, than to remain invisible, a body that did not register in any important way in the national imagination. Filmic images, taken alongside the range of other visual artifacts circulating in the twentieth century, therefore instilled some "life" through recognition and presence on the virtual reservation as moving pictures (in the sense of film's affective economy and its ability to animate communities that non-Indians perceived as dying or dead) for Native people who were considered doomed, defeated, vanished, or ghostly. This was particularly true in the early-cinema period when Indigenous-themed films were often set in the present, even as they simultaneously operated to homogenize very distinct tribal communities and portrayed tribal peoples along a "savage-noble" continuum.

Filmic images provided a kind of shield that protected Native American spectators from the burden of representation that would have forced them to lay bare often-private cultural practices (practices that for many were already marginalized within a marginalized field that privileged Southwestern and Plains Indian cultural identities as an Indigenous norm). While Native American spectators ambiguously empathized and identified with the caricatured portraits of Native Americans onscreen, these images flagged a broader, offscreen reality by the mere fact of their existence. They took some pressure off individuals to explain "Indian culture" to people who would have had a hard time understanding experiences that fell outside the hegemonic images of stereotyped Native Americans. The "reelism" of film resides in its ability to function as a placeholder: as a representational practice it does not mirror reality but can enact important cultural work as an art form with ties to the world of everyday practices and the imaginative sphere of the possible.

The very thing that makes early twentieth-century filmic Native American images so offensive to contemporary sensibilities was, ironically, what made them relatively unproblematic, even perhaps comforting, for spectators who were offered few alternative mass media self-representations. They could be visible in a culture that invested in the rhetoric of the vanishing Indian, given the western film genre's ubiquity and excessive, if highly vexed, attention to Native Americans. They could also remain anonymous behind the screen that the stereotypical images offered. These seemingly contradictory desires—to be both visible in a nation that had already written Native America's obituary and to be hidden from further violence in the face of overwhelming ignorance by non-Indians—coalesced around an understanding, through the liminal, physical space of the cinema, of Native American identity as a placeholder for visual sovereignty. This space could simultaneously screen some issues of importance to Native people as creative engagement rather than sociological effect and could connect with the critical work of sovereignty and decolonization that occurs offscreen (and often in spite of Hollywood).

Acknowledgments

This book would not have been possible without the generosity, encouragement, good humor, and support of a legion of colleagues, friends, and family. I have been truly blessed to bring this project to completion under the guidance of such wonderful people and I am eternally grateful. I am indebted to so many that it is difficult to single out individuals and I apologize to those whose names I have not included. I am fortunate to be a member of a collegial and supportive academic department. The English department at the University of California, Riverside (UCR) has consistently and unflaggingly challenged and encouraged this project. Sincere and humble thanks to Katherine Kinney—who served as a steadfast, skillful, and compassionate chair—and to Susan Brown, Kathleen Carter, Tina Feldman, Linda Nellany, and Cindy Redfield, staff members who make good things happen. UCR has been an intellectually rigorous and inspiring place from which to write this book. Special thanks to my wonderful and exceptional mentors, colleagues, and friends at UCR, many of whom graciously read chapters of this book and who all provided inspiration, support, and sagacity: Geoff Cohen, Stephen Cullenberg, Jennifer Doyle, Lan Duong, Erica Edwards, Keith Harris, Katherine Kinney, Monte Kugel, Molly McGarry, Dylan Rodríguez, Freya Schiwy, Andrea Smith, Cliff Trafzer, and Jonathan Walton. My most appreciative thanks to the brilliant members of my writing groups, who generously read and commented on versions of this book and encouraged me to continue when my enthusiasm for this project flagged: Amalia Cabezas, Tammy Ho, Jodi Kim, Tiffany Lopez, Vorris Nunley, Jacqueline Shea Murphy, Setsu Shigematsu, and Traise Yamamoto. To Lindon

Barrett, whose laughter, intelligence, and subversiveness I miss terribly. I am fortunate, also, to work with so many wonderful and engaged students in the English department and with members of the Native American Student Program at UCR who constantly encourage me to be a better scholar and person.

I would also like to extend my appreciation to many friends and colleagues who graciously read draft chapters, fielded frantic questions, helped refine my arguments, and produced the work that served as inspiration for this book. This list could stretch on endlessly but includes: Chad Allen, Berta Benally, Susan Bernardin, Blackfire (Clayson, Jeneda, and Klee Benally), Bill Brown, Dorothy Christian, Charlotte Cote, Denise Cummings, Thirza Cuthand, Philip Deloria, Anna Everett, Chris Eyre, Peter X. Feng, Christie Firtha, Stephanie Fitzgerald, Sandy Franks, Faye Ginsburg, Rayna Green, Alex Halkin, Sabine Haenni, Joanna Hearne, LeAnne Howe, Shari Huhndorf, Igloolik Isuma Productions, Jim Kreines, Daphne Lamothe, Shannon Leonard, Diana Linden, Carolyn Linn, James Luna, Joe Mancha, Elise Marubbio, David Martinez, Bunny McBride, Kathleen McHugh, Melinda Micco, Muriel Miguel, Rick Monture, Deborah Nelson, Shelley Niro, Chon Noriega, Eve Oishi, Michelle Olson, Kim Orlijan, Patricia Ploesch, Yeidy Rivero, Juana Rodriguez, Jeff Rhyne, Rob Schmidt, Audra Simpson, Jacqueline Stewart, Theresa Tensuan Eli, Jennifer Tilton, Gerald Vizenor, Robert Allen Warrior, Missy Whiteman, and Pamela Wilson. Michael Tsosie deserves a special note of thanks for hours logged as a brilliant interlocutor and best friend. He gave me the gift of laughter with his irreverent and acerbic wit when I needed it most. Thanks, too, to the hundreds of people who generously reached out to my family with support, love, prayers, and advice in November 2008 when collective local concerns about Thanksgiving costumes became national news.

This book owes its existence to the courageous Native American filmmakers and actors who participated in films from the silent era to the present and to their descendants. Thanks, especially, to Steve Smith, Heather Chorre Garcia, Shari Holland, Jean Archambaud Moore, Galina Mala Liss, Ted Mala Jr., and Ted Mala Sr. for generously sharing stories about and images of their relatives. My gratitude is also extended to the present and future producers of Indigenous media who continue to challenge and shape representations of Native people.

Gary Dunham deserves heartfelt thanks for believing in this project from its onset. I have been blessed with an astute and dedicated editor at the University of Nebraska Press, Matthew Bokovoy, who was encouraging and honest, thoughtful and rigorous. His unflagging support of the project and expertise is very much appreciated, as has been the assistance of Elisabeth Chretien and Ann Baker at the University of Nebraska Press. Ann Harrington, the press copyeditor assigned to this project, was also patient and thorough in her attention to this book. Thanks, too, to the anonymous press readers who reviewed the manuscript and provided incisive comments.

I am indebted to the Center for Ideas and Society and to the Academic Senate at UCR for providing me with fellowship awards and to UCLA's Institute of American Cultures/American Indian Studies Program for awarding me a postdoctoral fellowship, all of which enabled me to complete this work. The remarkable and energetic staff and archivists at the following research centers and libraries were also incredibly helpful in guiding me to invaluable archival sources and images: the Abbe Museum, the Autry National Center of the American West, the Braun Research Library at the Southwest Museum, the British Film Institute, the British Museum, the Denver Public Library, the Gary L. Friedman Archives, Marc Wanamaker/Bison Archives, the Margaret Herrick Library at the Academy of Motion Picture Arts and Sciences, the Motion Picture Broadcasting and Recorded Sound Division at the Library of Congress, the National Archives and Records Administration in Riverside and Washington DC, the Robert and Frances Flaherty Study Center, the Tómas Rivera Library at UCR, and the Yakima Valley Libraries.

My deepest appreciation is reserved for my family. Without them, this book would not have been possible. Although my mother did not live to see this book to its completion, her love of westerns inspired it, and she taught me that although film representations of Native Americans were disconnected from reality, they were nevertheless important. I like to think she would have seen herself in the pages of this book. Her sister always believed I would write this book and I cherish her fierce support. My father's passion for reading has always been infectious, and my brothers' generosity of spirit has always been unwavering. Lastly, words can never express my gratitude to Amar Raheja, unflagging source of strength, integrity, and patience. But, most of all, this book owes everything to my daughters for their love, courage, joy, and humor.

RESERVATION REELISM

1 Toward a Genealogy of Indigenous Film Theory

On November 17, 1940, John del Valle wrote an article in the *New York Herald Tribune* announcing a petition to what would become the Bureau of Indian Affairs (BIA) for recognition of a Native American tribe to be named the "DeMille Indians" whose membership was based on professional affiliation rather than consanguinity. Chief Thunder Cloud, the stage name of Victor Daniels, organized the effort and submitted the petition on behalf of a group of actors representing hundreds of Native American entertainers employed by Hollywood. "Hollywood has acquired a permanent colony of representatives of almost all tribes still extant," del Valle noted, "With the cinema as their melting pot, these expatriates are taking on the semblance of a tribe all their own—perhaps the largest tribal group not on any reservation."[1] Thunder Cloud, whose film career spanned twenty-five years, won acclaim as the first Tonto represented on film in the fifteen-part 1938 Republic serial, *The Lone Ranger*, as well as roles in many westerns, including *The Searchers* (1956).[2] He was one of several hundred Native American entertainers who made Southern California a temporary or permanent home in order to work in the film industry. The petition Thunder Cloud submitted may have been a publicity stunt intended to create a new Screen Actors Guild (SAG) of sorts for Native Americans and to draw attention to the already-established, nearly forty-year-old, transnational Hollywood Indian community in Southern California.[3] Or it may have been an ironic attempt to collectivize a group of Indigenous actors whose identifications had undergone a tectonic shift from the specific epistemologies of their multiple homelands to incorporating cross-tribal worldviews influenced by the film industry. The petition is important because it marks a movement from the Hollywood Indian as a constellation of visual images predicated upon white-generated stereotypes to a politicized understanding of the ways these images circulate in popular culture. It also demonstrates how these images are deployed by and in dynamic, often diasporic, contemporary Indigenous communities.

Most likely, it was a combination of both. Prior to 1978, when the Federal Acknowledgment Project was founded within the Department of the Interior (the BIA is an agency within the Department of the Interior), tribal recognition was not a uniform process. It was determined on an ad hoc basis, sometimes granted through congressional action, presidential decree, or individual cases brought before the courts. Recognition required proof of a group's long-standing residency in a particular geographical region and attendant visible and enduring (according to European American standards) linguistic, cultural, and spiritual traditions. Tribal recognition was and still is a very long and arduous process.[4] The group of actors petitioning what was at that time called the Office of Indian Affairs, whose residency in Southern California and whose traditions were very recent by the standards that typically determine a tribe's historical provenance, must have been aware that they would not qualify for federal recognition. Nevertheless, they utilized this legal venue as a platform to publicize their existence and to open up discussion on what constitutes Native American collective identity and sovereignty.

One of the most striking things about the petition is that it sought to legalize an identity of relatively recent origin (that of a transnational professional community living in or near Hollywood) but seemingly made no specific land claims and invoked no treaty rights.[5] Unlike other Indigenous nations whose sovereignty the United States and Canadian governments have recognized and whose identities are rooted in the pre-1492 era and appended to particular geographical locations with specific treaty rights, the DeMille Indians would be a new entity occupying a powerful, mass-mediated virtual reservation. By laying claim to this vexed social and imaginary geography where self-representation and stereotype collide and are continually negotiated, the DeMille Indians were members of a larger body of Indigenous people who have not mattered in the historical archive. But through an examination of the films they helped create and the cultural and pedagogical work Native American actors did off-screen through the production of activist and autobiographical texts, it becomes clear that Hollywood Indians were engaged in a complex dialogue with the prevailing forces of hegemony.

Although the actors did not come from a single tribe with unified linguistic, spiritual, and cultural customs, the petition for recognition is, in some critical ways, predicated on traditional Indigenous practice. Prior to 1492 Native American community identity was often flexible. Communities and families sometimes splintered for a variety of reasons and formed new bands, nations, and confederacies. With the codification of European notions of race in the eighteenth century and enforcement of laws alien to Indigenous people, Native Americans found it increasingly more difficult to maintain a system of creating new political and cultural entities, confederacies, and alliances. The establishment of the Federal

Acknowledgement Program in 1978 further drastically curtailed fluid and kinetic notions of Native American group identity.[6] This program set forth a series of stringent criteria for defining what constitutes a government-recognized tribe in the United States, much of which relies on European American archival records and a relatively simple understanding of Native American history. Without federal recognition, Native American communities do not have much of a voice in governmental decisions affecting them, nor do they benefit from policies afforded to recognized tribes based on their special government-to-government status. According to the National Congress of American Indians, there are currently 562 federally recognized tribes and several hundred more petitioning for recognition through a time-consuming and arduous process.[7]

James Collins argues that the acknowledgement process is unduly complicated and that the criteria are difficult for unrecognized tribes to meet. "These criteria appear reasonable at first glance," he contends, "but they pose a number of difficulties, for they demand multiple evidence of prior recognition, and they require forms of continuity that are exceptional rather than typical among colonized and dominated peoples."[8] The acknowledgement process essentially devalues traditional Native American forms of creating, recognizing, and sustaining community at the same time it imposes European American racial, political, and social definitions on Native people and privileges the invasion-contact period as the static and absolute moment of tribal organization. As the process now stands, it is virtually impossible to federally recognize a tribe formed in the post-eighteenth-century era, thus prohibiting a vital social, cultural, and political formation for Indigenous peoples. While the political exigencies of the current reservation system require the policing of the boundaries between Indians and non-Indians under settler colonialism, it is important to remember that the loss of earlier modes of identification and change is a loss of one of the creative powers exercised by Indigenous people since 1492.

Reservation Reelism

This is a book about (among other things) film, imagination, self-representation, identity, and perception. It describes the ways in which Native American actors, particularly in early North American cinema, interacted with hegemonic representational forces to engage with the image of the Hollywood Indian. I begin this chapter with the anecdote about the DeMille Indians in order to investigate how Native American actors performed critical work both on-screen and off-screen to create cinematic, cultural, political, and geographical spaces for the exploration of images by and for Indigenous communities as early as the turn of the twentieth century.

The DeMille Indians' stories and the narratives they helped create disrupted dominant discourses even as they sometimes, in trickster fashion, seemingly helped validate conventional narratives through the roles they played. The fate of Thunder Cloud's petition for federal recognition remains unclear. It was either never officially submitted, was declined, or never reached the appropriate bureaucrat within the Office of Indian Affairs.[9] Yet the DeMille Indians provide a provocative anecdote through which to explore how Native Americans have intervened in the public sphere via the medium of film and visual culture. They were not always the victims of corporate interests and ongoing attempts at colonization. Native performers were active agents whose work continues to influence, empower, and trouble contemporary Indigenous filmmakers and performers.

Most critically, Thunder Cloud's petition furnishes an early twentieth-century anecdote to counter the tendency in much scholarship on Native Americans to envision Indigenous peoples—particularly those involved in the entertainment industry—as the innocent dupes of capitalism, institutional power, patriarchy, and colonialism. Thinking about the DeMille Indians, whose fate as an unconventional tribe is unknown, compelled me to grapple with the relationship among the largely forgotten Native American actors who starred in a wide range of filmic genres, Native American filmmakers from the silent era to the present (whose work has intervened in the construction of Indigenous images), and North American film history.

Decoding Indigenous Inferences

Throughout this book, I examine how disenfranchised, nonpowerful groups in capitalist society participate in shaping media and consumption-based representations of themselves in the dominant culture, with a focus on Native American media-makers. I extend an invitation to think critically about how the images presented on-screen by Indigenous filmmakers and actors in narrative films not only pose key challenges to dominant discourses on film theory and history but also supplement crucial debates on sovereignty, identity, and Indigenous knowledge production. I look at the entire representational process from the production of representations, to the political concerns of the participants who helped create these formations, to the cultural and ideological work of the images in different sociohistorical contexts.

I examine a range of questions relating to the intersection of Native American subjects and visual culture, particularly film. Why did so many Native American actors play roles that presented negative images of Indigenous peoples? Did Native American actors who participated in Hollywood films have an impact on the number and type of roles available to them? If so, through what channels did they work to affect their desires, and are these self-representations visible on the screen?[10] What challenges do figures such as the DeMille Indians pose to our understandings of Native American identity and notions of sovereignty? How do Hollywood Indians help us better recognize Native American relationships to popular culture and the work of contemporary filmmakers who engage in this complex history of Indigenous performance? By expanding film studies scholarship to include the cultural work of Native Americans, how can we reconceptualize North American cinematic history?

This book traces out a genealogy of Native American representations from the inception of the motion picture industry at the turn of the twentieth century to the present in order to construct an Indigenous film theory unique to North American cinema through an analysis of key figures, films, and narrative artifacts of the period. I explore the influence of Native Americans on North American cinema and examine a range of narrative and performative strategies created by Native American actors and directors to intervene with and trouble mass-mediated images of Indigenous people. The work is by no means an exhaustive history of Native Americans in film; other books have covered that subject. I offer instead a blueprint for a reading practice for narrative films that Native Americans starred in and sometimes directed—from B-grade westerns to award-winning feature-length films—as well as the multiple contexts from which these films, actors, and directors arose. The narrative highlights Native American film practitioners from 1900 to 1940, bringing them into dialogue with contemporary Indigenous film, video, and new visual media artists through an engagement with the concepts of redfacing, the virtual reservation, and visual sovereignty. The project examines the relationship of Native American media-makers and their work with the broader historical, social, cultural, and political context in which they operated.

In order to contextualize my discussion of Native American filmmaking practices, the first three chapters of this book focus on how silent film actors negotiated representations of Indian images that were both self-generated and created by the dominant culture. I describe the ideological work they did both on-screen and off-screen as "redfacing," a complex practice that was at times transgressive but reified negative stereotypes at others. Using the DeMille Indians' petition as an interpretive lens, this chapter sets up the historical contexts and narrative strategies of Native American actors and directors who were involved in Hollywood film production during the first four decades of the twentieth century.

Chapter two analyzes how performances of gendered representations of Indians in visual culture from the contact period to the silent era complicate the visual logic of the sexualized "maiden" and the invisible drudge stereotype. As suggested in my analysis of films starring Native American actors Minnie Ha Ha and Molly Spotted Elk, the silent period offered up representations of Indigenous women that intervened in national discourses around race and gender in more visible and nuanced ways than occurred after the introduction of sound technology.

I propose a reconsideration of the cultural work of Iron Eyes Cody in chapter three as a bridge between the silent era and the late twentieth and early twenty-first-century's Indigenous cinema production. While not a Native American by birth, Cody's redface performance both on and off camera puts pressure on theoretical discussions of what constitutes Native American identity in general and how the identities of Hollywood Indians trouble conventional questions of community, identifications, and belonging. More specifically, I argue that as the most recognizable "Indian" actor, Cody underscores one of the most prevalent Native American stereotypes—that of the "vanishing Indian"—through his participation in the Keep America Beautiful Inc. campaign of the 1970s. At the same time, as an international celebrity, he opens up a space for public discussion of contemporary Indigenous issues and the political work of Native American representations.

This stereotype of the vanishing or ghostly Indian, as I suggest in chapter four, constitutes a pervasive legacy with which contemporary Native American filmmakers have had to contend. As an imaginative site of critical engagement, the virtual reservation serves as a space to counter such stereotypes while also articulating new models of Indigenous knowledge through visual culture. Using the films *Imprint* (2007) and *It Starts with a Whisper* (1992) as examples, I demonstrate how Chris Eyre and Shelley Niro collaborate with non-Native directors on experimental films that take up the question of the Native American ghost figure in order to suggest an alternative reading of Indigenous spirituality and prophecy.

Chapter five concentrates on visual sovereignty—the creative self-representation of Native American visual artists—as expressed in the film *Atanarjuat (The Fast Runner)*, a full-length feature film by the Inuit media collective, Igloolik Isuma Inc. *Atanarjuat* brings the discourses of ethnographic cinema and the history of redfacing into discussion with contemporary Inuit conceptions of oral storytelling and the productive space of film as a vehicle for thinking about Native American cultural production.

In the epilogue I connect the history of mainstream and alternative film production to recent experimental and "ephemeral" work by both professional and amateur Native American filmmakers on YouTube and other Internet sites through a discussion of the persistence of Hollywood Indian images. This work by contemporary media artists, which relies on continually changing technology, circumvents conventional circuits such as film festivals to provide innovative ways of accessing visual media by Native Americans. Because of the range of images presented by media-makers on these new sites, I suggest that these multiple outlets for articulating competing, often tribally specific notions of what constitutes visual Indianness have provided and will continue to offer alchemies of change in the representations of Indigenous people from stereotypes predicated on dominant culture fantasies to a reflection of the lived experiences and desires of Indigenous people.

I am indebted to recent work in Native American studies that complicates conventional notions of representations of Indigenous peoples. I have also been influenced by feminist, critical race, and queer scholarship on how gendered, raced, and queer spectators were constituted through decoding prohibited and stereotypical representations. Patricia White, for example, argues that under the Motion Picture Production Code (Hays Code) queer subjects, plots, and images were prohibited from the 1930s to the 1960s, much as Native Americans were rendered simultaneously highly visible and invisible through legal, representational, and cultural strictures during the same historical period. The Hays Code censored "sex perversion or any inference," a euphemism for any display of queer subjectivity, as well as miscegenation and "indecent movements" in dance sequences.[11]

As a result of the Hays Code, spectators employed imagination and fantasy to read "inferences" that were prohibited by law but nevertheless erupt on the screen to critique oppressive dominant values and power relations. White states, "The project of lesbian and gay readings of 'dominant' films is not simply a decoding process," but "a textual revision with the reader-critic as subject of its fantasy."[12] She discerns alternative spectatorial practices through close readings of films produced for female audiences. "While it remains difficult to conduct empirical work on lesbian and gay spectators," White claims, "we can reconstruct some of the discourses that intersected with film texts to broaden our analysis of how gender and sexuality were constructed by the cinema. Studies of stars, costuming, reception, source material, and authorship can all introduce traces of a lesbian historical presence that the narratives of the film exclude."[13] Likewise, a richer understanding of Native American involvement in Hollywood films as spectators, actors, directors, critics, and technicians requires textual analysis of films, archival materials, and autobiographical narratives. This methodology is speculative as it is impossible to intuit exactly what Native American actors, filmmakers, and spectators really thought about the films they watched and how these films impacted their communities. Yet we can still attempt to consider how cinematic images structured their experiences in order to explain cinema's place of importance among Native communities and the ways in which Hollywood was influenced by Native Americans.

Through subtle forms of aesthetic diplomacy, the many Native American actors who played racialized roles in the first half of the twentieth century and the spectators who read their "inferences" performed an important function by attempting to convince directors and production agents to alter aspects of film scripts to conform more closely to early twentieth-century Native American sensibilities. Through redfacing, Native actors performed the complicated role of human shields to absorb, deflect, redirect, and placate the fantasies projected on these "celluloid Indians"[14] by the dominant culture. It would be easy to judge Native actors harshly for bequeathing to us the array of stereotypes contemporary Indigenous people are called upon to grapple with and regard with contempt. The ideological and cultural work that redfacing enacts, however, complicates any easy reading of Hollywood Indians.

My project centers on the figure of the visually imagined Indian, a figure that has been crucial in serving as the universal foil against which European colonies and later the U.S. and Canadian governments have established legal and ideological claims of dominance in the "New World." The Native American performers who have helped create and critique the characterization of Indigenous figures in film have not mattered much in the dominant historical, literary, or visual culture narratives. Nevertheless, they have challenged (and sometimes complied with) hegemonic discourses of power in subtle and sometimes overt ways. Through archival research, close examination of a selection of films, and attention to the narratives produced by actors, directors, and their descendants, my research locates Native Americans not at the margins of cinematic history and culture but at its core, enmeshed in an evolving and sometimes paradoxical web of race, gender, citizenship, and sovereignty on the virtual reservation. This is especially true in the present as the proliferation and influence of narrative films by Native American media-makers attests. These films, which draw on earlier modes of self-representation and the strategies of redfacing, transform conventional cinematic genres to create a corpus of visual sovereignty whose importance is felt at all levels of Native American social, cultural, and political life.

The Only Good Indian Is a ~~Dead~~ Hollywood One?

To bring Indigenous film practitioners from the early twentieth century into dialogue with more recent film practitioners demonstrates how contemporary filmmakers fit within a broader history with roots in precontact performative traditions of creation, contestation, and collaboration on visual markers of identity and community. There is a strong confluence of performance, identity and identifications, and narrative in Native American visual culture and literary studies. For many scholars working in the field of Native American studies, images of the monosyllabic (if not absolutely silent), doomed American Indian in films from the turn of the twentieth century to the present are incorrect and irredeemable, representing the final chapter in the victimization of Indigenous peoples.[15] Ella Shohat and Robert Stam, for example, argue that the simultaneous absence and presence of Native Americans in early Hollywood films operated as "an ambivalently repressive mechanism [that] dispels the anxiety in the face of the Indian, whose very presence is a reminder of the initially precarious grounding of the American nation-state itself. . . . In a temporal paradox, living Indians were induced to 'play dead,' as it were, in order to perform a narrative of manifest destiny in which their role, ultimately was to disappear."[16] While most images of Native Americans in film have been overwhelmingly negative, there are more nuanced ways of looking at the performances of Native American actors who were involved in public spheres that take into consideration their own cultural and historical contexts.

Playing Indian roles provided these actors with class and geographic mobility, financial security, independence from the restrictions of white reservation agents, opportunities for political and social activism, and access to a limited range of institutional power. Some of these performers—notably James Young Deer, Princess Red Wing, Luther Standing Bear, Ray Mala, Molly Spotted Elk, and Jay Silverheels—joined their historical predecessors Matoaka-Amonute (Pocahontas), Samson Occom, Kahgegagahbowh (George Copway), and Tekahionwake (Pauline Johnson) as a growing number of international Indigenous celebrities. They used their privileged status in the service of their reservation or home nation, as well as broader transnational, urban communities.[17]

Other individuals employed film acting as a personal means to engage in activities that were illegal or not socially sanctioned. Lizzie Pablo, a Nez Perce elder from Kooskia, Idaho, told Harrold Weinberger, an assistant director scouting for Native American actors to star in *Northwest Passage* (1940), that she had starred in films previously and "would like to go back and kill soldiers."[18] Obviously the roles she anticipated were ones in which history would be rewritten from an Indigenous perspective, not the

1. Lizzie Pablo, a Nez Perce actor who auditioned for a role in *Northwest Passage* (1940). Photograph from the Harrold Weinberger manuscript collection at the Margaret Herrick Library. Courtesy of the Academy of Motion Picture Arts and Sciences.

more common ones where her gender and age would limit her to more sedentary and anonymous scenes. She noted that she was a widow and was "free to travel" with the film crew, demonstrating her eagerness to participate in filmmaking.[19] Her clear articulation of film as a means of imaginative and interactive revenge demonstrates how important entering the public sphere via cinema was for both prominent and uncredited Native American actors.

Philip J. Deloria employs the term "Indian modernity" to encapsulate this complicated social, ideological, and cultural position that Hollywood Indians inhabited as active agents negotiating new terrain while simultaneously reenacting scenes of violence and domination.[20] Native actors engaged in narrative pleasure to create new stories about Indigenous peoples that would not have been afforded them on reservations that offered limited options. They operated within what W. E. B. DuBois, an African American contemporary of early Hollywood Indians, called "double consciousness," which he describes as "a sense of always looking at one's self through the eyes of others, measuring one's soul by the tape of a world that looks on in amused contempt and pity."[21] For Native Americans the twentieth-century "problem of the color-line"[22] would be further complicated by the fact that the "amused contempt and pity" focused on Native Americans is coded as always already in the past. Native American actors and directors were forced to examine themselves through the eyes of others, but this necessitated a looking backward through the mists of history because Indigenous peoples had been written out of the present and the future of the United States through various forms of discursive genocide. Thus, they are ascribed the value of absence through assimilation and disappearance and the value of excess through the compulsion in Hollywood media to return continually to the scene of Indian-white contact.

One of the common assumptions made about Hollywood Indians is that they are an abject repository of the dominant culture's national visual fantasies about race, gender, legal discourse, and anthropological knowledge. As Ralph E. Friar and Natasha A. Friar contend in *The Only Good Indian . . . The Hollywood Gospel*, if the nineteenth century witnessed the culmination of nearly four hundred years of violence against Native Americans in a remark attributed to Indian fighter General Philip Sheridan: "The only good Indians [he] ever saw were dead," the twentieth century would, through visual representations of Native Americans, further contribute to the popular notion of the vanishing Indian through a rephrasing of the physical violence implied in Sheridan's declaration: the only acceptable, non-threatening way of existing as a Native American is to play one on the silver screen.[23]

Friar and Friar are representative of much of the scholarship on images of American Indians when they claim "Hollywood has continued to be a co-conspirator in committing cultural genocide by subverting the Native American's various ethnic identities and retaining him [sic] as a racial scapegoat," further arguing that "the cinematic assault upon the Native American is only comparable to the actual massacres at Sand Creek, the Washita, Summit Springs, and Wounded Knee."[24] Beverly R. Singer calls filmmaking "the white man's craft that betrayed Native Americans and promoted our demise."[25] While statements like these pack a kind of rhetorical punch that can be politically useful as a critique of stereotypes and public policy, the active participation of Native Americans in shaping North American cinematic history somewhat undermines (or at least problematizes) these claims. I agree with the general argument that the images created in Hollywood films of Indigenous peoples have been, at least to our contemporary sensibilities, inaccurate and negative, but in this study I attempt to offer up a more subtle consideration of the screened images and the agents behind them.

A number of important volumes on images of Native Americans in film have been produced in the past three decades that portray the figure of the Hollywood Indian as the site of harmful stereotype and victimization. Fortunately, recent scholarship has begun to move from a universal condemnation of images of Indians to a more complex (and, in my mind, more accurate) holistic understanding of the ways Hollywood constructs Native Americans and how these representations interact with other narratives about Indians, some of which are Native-produced. Angela Aleiss's *Making the White Man's Indian: Native Americans and Hollywood Movies*, for example, is an exploration of production materials that "sheds light on how Hollywood studios created its Indian characters."[26] While work such as Aleiss's is important because it illustrates the ambivalent images created by Hollywood, I am more intrigued by the interventions of Native Americans themselves on cinematic representations of Indigenous people.

My interest in the study of contemporary filmmakers' work was generated by the relative silence surrounding discourse on contemporary Native American filmmaking practices.[27] Two prominent filmmakers from the silent era—Edwin Carewe and James Young Deer—were of Indigenous heritage, and Native Americans have participated in various aspects of film production since the inception of motion pictures. But Native North American filmmaking and television broadcasting gained momentum, alongside the work of other minority groups, in the late 1960s.[28]

Although this study is limited to work that is being produced in Canada and the United States, in the past four decades Indigenous film, video, and television production has also proliferated in Latin America, Africa, Asia, Scandinavia, and Oceania. These filmmaking traditions constitute part of broader historical moves from cinema produced by European settler and colonial nations to what Fernando Solanas and Octavio Gettino term "Third Cinema" to a variety of Indigenous cinemas that incorporate local epistemes with new visual technologies.[29] While Third Cinema is a postcolonial movement that grew out of cultural and political changes in Africa, Latin America, and Asia in the 1960s to denounce Hollywood-style entertainment in favor of a national, popular, and activist vernacular, Indigenous cinema has its roots in specific Indigenous aesthetics with their attendant focus on a particular geographical space, discrete cultural practices, notions of temporality that do not delink the past from the present or future, and spiritual traditions.[30] Dorothy Christian, Jacquelyn Kilpatrick, Victor Masayesva Jr., and Steven Leuthold describe Indigenous aesthetics as grounded in tribally specific notions of place, the sacred, time, and orality.[31]

Maori filmmaker Barry Barclay has theorized this ideological and classificatory approach as "Fourth Cinema": "If we as Maori look closely enough and through the right pair of spectacles, we will find examples at every turn of how the old principles have been reworked to give vitality and richness to the way we conceive, develop, manufacture, and present our films."[32] Fourth Cinema, in Barclay's view, is a flexible space in which Indigenous filmmakers "may seek to rework the ancient core values to shape a growing Indigenous cinema outside the national orthodoxy."[33] Barclay cites the Saami director Nils Gaup; North Americans Zacharias Kunuk, Chris Eyre, and Sherman Alexie; and Pacific Islanders Vilisoni Hereniko, Merata Mita, Lee Tamahori, Don Selwyn, Tama Poata, Ivan Sen, Tracey Moffat, and himself as practitioners of Fourth Cinema. The ways these filmmakers operate "outside the national orthodoxy" is not only economic—most rely on inconsistent domestic funding sources and shoestring budgets—but culturally specific by incorporating an entire Indigenous framework into the filmmaking project from start to finish. Transnational Indigenous media production rethinks Audre Lorde's dictum that "the master's tools will never dismantle the master's house" by insisting that the very foundations on which the master's house is built are Indigenous and should be reterritorialized or repatriated.[34] Moreover, Indigenous filmmakers working within the framework of decolonization have found ways of appropriating some of the "master's tools," such as some forms of media technology, to Indigenous ends in order to rebuild their own houses.

As Barclay notes in his specific context, films are presented to local communities as part of the vibrant protocols of the people who produced them: "Maori filmmakers have been insistent on occasion that their films be accompanied to a new venue and be presented to the people of the area with full ceremonial."[35] One of the elements that sets this cinematic tradition apart is the filmmakers' continued investment in the public life of their visual product. Videos and films are often screened for home communities prior to the film's national and international release. This is done not so much to censor the content of the film but out of respect, to place the film back in relationship to the community. Indigenous-produced films serve as aesthetic objects that may or may not represent a particular community metonymically. At the same time, this work operates as a cultural ambassador of sorts, providing a space of mediation for an individual or community's artistic, cultural, and political concerns on Indigenous terms. The aesthetic diplomacy that the films enact complicates a colonial binary where the Indigenous subject is merely talking back to the metropolis, often through a non-Native interpreter. Not only does Fourth Cinema offer up a critique or revision of national and colonial cinematic practices, it also engages laterally with filmmaking traditions in other Indigenous contexts, allowing new aesthetic and political possibilities.[36]

This practice, which locates Indigenous cinema in a particular historical and social context while leaving room for individual, national, and tribal distinctions, is akin to the concept of visual sovereignty whereby Indigenous filmmakers take a holistic approach to the process of creating moving images. Visual sovereignty simultaneously addresses the settler population by creating self-representations that interact with older stereotypes but also, more importantly, connects film production to larger aesthetic practices that work toward strengthening treaty claims and more traditional (although by no means static) modes of cultural understanding.

The Cultural Work of Redfacing

Redfacing—the cultural and ideological work of playing Indian—is closely aligned with the traditional role of the trickster figure. Tricksters operate in the service of their community, albeit in an often clumsy, violent, outlier, sexualized, or humorous way.[37] The trickster serves a savvy, pedagogic function that predates European settler colonialism, often sacrificing something special in order to do good, or placing himself or herself outside the boundaries of the community in order to make a didactic point.

The Pueblo, for example, stage public performances that serve to take attention from private communal practices of sacred ceremonies. Santa Clara Pueblo anthropologist Edward P. Dozier notes that in the dances performed at these public ceremonies, "Novel forms are permitted, and improvisations are constantly made. Often these dances burlesque the whites, especially tourists, and their purpose is obviously for amusement and entertainment rather than to serve religious purposes."[38] These Pueblo performers also borrow from Plains Indian powwow culture by wearing costumes made of contemporary materials such as mirrors and colored feathers. These dancers may not perform in other ceremonials that take place simultaneously, but they enact important work in their communities as trickster figures, much as Hollywood Indians do, transgressing non-Native cultural mores in order to teach something new about the fluidity of Indigenous culture. They both shield other performative practices from non-Native eyes at the same time they critique European American spectators and dominant culture expectations. Pueblo performers demonstrate the social, cultural, and political transgression of the trickster by creating a pleasurable space where innovation and cultural appropriation can be tested and a critical site where colonialism can be mocked.

Likewise, legendary tales of Native American actors refusing to play dead when shot on film sets, replacing revolver blanks with live ammunition, and performing staged ceremonies incorrectly in order to subvert the potential power of the act attest to the on-screen and off-screen attempts on the part of Indigenous entertainers to subvert Hollywood hegemony.[39] Hollywood Indians, particularly those of the early twentieth century, function as trickster figures who are at times fully aware of the stakes of representation and from whom we can learn something about twentieth- and twenty-first-century spectators—ourselves, our parents, and our grandparents—even if they lead through what appears to be negative self-fashioning.

Redfacing refers to the complex performances of the Hollywood Indian both on-screen and off-screen. It resembles the ambivalent cultural and political work created by African American performers who appropriated the controversial and sometimes subversive valences of black minstrelsy during the Victorian and Progressive eras.[40] Hollywood Indians engaged in the same kinds of performative practices and felt similar conflicting pressures as early Asian American, Latino, and African American actors. Redfacing is a refraction of the image held up by Hollywood that foregrounds issues of uneven power relationships between Native Americans and European Americans. Redfacing describes a series of acts performed by Native Americans that draw upon Indigenous performance contexts and spiritual traditions but are staged under conditions controlled, more often than not, by white filmmakers using new technologies and often in conflict with Indigenous self-representations. At the same time, the term redfacing signals the ways in which the work of Indigenous performers, like that of the trickster, is always in motion and therefore creates acts that operate ambiguously, acts that open themselves up for further reading and interpretation.

Redfacing also provides a means of protection as a kind of virtual, visual prophylactic that keeps Native American cultural and spiritual practices somewhat sacrosanct, or at least hidden from the white tourist gaze. The pervasiveness and complexity of the image of Native Americans in film is not surprising given James C. Scott's work on what he terms hidden and public transcripts. "The greater the disparity between dominant and subordinate and the more arbitrarily it is exercised," he writes, "the more the public transcript of subordinates will take on a stereotyped, ritualistic cast. In other words, the more menacing the power, the thicker the mask."[41] The ways that subordinate groups confront and critique dominant forms of power more covertly constitutes, conversely, "hidden transcripts" by Scott, and these locations of resistance can be found in both narrative and nonnarrative forms such as dance, oral literature, private writing, and graffiti.

Traise Yamamoto discusses similar strategies in the autobiographical articulations of women who have been marginalized from both the public and hidden transcripts by dominant and racialized communities. She argues, "Through psychological, narrative, and metaphoric forms of masking, Japanese American women writers enact a mode of discursive agency that allows them to claim a viable and resistant subjectivity."[42] This form of "discursive agency" is similar to the redfacing strategies performed by Native Americans in film. I argue that in some key ways redfacing becomes a protective gesture—a mask, if you will—that takes the pressure off of tribal communities to perform dominant culture expectations in their quotidian lives.

Native American performers and directors (as well as spectators) have had an active, important, visible, and often-vexed role in the production and dissemination of Indigenous images throughout the history of North American cinema, especially during the first three decades of commercial film history. Many early twentieth-century performers launched their careers in film after working in other entertainment venues such as the Wild

2. Director Edwin Carewe (*center*) consults with actors Lupe Velez and John Boles on the set of *Resurrection* (1931). Photograph courtesy of General Photographic Agency/Getty Images.

West shows, world's fairs, vaudeville, the circus, federal Indian boarding school theater groups, the opera, sports (especially boxing and wrestling), and stage dance troupes. These figures include the two key Native American directors of the silent era: Edwin Carewe, a Chickasaw actor, director, producer, and screenwriter who created *Rio Grande* (1920), *The Girl of the Golden West* (1923), *Resurrection* (1927 and 1931), and *Ramona* (1928); and James Young Deer, an actor, director, and screenwriter of Ho-Chunk ancestry of over a dozen one-reel melodramatic western films.[43]

3. James Young Deer (*center*) and Princess Red Wing (*left*) in Fred J. Balshofer's *Young Deer's Return* (1910). Courtesy of the Museum of the American West, Autry National Center of the American West, Los Angeles; photograph #94.36.1.115.

During his brief but influential career, Young Deer was employed by several different film companies including Kalem, Lubin, Biograph, Bison, and Vitagraph. He was hired as West Coast studio director for Pathé Frères in 1910 and cut an impressive figure with his wife, Lillian St. Cyr (Princess Red Wing), in motion picture circles from the East Coast studios to Southern California. "Before *movie star* became an institutionalized identity," Philip J. Deloria notes, "Red Wing was a visible presence in American popular culture, the first widely recognized Indian actress."[44] Red Wing, a Ho-Chunk actor and graduate of Carlisle Indian Industrial School, starred in Cecil B. DeMille's *The Squaw Man*, among other key films throughout the 1910s and 1920s.[45] She and Young Deer would become one of Hollywood's first "power couples" alongside their contemporaries, Mary Pickford and Douglas Fairbanks.[46] Although Carewe and Young Deer were well known during the first two decades of the twentieth century, like many directors and actors of the time, they did not make the successful transition to "talkies."

Hundreds of Native American actors, consultants, screenwriters, and technicians also made their home in Southern California, drawn to the possibility of regular employment as well as the personal and professional pleasures and perils Hollywood afforded. Some of the most well-known Native actors of the silent era include: Charles Stevens, an Apache actor whose career spanned nearly fifty years and who starred in over two hundred television episodes and films, including D. W. Griffith's *The Birth of the Nation* (1915), where he was reportedly discovered by Douglas Fairbanks; Minnie Ha Ha (Minnie Devereaux), a Cheyenne actor who starred in comedies and westerns in the 1910s and 1920s alongside Roscoe "Fatty" Arbuckle and Mabel Normand; Ray Mala, an Inupiaq actor who began his career as a cameraman and actor with the Danish and Greenlandic Inuit explorer Knud Rasmussen, then moved to Hollywood in 1925, later starring in his most well-known film, W. S. Van Dyke's *Eskimo* (1933);[47] Luther Standing Bear, a Lakota actor, film consultant, and writer whose thirty-year entertainment career was launched with the Buffalo Bill Wild West Show; Chief Tahachee (Jeff Davis Tahchee Cypert), a Cherokee film and stage actor, stuntman, costume designer, and director who played a number of different ethnic and racialized roles from 1920 to 1960; Chief Thunder Cloud; Nipo T. Strongheart, a Yakima actor, camera operator, and technical advisor who began his career as a trick rider in Wild West shows and who starred in George B. Seitz's

4. Yakima actor Nipo T. Strongheart. Courtesy of the Yakima Valley Libraries.

The Last Frontier (1926) and William B. Wellman's *Across the Wide Missouri* (1951);[48] Jay Silverheels (Harold J. Smith), a Mohawk actor most famous for the role of Tonto in *The Lone Ranger* television series who spent the latter part of his nearly sixty-year career training Native American actors and advocating for the use of Indigenous actors in film and television; and Chief Many Treaties (William Malcolm Hazlett), a Blackfeet actor who starred in films in the 1930s and 1940s.[49]

While most of these entertainers migrated to the state from

5. Actor Jay Silverheels
as Tonto in *The Lone
Ranger* (1949).

elsewhere, the film industry attracted California
Indians as well, although in fewer numbers. The
demographics of the Hollywood Indian community reflect the racist attitude towards Indigenous
Californians during much of the twentieth century, many of whom were considered too dark to
play Native American roles except as extras and
whose Spanish surnames led them to be cast as
Mexican characters instead. It also illustrates the
ubiquity of the cinematic Plains Indian image.
Many Native actors were required to furnish
their own costumes on set. California Indians
who did not possess the standard war bonnet
and fringed buckskin costume could not compete

6. Joseph "Suni" Vance Chorre. Image courtesy of Heather Chorre Garcia.

with actors already trained to perform as the dominant culture's Plains Indian on the Wild West circuit.

One of the several California Indians cast in film roles, Tatzumbie DuPea, a Paiute actor born in Lone Pine, California, began her acting career late in life. She starred in at least two films, *Buffalo Bill* (1944) and *Across the Wide Missouri* (1951), both directed by William Wellman, in uncredited roles along-side Chief Many Treaties, Thunder Cloud, Tahachee, and Nipo Strongheart.[50] Suni War Cloud (Joseph "Suni" Vance Chorre), a Luiseño professional wrestler, dancer, and actor, is perhaps the most well-known California Indian from the early cinema period. During his twenty-two-year film career, he landed roles in films such as DeMille's *Union Pacific* (1939) and Michael Curtiz's *Jim Thorpe—All American* (1951).

Chorre attended Sherman Indian High School in Riverside, California, as did his brothers, Bennie and James, and sister, Marie, who also acted in films. Several Native actors used Sher-man as a place to live while performing on set or as a dormitory to house their children when they relocated to Hollywood. Joseph Chorre, whom Sherman administrators fault for taking too much time from school to devote to motion pictures, applied to live in a Sherman dormitory while attending Riverside Community College and continuing to act in films. Ira Walker, a Sac and Fox Carlisle graduate from Shawnee, Oklahoma, enrolled his son, George Lee Walker, at Sherman in 1924 so he could continue to pursue his acting career. George excelled at Sherman, where he played in the band, served on student council, and was on the honor roll. He also played minor roles in *Redskin* (1929) and was recruited by Richard Davis (Chief Thunder Bird) to star in *Battling with Buffalo Bill* (1931).[51] Joseph Chorre's mother, Gertrude Chorre, attended Sherman when it was located in Perris, California. When given the limited choice of a career as a domestic servant or as an actor, she chose Hollywood.[52] She starred in Allan Dwan's *Frozen Justice* (1929) as well as bit roles in other films. She also served as a language informant to linguist André Malécot.[53] As was the case with many Native American actors, she chose to live off-reservation in Riverside and Los Angeles. But the Chorres, like other Native American entertain-ment families, maintained contact with their tribal community through voluntary attendance at federal Indian boarding schools such as Sherman and frequent family visits.[54]

Native American actors and directors worked and lived within strict institutional, legal, and ideological parameters imposed by the dominant culture. They created, sometimes in collaboration with non-Native filmmakers, self-images that performed important work on-screen and in their respective personal and professional communities. These filmmakers and actors labored under the radar of mainstream culture, and their work also served the interests of tribal communities through visual sovereignty. Sovereignty in the filmic world emerged to challenge dominant representations of Native Americans created by the studio system. Randolph Lewis suggests that a "cinema of sovereignty" emerged in the twentieth century with the generative and important work of Indigenous documentary filmmakers.[55] He defines representational sovereignty to be "the ability for a group of people to depict themselves with their own ambitions at heart."[56] While this aligns with my own definition of visual sovereignty and is critical to understanding the processes by which Indigenous people rework and represent notions of sovereignty, visual sovereignty has a prehistory in the crucial practices of early Native American directors and actors, as well as in precontact artistic forms. It also extends past cinema, as Lewis anticipates in his study, to the fields of performance art, studio art, Internet media, and the televisual.

Native directors and actors have appropriated the narrative and visual conventions of the film medium stereotypes of themselves for their own interests and to their own ends and have strived to display tribally specific knowledge since the turn of the twentieth century. Through intervention in the production side of film representations of Native peoples in particular, such as the construction of identities, political activism, and language preservation, Native entertainers engaged the place of Indigenous communities in popular culture. Native peoples in the pre– and post–studio system shaped visual modes of sovereignty to reflect Indigenous knowledges through these activities.

Native American actors and filmmakers expressed visual sovereignty by creating performances of the "Indian" for various reasons, such as the search for economic opportunities to alleviate poverty, provide a decent living for their families, and escape oppressive conditions on their own reservations. One of the first scholars to ascribe agency to Native American public performers, L. G. Moses intimates that Indigenous employees of Wild West shows continued to live somewhat autonomous, traditional lives even while acting in staged plays that heralded their defeat and disappearance. Despite government policies to curtail their free movement off the reservation, Indian agents and administrators were "incapable on occasion of regulating the Show Indians' lives."[57] Deloria notes that Native performers traveled with Wild West shows and later relocated to film sets because they "felt a mission to serve as scouts charged with finding out about the United States" and the rest of the world.[58]

Native media-makers also wished to engage institutional power directly since most filmic representations of Indigenous peoples perpetuated stereotypes and were insensitive and untrue to the lived experiences of Native peoples in North America. When Native actors and filmmakers wore tribally inaccurate costumes or inverted the conventions of the ethnographic tradition in film, they performed important ideological and cultural work. They intentionally distorted the stereotyped filmic images of Native peoples through mocking white ignorance or offered affirmative and Native-centered film narratives as public pedagogy to change the dominant culture's attitude toward Indigenous peoples. In this project, I am less interested in situating specific performances of Indianness by Native American actors and filmmakers along an aesthetic and moral register than I am in thinking about the kinds of ideological and cultural work these embodiments perform and the complicated contexts that make archiving, accessing, or even imagining these moments (and their attendant aporias) difficult due to the shifting, legally and culturally unstable category of Native American identity and identifications. Native American involvement in both mainstream film and independent media production has been marginalized at best and completely elided at worst. This condition reveals much about film historiography, racial politics in the United States and Canada, and competing discourses around the concept of the nation and liberal white manifestations of guilt and its attendant forms of identity, belonging, and what Renato Rosaldo has termed "imperialist nostalgia." He defines this term as a strategy of ameliorating guilt on the part of European colonizers who express sadness for the disappearance of traditional cultures without acknowledging their hand in effecting radical change through violence in colonial and postcolonial communities throughout the world.[59] But even in this fraught environment, the complex, untidy, and tricksteresque performances of Native Americans such as the DeMille Indians deepen our understanding of the politics of race and representation in North America. Redfacing allowed Native directors and performers to exercise agency in participating in image production at the same time it revealed the powerful hegemonic forces Hollywood exerted in controlling those images.

The complexity of the lives that Native American performers created in Southern California also complicates conventional understandings of Indigenous identity. Most scholarship on Native urban diasporas focuses on the Urban Indian Relocation Program of the 1950s.[60] But the transnational Indigenous community in the Los Angeles area is much older, spanning from the precontact era through the first decades of the twentieth century to the present as Native actors moved to Hollywood to establish their careers. Native actors utilized their relatively privileged

7. Richard Davis Thunderbird. Courtesy of the Braun Research Library, Autry National Center of the American West, Los Angeles; photograph #P.36265.

positions as stars to forward activist agendas. Some, like Luther Standing Bear, advocated for the extension of voting rights to Native Americans prior to the 1924 American Indian Citizenship Act. Others pushed for better wages and working conditions for Native American media-makers, many of whom were paid less than animals used on the set. The ability to travel freely in a city that was much more diverse than their reservation hometowns must also have been enticing. For example, Richard Davis Thunderbird, a Cheyenne writer and actor whose film career spanned over three decades, owned a home in Pasadena that served as an intellectual and social hub for Native and non-Native organizations and individuals. Thunderbird maintained his identity as a Cheyenne while he also participated in the vibrant new urban community formed by Native American actors. Thunderbird assisted other Native Americans in the film industry and was a visible presence in Los Angeles.[61]

Reservation Reelism: Hollywood Indians and North American Film History

Few images are as ubiquitous and loaded as those of Native Americans in popular culture. With a genealogy rooted in a variety of Native American aesthetic media such as wampum belts and pictographs, these images also stem from non-Native portrayals in Medieval and Renaissance woodcuts and engravings of European invasions of the "New World"; painted portraits of prominent leaders; staged performances of Indigenous people in Wild West shows, public dances, world's fairs, and international expositions; and daguerreotypes and photographs.[62] Representations of Native Americans in moving pictures have been particularly pervasive and powerful. Recent films such as Terrence Malick's *The New World* (2005), Mel Gibson's *Apocalypto* (2006), Marcus Nispel's *Pathfinder* (2007), and James Cameron's *Avatar* (2009) demonstrate the continued popular interest in mainstream films with Native American subjects and films that metaphorize contact between Indigenous communities and invader-settlers.

Stoic and silent though hardly static, the Hollywood Indian became iconic with the advent of new visual culture technologies in the late nineteenth century. Since its inception, the commercial motion picture industry in North America has been fascinated with the image of the American Indian.[63] Hundreds of actualities featuring Indians engaging in putatively quotidian practices were shown in nickelodeons in the first decade of commercial filmmaking alone. Thomas Edison produced three kinetoscope films in 1894, *Sioux Ghost Dance*, *Buffalo Dance*, and *Indian War Council*, that featured Lakota performers employed by Buffalo Bill Cody's Wild West Show reenacting tribal dances on a stage at Edison's Black Maria studio in New Jersey. Although these films and others with Indigenous subjects from around the world permitted a new kind of endlessly available tourist gaze for the masses, recycling contemporary racist modes of understanding "exotic" cultures, they also challenged already prevailing notions of Native Americans as an extinct people relegated to dusty anthropological monographs and sepia-toned photographs.

This was particularly so during the silent film era when the representational focus shifted slightly from nineteenth-century reenactments of famous battles and "traditional" cultural forms, such as dance. These dances were popular with Wild West show audiences and fixed Native Americans as peoples in the past with an uncertain future.[64] Silent films of the 1910s and 1920s often presented Native Americans with contemporary roles and dramatized the ongoing tensions between Indigenous communities and European American invader-settlers.[65] Young Deer worked closely with his wife, Princess Red Wing, to create films that presented a more nuanced view of Native Americans within the limited confines of the silent western genre. He was recognized for his skill in negotiating both audience expectations and the limitations of the burgeoning studio system when he was appointed head of Pathé Frère's West Coast studio in 1909. According to Andrew Brodie Smith, Young Deer and Red Wing created and portrayed Native American characters "more sympathetically and in more complex ways than any other silent-era filmmakers."[66]

Yet even Young Deer's work presents stylized and often fanciful images of Native Americans to be consumed by North American and European audiences, including Native American movie-goers themselves. While much of his work attempts to underscore controversial subject matter such as miscegenation, racism against Indigenous peoples, and compulsory assimilation, according to Smith, "By the teens, Young Deer's Indian westerns had become indistinguishable from other filmmakers' similar product."[67] Jean Baudrillard's work on the "hyperreal" serves as a useful critical paradigm in thinking about how persistently these images bleed into the fabric of Native American lives off the page or screen as the Hollywood Indian has come to stand in for self-generated representations of Indigenous people: "Simulation . . . is the generation by models of a real without origin in reality: a hyper-real. The territory no longer precedes the map, nor survives it."[68] This simulation is not an "indiscriminate, inchoate condition," as Baudrillard supposes, but an everyday practice that Michel de Certeau would locate as "the place from which discourse is produced."[69] The cinematic Indian is what Meaghan Morris calls a "banality" that continually reproduces itself like the Land O'Lakes butter maiden who holds up an image of herself that reflects endlessly but has no stable point of origin.[70] It is predicated on constantly shifting binary oppositions and paradoxes along a vast circuitry of representations: noble vs. bloodthirsty savage, faceless horde vs. lone warrior in defeat, beautiful maiden vs. shapeless drudge, inscrutable enemy vs. loyal sidekick, assimilationist vs. traditionalist, sexual predator vs. emasculated "last of his breed," to name just a few. The "excess" of such images, Gregory J. Seigworth contends, "finds the *potential* of its politics within that virtual space" that I call the virtual reservation.[71]

And in the end, with the tension between and overlapping of the discourse-generated representations of Native Americans through the texts of literature and visual culture and the embodied, material world beyond the page or screen—what Craig Womack has described as the vexed "intrinsic and extrinsic" relationship between "the world of literature and the very real struggles of American Indian communities"[72]—the representations have come to serve as the markers of Indigenous identity and identifications for both non-Natives and some Native American people. In many ways the Hollywood Indian can serve as a kind of ground zero for the kinds of critical work on the multiple nodes of identity, performance, and race in which postmodern and post-postmodern theorists have been engaged.

In *Making the Movies* (1915), one of the first histories of early U.S. cinema, film critic Ernest A. Dench argues, "To act as an Indian is the easiest thing possible, for the Redskin is practically motionless."[73] In contradistinction to cultures depicted as within the bounds of modernity, cultures that were becoming more kinetic and active through new motion picture technologies, Dench's assertion demonstrates how Native Americans in the twentieth century were portrayed as nearly static, receding to the vanishing point of national history. Despite the European American impulse to eradicate the Indian, Native Americans have still been influential in both North American mainstream and independent cinema since the inception of motion pictures in both obvious and less visible ways. The drive to subdue the wilderness began as "regeneration through violence," a myth that "became the structuring metaphor of the American experience."[74] Conquest is conjoined to twin desires that seek to simultaneously celebrate Native American cultures by domesticating them for mass consumption and, in a more literal form of consumption, embody in European Americans the desire to be Native American.

Actors, particularly in the silent era, worked within and against this hegemony by influencing the way Indigenous people would be portrayed through professional relationships with filmmakers and through their work as film consultants. For example, Luther Standing Bear, whose fascinating life led him from the Oglala

8. Luther Standing Bear in regalia. Courtesy of the Denver Public Library, Western History Collection, call number x-31857.

Lakota Reservation in South Dakota to Carlisle to London with
the Wild West show to Hollywood, argues in his autobiography, *My People the Sioux*, that although films featuring a Native
American plot were overwhelmingly based on stereotype and
the industry often exhibited a hiring preference for non-Indian
actors, well-known directors of the period were amenable to,
and even welcomed, criticism.

In 1912 Standing Bear wrote that when he first arrived in
Southern California, he and director Thomas H. Ince spoke at
length about representations of Native Americans. "I told him
that none of the Indian pictures were made right," Standing Bear
notes. "He seemed quite surprised at this and began asking me
questions. I explained to him in what way his Indian pictures
were wrong. We talked for a long time, and when I arose to
leave, he said, 'Standing Bear, some day you and I are going to
make some real Indian pictures.'"[75]

Standing Bear, who died on the set of *Union Pacific* in 1939,
never had the opportunity to collaborate with Ince on any "real
Indian pictures," although Ince recruited Native Americans
from reservations in South Dakota to star in silent melodramas
and westerns that were sympathetic, by early twentieth-century
standards, to Native Americans.[76] Nevertheless, he did continue
to struggle on behalf of his community through his activism for
universal suffrage for Native Americans and his behind-the-scenes
work on film sets, including founding an "Indian Employment
Agency" in 1927.[77] Standing Bear serves as an example of the
many Native American performers and show business workers
who complicated representations of Native Americans in the
first years of film production.

For Standing Bear and other Native American actors, acting
in films permitted a socially acceptable way of talking back to
colonialism. In his autobiography he recalls an anecdote about
being forced to receive a European American name to replace his

Lakota name, which school administrators found unacceptable. "When my turn came," he wrote, "I took the pointer and acted as if I were about to touch an enemy. . . . The first few times I wrote my new name, it was scratched so deeply into the slate that I was never able to erase it. But I copied my name all over both sides of the slate until there was no more room to write . . . then I took a piece of chalk downstairs and wrote 'Luther' all over everything I could copy it on."[78]

In a world where Standing Bear could no longer complete a culturally sanctioned process of attaining manhood through traditional Lakota practices, he initiated his own ritual of adulthood in the midst of an incredibly alien and oppressive context. He not only defused the new name's power over him by touching it according to a Lakota test of bravery and possession, he reinscribed the name with power by making it his own, engraving it so deeply on everything he could find that it could not be erased. By counting coup on his "enemy"—his new European American name and institutionalized education—he fulfills his promise to his father to "do some brave deed, and then come home again alive,"[79] demonstrating how his Lakota worldview served as a guidepost to lead him through the complex and difficult program of assimilation relatively unscathed. Acting in films could function for him as an extension of this innovative way of counting coup and making an unfamiliar representational world his own, even if the motion pictures he starred in did not necessarily reflect his views on Native Americans.

Native American spectators also engaged in public debate about Indigenous images in films. By the first decade of the twentieth century there were movie theaters near or on many reservations, and Native American spectators filled the seats.[80] The majority of Native American spectators who entered the public sphere via letters to the editor of newspapers were concerned with verisimilitude and authenticity of visual iconography, particularly costumes. John Standing Horse, a Carlisle student, for example, critiqued representations of Native Americans in motion pictures as well as studio hiring practices. He wrote in 1911 to the trade newspaper *Motion Picture World*:

> If the directors of the moving picture companies knew how foolish their women and girls look in the Indian pictures, with from one to three turkey feathers stuck in the top of their heads, they would be more careful. . . . We always laugh and think it a great joke when we see the leading girls in the pictures made up as Indians, with the chicken feather in the hair. It is funny, but they would all look much better without them. The braves wear the eagle feather, one or two, after they are braves, but they have to earn them. The chief and council-chief have the war bonnet. Have also seen pictures with all the made-up Indian men with big war bonnets on their heads. Another big laugh, but don't think the managers know this; if they did, they would do different. Then again, they should get the real Indian people.[81]

Not only does Standing Horse provide ethnographic information that would correct "inauthentic" costuming and argue for hiring practices that would privilege Native American actors, but he also deflates the dramatic import of silent movies with Indian themes by suggesting that he and his friends laugh at these films. Native Americans are considered in popular representations to be a group of people utterly devoid of humor; however, Standing Horse corrects this stereotype by arguing that Native Americans are not only capable of humor, as active spectators they laugh at dominant portrayals of Indigenous people. In her study of Indigenous film reception, JoEllen Shively notes that Native American spectators "liked humor and wit in western movies and valued this trait in their friends. Humor is a source of joy for them—a gift."[82] Humor is deployed by spectators not only as critique, but as a mechanism of survival.

Laughter becomes the strategy of the oppressed in Standing Horse's critique. It encapsulates a dual purpose that Keith Basso calls "a form of play" and "a negative statement that contains within it an implicit negative metastatement."[83] The representations Standing Horse mocks are both "funny" because they are inaccurate and "dangerous"[84] because the act of calling into question these representations could have dire consequences in a settler colonial nation state that Dylan Rodríguez characterizes as the site of "biological and cultural genocides, mass-based bodily violence, racialized domestic warfare, and targeted, coercive misery."[85]

Native American critiques of images of Indians suggest that Indigenous people were not only laughing at what they interpreted to be ludicrous caricatures of Indian subjects, but publicly protested against them as well. In 1911 a delegation of over thirty Anishinabe (Ojibway) men from Minnesota traveled to Washington DC to join "in an 'uprising' against the motion pictures," according to a *Motion Picture World* article entitled "Indians War on Films."[86] Members of the delegation charged that even those films that portrayed Native Americans as figures in larger twentieth-century dramas such as the boarding schools still perpetuated stereotypes and were "grossly libelous."[87] Their activism suggests a sophisticated response to dominant culture paradigms of representation that welds a negotiation of compulsory assimilation practices on the part of the U.S. government to Indigenous ways of making meaning out of the unfamiliar, a means of counting coup in much the same way Standing Bear took charge of his name and new social context.

Following so closely on the heels of the violent massacres of Indigenous communities by U.S. troops all over Native America, a military uprising against those who created unacceptable images would likely have been immediately suppressed. Instead, the Anishinabe delegates from Minnesota fought motion picture representations on the dominant culture's discursive terms. They counted coup on their enemy through a means that registered to European American culture. According to the newspaper account, they circulated a signed petition and were considering "a call at the White House . . . to lay the case before President Taft, and may ask for congressional action looking into the regulation of moving pictures in which Indians are shown." Whether or not the petition reached its intended audience, Native Americans since the inception of the motion picture industry—from spectators to filmmakers—have found various ways of counting coup on Indian representations and rendering these images acceptable on their own terms.

Life on the Virtual Reservation

Native American media-makers and spectators have enacted agency in Hollywood through functioning as trickster figures and transforming their experiences with visual media into Indigenous epistemes, as Standing Bear and the Anishinabe delegation demonstrate by counting coup on film stereotypes of Indians. The space in which Native Americans create and contest self-images and where these images collide with mass-mediated representations of Indians by the dominant culture can usefully be thought of as a virtual reservation, a topic I take up at length in chapter five.

From their creation, reservations have been often-perverse tourism sites where non-Indians would travel to experience a glimpse into a purportedly "vanished" culture. Reservations became living dioramas where tourists could putatively step outside of time and space to see "real" Indians (or what passed for the "real" in the settler nation's national mythology). By relocating the Native American experience to celluloid, film became a virtual reservation for a viewing public eager for Indigenous images, but lacking the spare time and money to visit a geographical one. This would prove to be especially so for European immigrants and the working class in the early twentieth century, for whom, as Miriam Hansen argues, silent cinema created a space for imagining a unified national spectator.[88] Reservations, of course, continued to bear the brunt of this fascination with Indians, as roadside attractions near Indian communities would demonstrate, but the presence of films with Native American plots and subplots helped ameliorate the situation in some important ways by diverting the gaze from reservation communities to the virtual reservation of the filmic space.

Drawing from the work of Marcel Proust, Henri Lefebvre, and Henri Bergson, Gilles Deleuze defines the virtual as "real without being present, ideal without begin abstract."[89] Seigworth elaborates on this idea, "More exactly, the virtual gives account to the contextual space of an actual moment in time without necessarily abstracting or arresting this moment in time."[90] Cinema as virtual reservation exemplifies this space in between "real" conceptions of space, physicality, and time and the purely imagined.

Native American actors, particularly those living and working in Hollywood, would have sustained access to philanthropists and policy makers located far from reservation communities, thereby creating opportunities for social change that would have been much more limited otherwise. Reservations would come to signify both the space of confinement and disempowerment and, paradoxically, liberation and the retention of tradition. Virtual reservations sequester Native Americans (as visual and imagined representations) but also provide Indigenous people with an organizing principle that allows communities and individuals to coalesce around commonly held as well as contested ideas and objectives.

Conclusion

When the DeMille Indians sent in their petition in 1940 they were expressing their visual sovereignty. Even though the group's traditions were recently established and would most likely disqualify them by the European American standards typically used to determine whether or not a tribe would be federally recognized, they united in their common condition as Indigenous actors, and they utilized the resultant power their images on the silver screen had to capture the imagination of the public. The DeMille Indians effected reverse frontier expansion by staking out their territory in Hollywood, a powerful imagined space on which they could create a virtual reservation. Their acts of visual sovereignty in the films they starred in and their work organizing a collective Hollywood Indian community set the stage for later generations of Indigenous artists who would borrow from, contest, and operate in dialogue with images produced by this first generation of film actors and directors.

2 Ideologies of (In)Visibility

Redfacing, Gender, and Moving Images

Historically, motion picture companies have hired fewer Native American female actors than their male counterparts. Because the politics of representation in films with American Indian plots and subplots privilege the frontier as an imagined site where Native American warriors must be conquered, secured, and surveilled, especially in westerns, male characters have been more visible. Silent film, in particular, supported Frederick Jackson Turner's privileging of the frontier as the primary lens through which to view North American history, allowing spectators to render genocide natural and inevitable, even as this era in cinematic history witnessed a record number of films with Native American storylines, some of which feature sympathetic portrayals of Indigenous people.[1] "If Turner's thesis was a blueprint for a compelling shape for American identity," Paula Marantz Cohen argues, "silent film was the form of its realization. The oscillation between the civilized and the primitive could find conceptual correlatives in the still and the mobile shot . . . which were fundamental to the lexicon of film."[2] Although the silent era featured hundreds of films with Native American characters and contexts, the majority of these images fixated on the frontier as a metaphor for the doomed, static present of Native Americans set against the kinetic, animated future of the dominant culture and constitute what Ella Shohat and Robert Stam have called "a kind of national obsession."[3]

Within this masculinist paradigm of the western, film and literary plots often center on queer and what Eve Kosofsky Sedgwick calls "homosocial" relationships between men.[4] In plots that feature raced relationships, Native American men are often emasculated and primarily invested in conditions of "friendship" and "love." In *Sitting Bull* (1954), a western directed by Sidney Salkow that attempts to narrate a complicated history of the frontier, for example, the title character (played by J. Carrol Naish) repeatedly invokes the language of "friendship" and "love" rather than, say, sovereignty and treaty rights in his interactions with the U.S. cavalry. He forms a homosocial triangle with Major Robert "Bob" Parrish (Dale Robertson), an officer determined to recognize Lakota land claims, and Charles Wentworth (Bill Hopper), a newspaper reporter who becomes engaged to Parrish's ex-fiancée, an unlikeable, superficial general's daughter. Parrish is loyal to Sitting Bull, although he is court-martialed and almost executed, and exchanges intense, sexually charged glances with Wentworth, whose company he seems to enjoy more than his former fiancée's. He also develops a homosocial relationship with Sam (Joel Fluellen), a runaway slave who has been living among the Lakota and voluntarily becomes a loyal servant to Parrish, underscoring a flawed conventional narrative that assumes that forms of slavery can be predicated on a relationship equally beneficial to both parties. These complex relationships reflect Leslie Fiedler's assertion that "the western glorified pure, same-sex love."[5] Blake Allmendinger character-

9. *Nova Reperta (New Inventions of Modern Times)/America.* Print made by Theodor de Galle after Jan van der Straet, Antwerp, ca. 1588–1612. Image courtesy of the Trustees of the British Museum.

izes the western as "the queer frontier": "at the heart of most westerns are male friendships and rivalries, both of which constitute complex love-hate relationships."[6]

When Native American women were represented, they tended to embody what M. Elise Marubbio terms either the helpless "celluloid maiden" or the destructive "sexualized maiden," both of which served the colonial interests of the westward-moving frontier.[7] As early as the fifteenth century, the Americas were imagined by conquistadors, explorers, potential settlers, and bureaucrats in European print culture as a metonym for an Indigenous female body that was readily available for conquest. Jan van der Straet's print of Theodor de Galle's late sixteenth-century image below epitomizes what Anne McClintock describes as colonial "porno-tropics": "Roused from her sensual languor by the epic newcomer, the Indigenous woman extends an inviting hand, insinuating sex and submission."[8] The reclining, naked figure of the Indigenous woman standing before the fully clothed, authority- and technology-bearing European man metaphorizes the scene of colonial dominance by suggesting simultaneous sexual and military penetration.

The image also inaugurates the trope of the Indigenous whore-traitor exemplified by Malintzin (La Malinche or Doña Marina), Pocahontas, and Sacajewea, women who have borne the onus of being considered betrayers of their communities, an image that fortunately has been revised in recent years.[9] Despite her nakedness, the reclining figure in this engraving seems less sexually aroused by than protective of the solitary European explorer. She raises her hand and opens her mouth in warning, drawing his attention to the background images that form the center of the print and stand between them: "In the central distance of the picture, between Amerigo and America, a cannibal scene is in progress."[10] While her sisters are dismembering, roasting, and ingesting a human body, perhaps an ill-fated European colonizer, America is napping, physically and psychologically distancing herself from the violent scene.[11] Her unwillingness to take part in a practice that has often been considered the dividing line between the human and the savage, the commensurable and the incommensurable, indicates her status as a figure open to all the "benefits" colonialism might entail. Cannibalism forms the literal dividing line between these two figures and epistemic knowledge, a dividing line that America, as rendered in this image, appears ready to cross. In fact, she seems to be waiting for the opportunity to escape from her community's putative barbarism. America does not reach for her wooden club as a weapon against the European invader, although the image suggests she might take up arms, alongside Amerigo, who is armed with a dagger and sword against the unarmed women in the scene intended to represent pastoral perversion beyond.

It is not surprising then that the western film's narrative precursors—images such as van der Straet's, the dime novel, and Wild West shows—relied on imagining the frontier as a site of masculine opposition wherein the individual, traitorous Native American female betrays her race to save European Americans and thus symbolically redeems herself while Indigenous men either lose to technologically superior opponents or recede with the rest of the race en masse to the vanishing point on the horizon.[12] The dominant story that emerges in the majority of texts whose plot centers on contact with Indigenous peoples in North America reifies a past that privileges European American invasion and settlement history as well as patriarchal dominance.[13] A European inability to see—much less accept—gender ideologies that were different than its own "served to naturalize conquest," according to Virginia Marie Bouvier. "Myth, language, and culture worked hand-in-hand to reinforce a gender ideology that dictated male domination of women. . . . Land was considered to be female and was often depicted and judged as worthy of possession."[14] Hollywood films created a spectatorship among new European immigrants that served as a primer on how to identify with Anglo-American colonialism and its cultural heroes, further erasing Native American agency and subjectivity from the historical and popular archive.[15] Hollywood's version of American history relies on solidifying a national identity among divergent European ethnic and religious groups against a common, usually male Native American "Other."

In spite of this, many female actors starred in films from the silent era to the present as extras and in rare yet important cases as lead characters. This chapter examines the personal and professional performances of two Native American female actors,

Minnie Ha Ha (Minnie Devereaux) and Molly Spotted Elk (Mary Alice Nelson), who starred in genres as wide-ranging as comedies, melodramas, docudramas, and westerns. Through a discussion of "sympathetic" silent films, the critical contours of redfacing, and a close reading of three films and one contemporary performance piece, I demonstrate how their lives and work illustrate a reading of redfacing in complicated and nuanced ways that illuminate the tension between their own complex ideological investments in playing Indian characters and the types of roles offered to them within a patriarchal labor and representational system.[16]

As people who have not historically mattered, there is a lack of substantial material in the official historical archive that provides witness to the lives of early Native American female film actors. Yet there is also an ever-increasing abundance of anecdotal material—gossip, family stories, and stage performance around the recorded facts in the informal, noninstitutional archive that supplement the absences in profound and meaningful ways. Since much of the historical information we have for these early twentieth-century female performers is unseen, peripheral, and often ephemeral, my approach to writing about moments when aporias become visible and voiced is illustrative of the practice of Indigenous consciousness within dominant structures of knowledge and power. This chapter enlists questions and concerns that lie between literary and filmic texts and the broader, unexamined discourses surrounding Native American female performers in the first half of the twentieth century. Such a history should necessarily be attentive to gender and the female actors whose work laid bare the conditions of possibility for the complex practice of visual sovereignty present, however unevenly, in these early films. This movement from domination to agency comes to fuller fruition in the more contemporary context as Indigenous artists and communities gain greater control over all aspects of the filmmaking process.

An examination of both the texts and contexts of Native female actors is key to understanding how visual culture has been both the site of the most visible forms of discursive violence committed against Native people and a space where Indigenous directors and actors have created virtual reservations that have fostered a complex grid of agency and empowerment.[17] These actors negotiated what Diana Taylor terms the "so-called ephemeral *repertoire* of embodied practices/knowledge" and the historical record on the eve of the sound revolution in film.[18] They did so through the off-screen cultural work the films generated and the roles they engendered on-screen. The texts these actors created help forge a genealogy of Hollywood Indians, but also form a body of work that contributes to our practical and theoretical conceptions of Indigenous identity, identifications, and the politics of performance.

The importance of what might be called ephemera—photographs, autobiographical fragments, family stories, largely forgotten silent films, and the flotsam and jetsam of personal lives that wash up both in public memory and in the archive—created by women generally unknown outside their own communities reveals how their work alternately disrupts, complicates, and conforms to dominant conversations about Native American representations in films and North American film history. Recent scholarship on the silent period in general and Native American performers in particular has opened up a discursive space in which to rethink Indigenous relationships to the film industry and the performance of race, gender, and identity in both the United States and Canadian public spheres.[19] This chapter is an exploration of the space in between the often-complicated social and cultural contexts of the actors (and what counts as evidence when reconstructing these contexts), the ways in which their work has either been ignored or deployed strategically by the film and media industry, and how contemporary Indigenous scholars and artists imagine their relationship to the legacy of intergenerational trauma, empowering modes of performance, and challenging subjectivities these actors leave in their wake. In what follows I demonstrate how Native American women actors participated in redfacing. I focus on Minnie Ha Ha and Molly Spotted Elk in order to contextualize their work as both a critique of the representational regime of Hollywood and as a vehicle for screening Indigenous subjectivities. I also examine how contemporary Native American filmmakers and artists are in the process of revising understandings of the figure of the Hollywood Indian in ways that provide a more nuanced and vibrant history of Indigenous entertainers and their complicated relationship to gender, writing, and identification. These filmmakers and artists do so by exploring the connections among bodily practice, autobiography, memory, and the meager historical archival materials that exist on these figures.

How Native American female actors intervened into a representational regime dominated by both colonial and gendered restrictions is similar to the work created by racialized subjects in other contexts. Silent cinema and early sound-era African American, Asian American, and Latino/a directors and actors such as Josephine Baker, Louise Beavers, Sessue Hayakawa, Dolores Del Rio, Nobel Johnson, Hattie McDaniel, Oscar Micheaux, Etta Moten Barrett, Lotus Pearl Shibata (Lotus Long), Lupe Velez, and Anna May Wong also negotiated Hollywood hegemony in order to carve out space to challenge dominant representations.[20] Given this broader history and context, this chapter is informed by Clyde R. Taylor's provocative questions about African American cinematic self-representation and agency:

> Given the prohibitions against picturing blacks as humans, which also implied the muzzling of attacks against their dehumanization through racism, how did the various framers of black imagery "make waves?" In other words, when we look

at this body of representation, particularly the self-portraits of blacks in silent race movies, what is a direct projection of unequal development . . . and what is . . . the self-censorship of the oppressed?[21]

Taylor's critical questions about African American agency and self-representation mirror Native American cinematic history. In the face of governmental policies (such as the Dawes Act), various attempts to enforce assimilation, and laws against universal citizenship designed to institutionalize Native Americans' absence from demographic and representational realms, how did Indigenous actors, particularly women, represent themselves, and how can we develop a reading practice that takes into account the kinds of work these actors were doing behind the scenes, the pre-representational work that may not be explicit on the screen?

Reservation Reelism: Native Americans, the "Usable Past," and Silent Films

Marubbio argues that cinematic representations of Native American women from the silent era to the 1990s are arrayed along a register of "the squaw, the young maiden, and the hag."[22] She centers her study on the "celluloid maiden," a figure most visible in silent films from the 1920s to the mid-1930s who "stands metonymically for Native American acquiescence to the sovereignty of the United States," and the "sexualized maiden," prominent in films from the 1940s to the 1960s who "represents the ramifications of interracial mixing on American society."[23] While the "celluloid maiden" may be present in many twentieth-century films, the actors whose work is examined in this chapter stand as significant complications of this representational field. Neither Minnie Ha Ha nor Molly Spotted Elk played on-screen or off-screen roles that could easily be represented in either of these ways.

10. Minnie Ha Ha (*left*) and Mabel Normand from *The Mack Sennett Weekly* (1917).

Minnie Ha Ha—who was also known as Minnie Prevost, Indian Minnie, and Minnie Devereaux during her career—was a subtle and accomplished comedic actor born ca. 1868.[24] She starred in more than fifteen films, most of which were silent slapstick comedies directed by Mack Sennett, in roles that are surprising in their complexity. These films include *Old Mammy's Secret Code* (1913), *Fatty and Minnie He-Haw* (1914), *Mickey* (1918), *Rose of the West* (1919), *By Right of Birth* (1921), *The Paleface* (1922), *Suzanna* (1923), *Painted Ponies* (1927), and *The Miracle Rider* (1935). Both Mabel Normand and Roscoe "Fatty" Arbuckle considered her a friend, although she never achieved the fame (or, in Arbuckle's case, notoriety) of either of those actors. In a 1917 interview published in the *Mack Sennett Weekly*, Ha Ha states that she was born to Cheyenne parents who fled George Armstrong Custer's army during the Battle of the Little Bighorn, an event that took place when she was eight years old.[25] She identifies her father as Chief Plenty Horses and she translates her Cheyenne name to mean "Earth Woman."[26] Although Ha Ha was not a U.S. citizen for much of her career because the Indian Citizenship Act, which granted universal citizenship to Native Americans, would not be passed until 1924, she must have found life outside the oppressive structures of the reservation appealing.

Nevertheless, she still critiqued the written accounts of Indigenous history that informed cinematic representations of Native Americans. She tells the interviewer, "White man's history. They do not tell the truth."[27] Ha Ha realized that the end result of her labors as an actor would lead to films that bore little resemblance to the lived reality of her community, yet she still participated in the creation of the Hollywood Indian. Her statement indicates that not only were Native actors aware of the representational structures and pressures that were in place in Hollywood, governing cinematic characterizations of Indigenous peoples, but that individual actors such as Ha Ha chose to exert their influence on films with Indian plots rather than choosing to be completely excluded from the film industry.

Spotted Elk was born Mary Alice Nelson on the Penobscot Reservation in Maine in 1903. She performed Native American dances for tourists as a child and as an adult became a vaudeville dancer in New York and a burlesque dancer in Europe. She took the stage name "Molly Spotted Elk" as a marketing tool to more clearly identify herself to potential employees and audiences as Native American. *The Silent Enemy* was the only film in which she received star billing, although she and her sister, Aphed Elk,

11. Mildred Nelson, Molly Spotted Elk's younger sister, who also was a silent film actor. Photograph courtesy of Jean Archambaud Moore and the Abbe Museum.

were extras in several Hollywood productions, including works by Bison and Henry King's *Ramona* (1936). Elk also had an uncredited role in W. S. Van Dyke's *Laughing Boy* (1934).[28] In addition to her engagement with the performative arts, Spotted Elk studied journalism and anthropology at the University of Pennsylvania[29] and cultivated her writing throughout her life.[30]

Spotted Elk's life was punctuated by her aspirations to become a writer and the reality of having to perform often highly sexualized Indian stereotypes on both screen and stage. But unlike the "sexualized maiden" who embodies miscegenation fears and fantasies, Spotted Elk's burlesque performances hint at a more ironic striptease that acknowledges both the primitivism inherent in her roles on screen and stage and her own work to counter dominant narratives of Native people. She traveled to Paris with the United States Indian Reservation Band, a State Department–sponsored musical troupe that was commissioned to play at the 1931 International Colonial Exposition. After the Exposition ended, Spotted Elk stayed in Paris to perform in cabarets and nightclubs, appealing to Parisians in much the same way as Josephine Baker, who arrived in Europe six years previously. Molly was "struck by the relative lack of color prejudice in France," which stood in stark contrast to her experiences in the United States.[31]

In France she also capitalized on her exotic image, as had Baker. Baker engaged what Wendy Martin calls "conventions of the burlesque to create a *danse sauvage* that played with the paradigm of the black exotic in the context of white colonialism."[32] Primitivism moved Indigenous peoples outside of history at the same time it made them available as sexual objects as an effect of modernity, a fact of which Spotted Elk was no doubt aware and mobilized in her favor. Lisan Kay Nimura, a European American dancer who often performed alongside her husband, Yeichi Nimura, "naturalizes" Spotted Elk's success as a performer: "After all, she was an American Indian and looked that way every inch. She wore an Indian coat and braided her long black hair. . . . [On top of this,] she moved exquisitely."[33] Spotted Elk's career in France was launched on her exotic, sexualized image, but she steered her course in directions that allowed her to revise representations of the Native sexualized "savage." She procured opportunities for herself to lecture on American Indian history in public venues; performed her version of traditional Penobscot dance on concert stages; and befriended philanthropists, politicians, and intellectuals from all over Europe, as well as U.S. expatriates.[34]

The tension between the economic and social benefits of a career in film and Native American revisions of the past and dominant cultural historiography was evident in government policy regulating film plots. Writing to the Selig Polyscope Company in May 1911 in response to their request for permission to employ Native American actors and to film on reservations, commissioner Robert Valentine stipulated that Native Americans recruited from reservations to act in films needed to be disciplined in appropriate uses of the past. He wrote, "There is a great deal of danger that, through the taking of pictures of Indians in their old dress and engaged in their old-time customs, the Indians are led to believe that that is the side of them which interests both the public and the Government."[35] For Valentine, the "danger" of cultural and historical reenactments via redfacing on the part of Indigenous practitioners was that they reanimated Native American history as vibrant, viable, and in dialogue with the present and future. Richard Abel notes that western films mined the "usable past" as part of the myth-making enterprise that served the project of colonialism, often even in the most sympathetic of films.[36] What white filmmakers and government officials considered the "usable past" were those narratives that upheld the colonizing goals of the United States. This conception and use of Native American history differs significantly from how Native American actors considered the past as engaged in dialogue with the present and future.

For Native actors, performances of "old-time customs" deconstructed a teleological trajectory that rendered the past "savage," undesirable, and inaccessible. These performances thus troubled how European Americans had narrated nearly three hundred

years of government-sanctioned colonialism and cultural genocide. Filmic performances by Native Americans challenged the
dominant culture's will to believe that Indigenous people were
eager to eschew their cultural heritages and identities for a European American one through the policies of enforced assimilation.
These performances also offer up a reading of film in some cases
as a technologically mediated extension and revision of the Ghost
Dance religion, a late nineteenth-century practice that sought
to erase colonial history and thereby return to a pre-invasion
period through collective dance performances and a revision
of Western notions of history and teleology.[37] In his study of
Native American documentaries on the Wounded Knee massacre, Steven Leuthold suggests, "The revival of the rhetoric of
the Ghost Dance at Wounded Knee exemplifies how traditional
expressive forms serve a rhetorical function in the context of
the new media environment."[38] Film as Ghost Dance serves as
a powerful collective metaphor to reinvigorate Native American
epistemic knowledge and practices in the service of Indigenous
communities rather than as a technology that would erase colonial
histories. While not all actors aligned their work with those of
Ghost Dance practitioners, interpreting film through this lens
provides a conceptual tool for contemporary scholars looking
back at these early film productions to envision how Native actors
may have viewed the relationship between their profession and
their social lives.

Native Americans seeking employment off the reservation
from the mid-nineteenth century through the first decades of
the twentieth century needed government permission to do so in
most cases. They also had to negotiate the ambivalent discourses
of federal policies of assimilation that mandated "compulsory
Christianity,"[39] dominant social norms, and education in boarding schools, on the one hand, and popular and anthropological
interest in what was considered the Native American past and

tradition on the other.[40] Native peoples were compelled to embrace competing and incongruent discourses of the present and future with those of the past and to adhere to European chronotopic notions of time and space that may have been unfamiliar to them. For many Native American actors, film thus provided an array of opportunities to protect and utilize Indigenous epistemologies, critique colonization, engage with modernity, and ensure economic survival.

During the silent era, hundreds of films were produced with primarily Native American plots, and these films are often striking in their sympathetic and sensitive portrayals of Indigenous themes.[41] Andrew Smith Brodie argues that especially in the first decade of film technology "Native Americans, Mexicans, and white women were as likely to be central protagonists as were white cowboys. Moreover, Indians who were involved in the production of early westerns created sympathetic nonwhite characters and wrote screenplays that dealt with racism and assimilation."[42] Some film companies, such as Kalem and New York Motion Picture, "specialized in the production of pictures that featured only American Indian characters."[43] This is not to suggest that early twentieth-century Native American spectators embraced them as flawless or that twenty-first-century spectators would find these representations acceptable.

Native Americans were clearly active participants engaged with critiques of film production and the multiple valences of spectatorship. Within their own historical context, however, many of these silent films fleshed Native Americans out as human beings who interacted with a whole web of contemporary social, political, and cultural networks, not as historical anachronisms frozen and doomed to a ghostly past. The fact that Native American plots and subplots were prominent in so many silent films stands in stark contrast to the virtual invisibility of Indigenous people in popular media today.

In recent years there have been very few major network and cable television shows featuring prominent Native American characters, and of these very few have been women. *Northern Exposure*, a CBS series that ran from 1990 to 1995, featured Umatilla actor Elaine Miles, who played Marilyn Whirlwind, a Tlingit physician's assistant and traditional dancer.[44] Whirlwind was the only prominent female Native American television character of the twentieth century in the United States. After *Northern Exposure* the only conspicuous Native American network television character was John Redcorn on *King of the Hill*, a Fox animated series that first aired in 1997. Redcorn was originally voiced by Yaqui actor Victor Aaron until his death in 1996 and is currently voiced by Jonathan Joss, a Comanche actor and director. Another CBS series, the short-lived *Wolf Lake* (2001–2002), starred Oneida actor Graham Greene as Sherman Blackstone, a mysterious biology teacher who is the keeper of the town's lycanthropic secrets. NBC's 2008 season of *Law and Order: SVU* introduced one of the most nuanced Native American television characters, Mohawk police detective Chester Lake. Played by Saulteaux actor Adam Beach, Lake grew up in Brooklyn, descended from a long line of high-steel workers. Not only does his intimate knowledge of New York City surprise his coworkers, he also collects rare books, was a foster child, and participated competitively in mixed martial arts.[45] Despite these rare exceptions, contemporary U.S. broadcast television and Hollywood films feature very few representations of Native Americans. According to Roscoe Pond a 2009 Screen Actors Guild report demonstrates that "American Indians held steady at 0.3 percent of all roles for each of the last two years. These statistics are not good. It is now 2010, and still there are no lead acting roles for Native men and women on primetime television. The same can be said of no lead characters in major studio films."[46] The situation in Canada is slightly better given the rise in self-representations of Indigenous people through the creation of the Inuit Broadcasting Corporation (IBC), Television Northern Canada (TVNC), the Aboriginal Peoples Television Network (APTN), and Isuma TV.[47]

Silent "Sympathies" and Narrative Gestures

In stark contrast to the late twentieth and early twenty-first centuries, Native Americans were much more visible in the silent era in both feature-length fiction films and nonnarrative cinema.[48] Nonnarrative films of the silent period document a range of Native American experiences at the turn of the twentieth century, from the lives of children in federal Indian boarding schools to those of actors who were involved in the Wild West Shows, as well as the oppressive and impoverished conditions of reservations. Pre-cinematic actualities and silent films, created by both Native and non-Native directors, present a snapshot of the often-contradictory attitudes towards Native Americans from the turn of the twentieth century to the sound revolution of the late 1920s. Nonfiction films exemplified a representational field that ranged from one-reel movies in the salvage anthropology vein to those that presented Native American experiences in a social justice light. *Esquimaux Village* (1901), filmed at the Pan-American Exposition in Buffalo, New York, features a simulated Inuit village in order to present an "authentic" image of Indigenous people to fairgoers and cinema spectators, an image that fixed Native Americans in the past as part of a premodern, preindustrialized world with no viable future.[49] *The Vanishing Indian* series by Sioux Super Films produced in the 1920s foregrounds "traditional" ethnographic practices and material artifacts of Native Americans (a Navajo wedding, Apache wickiups, Taos Pueblo dances) in order to preserve, at least on celluloid, the so-called vanishing cultures of Indigenous people for anthropological study.[50] *Serving Rations to the Indians, No. 1* (1898) is an abject view of Indigenous people in the Southwest receiving government rations in front of their log cabin. This film underscores the poverty and misery of Native Americans on reservations at the same time it presents an image of Indigenous people as domesticated and nonthreatening, receiving "civilizing" foods (sacks of grain and flour) from "benevolent" white agents of the government and Christian churches.

Narrative films reflect this same ambivalent impulse to contain Native Americans in a Social Darwinist reading of history and present them as complicated figures in a broader national drama. These films often foregrounded the national policies, attitudes, and events that shaped Native American lives, such as the institution of the federal Indian boarding school system in the United States and the residential school system in Canada, the fallout from the General Allotment/Dawes Act of 1887, exploitation of natural resources on tribal land, and government-sanctioned discourses surrounding race and gender.[51] While these films did not significantly alter damaging stereotypes that were already in place by the end of the nineteenth century, they did bring contemporary Native American experiences to the fore and opened them up for public discussion. Joanna Hearne argues that Hollywood silent films "did not change the prevailing negative cultural stereotypes about Native Americans, but they did produce a large number of westerns and documentaries that offered alternative viewpoints influenced by the Indigenous writers and filmmakers, reform movements, and racial theories that were widespread at the time."[52] I argue that these counterreadings can be accounted for in two ways. The highly theatrical dimensions of silent film—the spotlighting of the actor's body, costuming, and gestures, for example—focus our attention outside the verbal narration of the plot. The intertitles of silent films also permitted Native American speech in ways that would be disallowed with the advent of sound and the monosyllabic, pidgin forms of imagined Indigenous language that would later dominate mid-twentieth-century western films. Secondly, production companies in the silent era hired more Native American actors than "talkies" would, and these actors left their imprint on films in ways that have yet to be fully recovered.

Most of these films that scholars have characterized as "sympathetic" (if problematically so) can be divided into three main interrelated categories: miscegenation plots, narratives of the plight of Native Americans upon graduation from federal Indian boarding schools, and attempts to make Indigenous people commensurable and sympathetic to a white spectatorship, through representations of "authentic," unadulterated Native American culture. Films with Indian plots featuring Native American actors and directors from the early cinema period through the 1950s mirrored the state of mind that DuBois characterized as "double-consciousness" in *The Souls of Black Folk*. For the Native American participants, participation in these films constituted an experience of double consciousness, an act of being compelled to self-examination through the eyes of the dominant culture while also attempting to self-represent in ways that were consistent with Indigenous practices. Given the complicated history of Native American relationships with invader-settler states and European American law, this state might more usefully be thought of as what Audra Simpson calls "a tripleness, a quadrupleness, to consciousness and an endless play."[53]

An early film about miscegenation, *White Fawn's Devotion* (1910), directed by James Young Deer, is a subtle study of a family composed of a white frontiersman, his Native American wife, and their mixed-race daughter. After a series of events sparked by a misunderstanding almost leads to the family's dissolution and death, the family is reunited. This film is unique in the history of visual images of miscegenation because it does not pathologize the mixed-race heteronormative union.[54] The conclusion of the film is marked by a romantic reunion of the mixed-race couple with their daughter, who shuttles, seemingly effortlessly, between her mother's Lakota community and her father's European American culture.

Like the melodrama *White Fawn's Devotion*, *Little Dove's Romance* (1911), a film starring Young Deer and his wife, Princess Red Wing, foregrounds the consequences of misreading. When Little Dove sustains a horse riding accident, a party of two white hunters and their Indian guide (played by James Young Deer) nurses her back to health. When her generic Plains Indian camp eventually finds her, they mistakenly believe she has been harmed by the hunting party. When Little Dove returns to thank the white men, she falls in love with one of them, but her affection is unrequited. While the hunters save her from their Native American guide, who attempts to rape and kidnap her, she is returned to her Indian fiancé. *Little Dove's Romance* undermines western film conventions by narrating the film from the point of view of Native Americans (the subjects of most of the camera's visual interest), by centering the romantic resolution on a Native American couple, by imagining the Native American community in the film to be intact and flourishing, and by focusing on the white hunters as interlopers in Indian territory rather than representing Native Americans as aliens.[55] Yet the film also advocates a Jacksonian paternalistic attitude towards Native Americans. It suggests that the two communities should remain relatively separate from each other, that miscegenation is undesirable, and that Native individuals who come into too much contact with European Americans are dangerous and pathological. This last point is illustrated in the film when the Indian guide (who is clothed in the same manner as the white hunters, as opposed to the other Indian characters who wear buckskins, beads, and feathers) attempts to rape and abduct Little Dove. Although the U.S. government was carrying out a large-scale, devastating policy of assimilation through often-compulsory boarding school education for Native American children predicated on visually erasing tribal identity through a series of before and after photographs, the film upholds the need for a racial-optics system whereby Native Americans are policed through the dominant culture's ability to recognize them as Indigenous through their dress and physical and cultural separateness from other communities.

Other "sympathetic" films of the period with miscegenation plots do not criminalize heterosexual mixed-race marriage, but nonetheless portray it as either a tragic impossibility given the dominant culture's racism or something that is unpalatable to Native American communities. These include *Ramona* (1910), *The Chief's Daughter* (1911), *The Tourists* (1912), *The Squaw Man* (1914), *Just Squaw* (1919), *The Heart of Wetona* (1919), and *The Vanishing American* (1925).

In narratives about education, Native Americans (usually male) return to their reservation communities after attending federal Indian boarding school or university and find themselves caught between two worlds, an experience of double-consciousness. A rare portrayal of a Native American woman as lead protagonist, *Maya, Just an Indian* (1913), features a young woman who returns to her community after graduating from Carlisle Indian Industrial School in Pennsylvania and falls in love with and marries a white prospector, ostensibly because she has adopted European American values and no longer feels accepted by her community. The prospector abandons her for a white woman after she shows him where to pan for gold. The film critiques Maya's poor treatment by her white husband at the same time that it casts her in a tragic role as "just an Indian," the "Celluloid Maiden" victim of colonialism and assimilation. *Strongheart* (1914), another complex film about assimilation, narrates the story of Strongheart, a college graduate and football star who falls in love with a white woman. After his father dies, he leaves his life in the East to return to his tribe, an act he does out of filial duty, which represents a tragic fate in the eyes of European American spectators.

Both *Red Love* (1925) and *Redskin* (1929), however, center on less tragic readings of the boarding school experience. *Red Love* is animated by a heterosexual love triangle between two men: Thunder Cloud (John Lowell), a Lakota Carlisle graduate and horse and cattle thief; and James Logan/Little Antelope (F. Serrano Keating), a Lakota police chief; and a young woman, Starlight (Evangeline Russell), whose father is a white sheriff and whose mother is Lakota.[56] This independent film is remarkable for its representation of the reservation not simply as a site of unmitigated misery and anachronism, which prefigures the findings of the Merriam Report of 1928, but also as a space where Native Americans respond in sophisticated ways to modernity, invader-settler society, and flexible characterizations of Indigenous culture in the early twentieth century, despite the fact that none of the lead characters are played by Native American actors. *Red Love*, released a year after the American Indian Citizenship Act of 1924, provides no point of entry for a white spectatorship as its romantic plot centers on Native American characters.

Similarly, *Redskin* (1929), released at the dawn of the sound revolution in film, provides a more nuanced view of assimilation and Native American interfaces with imposed Western educational systems. *Redskin*'s diegesis centers on Wing Foot (Richard Dix), a college graduate who returns to the Navajo reservation but has trouble reintegrating into life there. After breaking several social taboos, including falling in love with a Pueblo classmate, Corn Blossom (Julie Carter), who has also returned to her community, he discovers oil on the reservation and finally finds acceptance by ameliorating the tribe's impoverished condition as a result. Unfortunately, like *Red Love*, *Redskin* features no Native American actors in lead roles, despite the large number of Indigenous actors who were available.

The third main category of silent narrative films that features Native American plots focuses on representing Indigenous people as sympathetic, human, and humane characters who struggle to survive in the face of multiple forms of violence perpetrated by European American invader-settlers. These films attempt to foreground issues of social justice (even if the terms and boundaries of what constitutes justice are dictated primarily by white directors through Western ideologies and epistemologies) by rendering Native Americans commensurable to white spectators. These films do not necessarily endeavor to present Indigenous culture through a Native American perspective, but they do try to challenge the prevalent stereotype of the bloodthirsty savage through drawing parallels between European American and Native American values. Several of these films exclusively feature Native characters within a tribally specific representational field but still provide a point of entry for a white audience by underscoring putatively universal plots centering on issues such as heterosexual romance, heroism, Christian-influenced self-sacrifice, and loyalty.

Films within this category include D. W. Griffith's *The Redman's View* (1909), which attempts to narrate the history of colonization through an Indigenous lens and is clearly sympathetic to Native American perspectives even if its diegesis is part of a broader representational fantasy and, unlike many other silent films, it features no identifiable Native American actors in key roles. The film opens in a peaceful Kiowa camp, and the first scenes introduce a romantic plot that centers on two young Native Americans, Silver Eagle (played by Owen Moore) and Minnewanna (played by Lottie Pickford, Mary Pickford's sister). After a violent attack by white men who covet Kiowa land, Minnewanna is taken captive to prevent a massacre. The film places the spectator in the position of identifying and sympathizing with the romanticized Kiowa characters. Yet it still works ideologically to situate the historical context of the film as a series of events well within the scope of the past and is not aware of the problematics of telling "the redman's view" through a white director's voice and casting choices. While it compels the spectator to think critically about colonization, it does so through focusing its critique on greedy European American individuals rather than implicating more widespread governmental policies that eroded Indigenous land bases.[57] According to Gregory S. Jay, D. W. Griffith's representation of Native Americans, like those of African Americans that would follow in works such as *The Birth of a Nation*, "still adheres to the logic of white supremacy" through its indexical references to racist discourses surrounding Indigenous peoples that work to close off access to a viable present or future.[58]

Redfacing On and Off the Silent Screen

Redfacing is remarkably similar to, but also profoundly different from, blackface minstrel stage and screen performances. Historically, it preceded and was concomitant with blackface performances in North America as evidenced by, for example, the Boston Tea Party participants dressed as Mohawks in the eighteenth century and Edwin Forrest's popular stage characterization of Metacom, a Wampanoag sachem, in the nineteenth century.[59] Both racial performance styles engage in what Eric Lott has termed "a mixed economy of celebration and exploitation" that simultaneously underscores social, economic, and cultural differences between races and facilitates movement across these divides "in which transgression and containment coexisted, in which improbably threatening or startlingly sympathetic racial meanings were simultaneously produced and dissolved."[60] This ambivalent act of what Lott calls "love and theft" is mirrored in redface performances that enable a complicated form of appropriation through both white working-class and middle-class desires to play Indian. Through redfacing, the Indian is primarily imagined as a marker for values associated with the mythologized version of America (freedom, justice, strident individualism, etc.) and the "natural rights" philosophy popularized by Jean-Jacques Rousseau and Thomas Jefferson that "ennobled" Native Americans in order to discursively deprive them of land and life. Eighteenth-century discourses on natural rights, wedded to Victorian notions of the individual, led to governmental policies in the late nineteenth and early twentieth centuries that deemed Native Americans morally and spiritually deficient, ill equipped to "appreciate" European American understandings of opportunity and mobility.

In his work on blackface minstrelsy in Hollywood, particularly as it was performed by Jewish American actors, Michael Rogin argues, "Minstrelsy claimed to speak for both races through the blacking up of one. [Al] Jolson's blackface 'My Mammy,' in the service of Americanizing immigrants, pretended to the absence of conflict between black and white."[61] Likewise, redface performances by white actors who were spray painted with pigments to give their skin a reddish tone also elided the incredibly violent and complicated realities of North American history. Yet these performances did so in order to herald the success of genocidal policies against Indigenous peoples. Redface ostensibly became necessary in the film industry as the nation rendered Native bodies invisible, vanished, and extinct. If there were no Native Americans available to play these roles, the logic of redface suggests, then white actors were required to perform American Indian characters. Despite the early successes of Young Deer and Carewe, discursive redface also allowed non-Native scriptwriters and directors to have a large sphere of control over how Native Americans would be represented. On the broader national stage, the erasure of Native Americans, represented as more or less conceding their homelands to European invader-settlers, conjoined with these filmic representations to create a national fantasy wherein European Americans could perform as autochthonous by stepping into territories and roles ceded to them through putative Native absence.[62]

Unlike blackface, redface performances by white actors operated significantly under the assumption that Native Americans as a distinct group of peoples had disappeared and therefore were not available to fill "Indian" roles. This "vanishing" of Native Americans occurs as early as 1000 CE in the *Vinland Sagas* where Indigenous people along the northeastern seaboard of the future United States briefly appear and disappear, leaving behind narratives of mythological figures that always recede to the horizon.[63] In colonial texts, Hollywood cinema included, the myth of the "vanishing Indian" becomes so concretized that it gives rise to the question of whether Native Americans existed at all. Official and unofficial discourses of the dominant culture bolster this view, from the fantastic tableau of the imagined first Thanksgiving to the irony of the name of the post-9/11 Office of Homeland Security.

According to Roland Barthes, "Myth is speech *stolen and restored*. Only, speech which is restored is no longer quite that which was stolen: when it was brought back, it was not put exactly in its place."[64] This displacement accounts for the vertiginous quality of historiographies of the United States where foundational myths continue towards discursive violence through the substitution of concepts like "vanish" for "genocide" and where the devastating history of the mission system in California can be replaced by popsicle stick dioramas empty of Native presence, suffering, and labor in public schools. Yet much like the Wizard of Oz carefully orchestrating his power from behind the curtain, myth does not permanently delete history, but rather alters it. Barthes writes, "However paradoxical it may seem, *myth hides nothing*: its function is to distort, not to make disappear."[65] Native American actors who participated in redfacing puncture the work of myth by projecting an image that points to the distortion, calling attention to the place where speech was stolen, but never substituting the counterfeit for the original. Poet Carolyn Dunn considers the placeholder status of Native Americans in the cinematic myth machine: "I am the real Hollywood Indian / a blessing and a burden of myth."[66] The ironic oxymoron—real Hollywood Indian—stands in for a tricksteresque, self-conscious, sometimes-anguished play with language and performance on the part of Native American actors. Native Americans in redface countered the national narrative that Indigenous people had vanished, and they also subverted representations of Indians in colonial discourses through their divergence from stereotype.

Since the inception of film, there have been hundreds of non-Native actors who have played Native American roles in redface, thus fulfilling the dominant culture's desire to efface Native American traces to the point that they never seemed to have existed at all.[67] Yet what do we make of the many Indigenous actors who played Native American characters, some of whom also wore heavy makeup to ensure their skin took on a reddish cast or were fitted with prosthetic features to appear more "Indian"? These individuals enacted the prevalent discourses of the vanishing Indian by taking roles that were racist characterizations of Indian-white relations created by non-Native writers and directors, while at the same time they tested, critiqued, complied with, and attempted to overturn these stereotypical images both on-screen and off-screen. Their work as film actors and activists set the stage for late twentieth and early twenty-first-century Indigenous actors and directors who would take up the same issues, often by repudiating both the successes and failures of previous generations.

In his study of Bert Williams, a popular turn-of-the-twentieth-century Caribbean performer who played blackface roles, Louis Chude-Sokei describes the work of African diasporic actors as engaging in "black-on-black minstrelsy."[68] Chude-Sokei characterizes Williams's work as follows: "As a black performer who worked within the now universally despised yet still resonant space of blackface minstrelsy, he left a legacy as fraught as it was complex, as troubling then as it is productive now for a reevaluation of contemporary thinking about that crucial period of American and transatlantic modernism."[69] In their self-conscious interactions with film performance and its myriad possibilities for on-screen and casual, back-lot negotiations of racial representation through redfacing, Native American actors attempted to make a register of images not necessarily of their own creation. Like Williams, Minnie Ha Ha, Molly Spotted Elk, and a host of other Native American actors enjoyed national and international renown during their lifetimes yet fell into obscurity with the advent of sound technology and film histories that excluded Native American participation from North American cinema studies.

Minnie Ha Ha Gets the Last Laugh: Gender, Comedy, and Silent Smoke Signals

In a nearly eponymous role in *Fatty and Minnie He-Haw* (1914), a Keystone-Mutual slapstick western production directed by Roscoe Arbuckle and Eddie Dillon and produced by Mack Sennett, Ha Ha plays Minnie, the Native American love interest of Fatty (Roscoe Arbuckle), a grifter who is ejected from a passing train. This role is rare in the history of cinematic representations of Native American women because it represents a central figure who not only holds a high position in her own community but is treated with esteem by local white townspeople. She possesses a clear sense of sexual agency that is not predicated on the looking relations that dominate most gendered and raced viewing practices. She is unambiguous about her desires and she does not conform to most Western standards of beauty (she is overweight and dark-skinned), therefore atypical in relation to other roles that typify Marubbio's "Celluloid Maiden." Neither does Minnie epitomize the "hag" or "drudge" figure "notable for her many children and haggard body."[70] While she is eventually thwarted in her desire to marry Fatty due to his predilection for fraud, she neither dies at the end of the film, as many other Indigenous female figures do, nor does she place herself outside the conventions and geographic space of her community by her desires.

While the miscegenation plot is foiled, it is not because of a larger anthropological discourse on race wherein Native Americans are pathologized, but rather the product of Fatty's own character flaws. Miscegenation in the space of the film becomes a possibility because of the Native community's seemingly flexible notions of race and belonging. The community welcomes Fatty as Minnie's potential husband, but on their own terms (the wedding is conducted in the community in a non-Christian, putatively "Indian" fashion), and it is clear that it is Fatty who will be adopted by and have to assimilate into the community, not vice versa. Part of the supposed comedy of this plot is that Fatty is confronted with the choice of surrendering his dominant position in society vis-à-vis his whiteness in return for safe harbor from the U.S. legal system. This plot overturns other silent films whose premise is that while miscegenation is possible, it requires the Native woman to eschew her cultural values to live within a non-Indian paradigm. Ironically, while the conventional miscegenation plot affords the Native woman the possibility of upward social mobility through disavowing her community, this rarely occurs as the Native female character often dies before her subordination to dominant transformation is achieved.

Minnie stumbles upon Fatty while gathering firewood when he feigns distress to get Minnie's attention, acknowledged in the intertitles as "A ruse to get some sympathy." She escorts him back to her village, a generic Plains-style camp of tipis. Minnie's community, composed of Native actors (possibly Wild West show performers hired by Keystone) greets them. From her simple cloth dress, which stands in stark contrast to the other women's more elaborately decorated and tailored dresses, it appears that Minnie is both unmarried (she has no husband who can provide her with deerskin dresses) and is a prominent figure in the community (the chief of the camp appears as a kind of father figure to her).[71] Minnie's costume opens up the possibility of a double reading.

As a marker of her single and elevated status in the community, it can be read as a form of Indigenous-generated public pedagogy for the white spectator who equates ostentatious dress, wealth, and slimness with power. Or, conversely, her simple dress can be read as conventional visual proof of her unattractiveness, as Minnie's overweight, unmarried, plain-costumed character does not fit norms of standard beauty in the dominant culture. The possibility of a double reading of Minnie's character via an analysis of her costume demonstrates the double consciousness of Native American representations. Both Native and non-Native actors and directors must have been aware of the ways the dominant culture interprets Indigenous people, at the same time many of the films from this era parody stereotypes of the American Indian in order to display a counterreading from an Indigenous perspective.

Minnie soon begins to seduce Fatty inside her tipi in a scene entitled "The Allurement." Here Minnie begins to hug and kiss Fatty, to his mortification, as the con artist realizes that his plot to escape punishment on the train may lead to imprisonment in the form of marriage. When it becomes clear that their bellies are too large to accommodate a passionate embrace, Minnie becomes inventive, standing in front of him and craning her neck so that they can kiss unencumbered by their bodies. Encouraged by his response, Minnie proposes to him (the intertitle reads: "She offers her maiden heart in marriage"), but when Fatty hesitates, she "encourages" him at knifepoint.

The intertitle eschews a reading of Minnie as promiscuous (she offers her "maiden heart"), while at the same time it opens up the possibility that she may be offering a maiden heart, but not a virginal body. This suggests that Minnie may have tricked Fatty into marriage, proving that she is a more adept grifter than he is. This scene overturns the conventional western plot where the gullible Native American loses land or life at the hand of a cunning white character. In these standard scenes, the spectator is privy to the fraud while the Native character remains unaware until it is too late. In *Fatty & Minnie He-Haw*, however, Ha Ha is cast as an intelligent character who not only acts on her desires but also possesses the agency to effect a marriage on her own terms.

Minnie is not the damsel in distress who relies on male characters to chart her life course. She is also not a grim, stereotypical Indian figure in that she possesses a sense of humor. In a 1936 critique of the "Hollywoodean Indian," historian Stanley Vestal argues that cinematic portrayals of Native Americans are false and lifeless. He suggests altering the stereotypical image for a more sophisticated array of representations: "the Indian is actually a very human person—humorous, sexy, sensitive, tough and quick-tempered, a great gossip and practical joker, a born mimic, a politician from intimacy, and an incorrigible lover of human society."[72] While Vestal inserts some stereotypes at the same time he wishes to overturn others, his more expansive, multidimensional description of Native Americans, particularly in terms of his characterization of a tribal sense of humor, is mirrored in the film.

After Fatty is coerced into marrying Minnie, he realizes that the wedding preparations will involve a feast and that one of the dishes that will be served is roasted dog. Part of the humor of the scene is Fatty's unwillingness to eat a freshly killed dog, what spectators might view as a "savage" custom.[73] The in-group humor of this scene, however, revolves around the fact that the community does not select the white dog that passes in front of the camera to slaughter, but a brown one.

Reports of dog sacrifice in North America usually indicate a preference for white dogs, so the choice of the brown dog can be read in multiple ways.[74] Because the film is set in the West somewhere and the characters are clothed in Plains-style dress (see the chief's headdress) and live in tipis, perhaps the actors did not want to degrade through visual representation the spiritual practice of the Sun Dance, with which dog sacrifice is sometimes associated, by choosing the white dog. By serving dog at a marriage feast rather than as part of a Sun Dance ceremony, the actors may have capitulated to the representation of Native culture as alterity rather than enacted a form of mimesis that followed too closely spiritual practices performed on reservations.

This scene not only pokes fun at European American spectators' expectations, but also at intra-ethnic relationships. While some Native Americans engage in dog sacrifice rituals, others do not. Ernest Wallace and E. Adamson Hoebel note, "Dog meat was regarded as an almost sacred dish by the Sioux, and to the Cheyennes. . . . But the Comanches did not eat dog meat."[75] Their anthropological informant, Medicine Woman, related that "A nice, fat, boiled puppy is just like a turkey on Thanksgiving to you white people."[76] This scene opens up a space of multiple readings that is illustrative of the limits of the archive since interpretations of these films must rely so much on the films themselves. If the Native American actors in the film had control over the creation and staging of this scene, perhaps they were demonstrating that their characters were from the northern Plains, thus members of communities who participated in dog sacrifice. If the non-Indian director had full control over the scene, perhaps he wanted to mark the Indigenous community as utterly alien, capable of eating a meal that would be taboo in the West. This reading would indicate how much Arbuckle's character would have to lose if he chose to join Minnie's family through marriage.

Perhaps, too, in response to the conventional narrative of assimilation wherein the Native American character always chooses white culture over his or her own, the dog sacrifice can be read in metaphoric terms. The community serves up the brown dog rather than the white one in order to instruct Fatty on his future allegiances and the trajectory of his future life. He will remain with Minnie's family and assimilate into their culture rather than return to his own with his new bride.

What is most clear, however, from the smiles on their faces and their unheard yet visible laughter, is that the Native characters are aware of their double-consciousness: Fatty's on-screen revulsion, the anticipated spectators' response, and their own desires to screen elements of Indigenous experience. The Native characters seem to be testing Fatty's capacity for assimilation by offering him a feast item that challenged the West's anthropomorphism of dogs. They were also laughing at what Ha Ha noted in her interview was Hollywood's inability and unwillingness to "tell the truth" of Indigenous experience. The characters demonstrate that they are in on the joke that the dominant culture's cinematic representation of Native Americans was always already ridiculous and inaccurate for dramatic effect.

Cinderella in Moccasins: Race, Gender, and Class in *Mickey* (1918)

Ha Ha plays a similar uncredited role in the "genteel comedy"[77] *Mickey* (1918), a film released by the Mabel Normand Feature Film Company.[78] Directed by F. Richard Jones and James Young and produced by Mack Sennett, this two-reel romantic comedy that Simon Louvish calls a "sentimental 'Cinderella' tale"[79] stars Mabel Normand as Mickey, a playful, adventurous young woman from the outpost of Feather River, California, who falls in love with Herbert Thornhill (Wheeler Oakman), a cosmopolitan young man from Long Island who travels to California in the summer of 1917 to check on his gold mine.

Mickey's adoptive father, Joe Meadows (George Nichols), operates the Tomboy Mine, a gold mine that abuts Herbert's and has not been lucrative. Mickey and Joe live in a dugout cabin with "Joe's Housekeeper," played by Minnie Ha Ha, who is not listed in the film's credits. In an effort to expose Mickey to "appropriate," which in the space of the film means "urban and non-Native" female influences, Joe sends Mickey to live with her aunt, Mrs. Geoffrey Drake (Laura Lavarnie), and her family on Long Island. However, once the aunt realizes that Mickey's inherited mine is worthless, she forces her niece to serve as a maid in the household.

Ha Ha's role in *Mickey* is a complicated one. She epitomizes the role of alterity as the opposite of Marubbio's "Indian Maiden" popular in films of this period: she is the desexualized, dark-skinned, corncob pipe–smoking woman employed as housekeeper in the very poorest of white households. Yet her role also suggests that she is matriarch of a family that cannot be recognized as such given its historical context and locality. Ha Ha's ambivalent role resists mass-mediated images of Indigenous women as well as critiques the social conditions under which Native American women operated at the turn of the twentieth century.

Minnie is both Joe's common-law wife and possibly Mickey's biological mother, two roles that would have violated social taboos in the representational world of the film's historical, geographical, and cultural context. In the opening scene she is the second character to be introduced, after Joe. She strops a straight razor, preparing to give Joe a shave. This scene is intercut with a shot of

12. Minnie (Minnie Ha Ha) tries on a hat in *Mickey* (1918).

a cat hunting and killing a frog, evoking images of tomahawk-wielding, Native American scalping practices and "savage" violence. When the shot cuts back to the cabin's interior, the spectator expects to witness Joe's lifeless body rather than the clean, bloodless shave he receives.

This scene conjures up another key image in the lexicon of North American racialized fears: the shaving scene from Herman Melville's novel *Benito Cereno* (1855). Captain Amasa Delano's misreading of the scene of a slave rebellion offers up what Jonathan Elmer has called a "pedagogy of the misrecognized event."[80] Like the African slave Babo, Minnie appears to be trapped in an economy of servitude out of which she cannot escape. The key difference, however, is that her servitude is compounded by gender and her seemingly sexualized relationship to Joe. Also, she does not share a community with which she can stage an uprising—as does Babo—as she has no visible social contacts outside the Meadows family.

After the Tomboy Mine yields gold, Joe plans a trip to Long Island with Minnie to deliver the good news to Mickey. To prepare for the journey, he takes Minnie to the dry goods store in town to buy her new clothing and a fancy hat. She is fitted by a white, female store employee and sits with Joe in the same train car, suggesting Joe's intimate relationship with her; the complicated place of Native Americans within a segregated racial matrix that depends on the binary categories of black and white; and the ways in which Joe's whiteness and gender serve to afford Minnie temporary race privilege and protection while she shops and travels with him. In effect, Minnie undergoes a process of domestication through the acquisition of the hat that renders her potential for violence and revenge, as staged in the shaving scene, no longer possible or desirable. Minnie's assimilation is effected through her surrendering of the symbolic tomahawk (the razor) for the accoutrements of white femininity (the hat). Later, on the train, while Joe plays cards with other male passengers, he looks with affection at Minnie, who is seated across from him. He does not identify Minnie as his housekeeper on the train and enters the front door of the Drake mansion with Minnie rather than requiring her to use the servant's entrance, suggesting a will on his part to acknowledge Minnie's complicated social position.

While Minnie is described in the intertitles as "The only mother Mickey ever knew," the film intimates that she may be Mickey's biological mother, not just a surrogate maternal figure. While Mickey's father, Joe's best friend and co-owner of the mine, is acknowledged as deceased, no explicit mention is made of her mother. Minnie constantly watches Mickey from doorways and windows, always remaining hidden, but witness to Mickey's comic pranks, of which she tacitly approves by her smiles. After Mickey meets Herbert she confides in Minnie in an intimate scene outside the cabin, and later Minnie gives Mickey an elaborately beaded pair of moccasins when she leaves for Long Island, indicating her desire for Mickey's mixed-race identity to be remembered and acknowledged. The ideology of miscegenation in the film is complicated. Children of mixed-race unions appear to pose little threat to the dominant culture as Mickey is the film's heroine. Yet there is a subtler specter of a gendered threat as Mickey refuses to trade her moccasins, the external repository of her cultural heritage, for the Victorian high-heeled shoes that would limit her freedom of movement and thus provide her a more conventionally feminine image.

When Mickey's economic status is revealed to the Drake family, she is forced into becoming a maid for the family and is sexually assaulted by Reggie Drake (Lewis Cody), her cousin. The film engages in social critique as the upper-class Drake family is later revealed to be both morally and economically bankrupt. In an attempt to save the family from financial ruin, she forces Mickey into indentured servitude in order to preserve the illusion of social status on the eve of an important party for the local gentry, an act that closely mirrors Minnie's condition. Conversely, in fairy-tale fashion, Mickey is rewarded for her good deeds (she tries to save Herbert from financial collapse by jockeying his horse anonymously during a race) when the Tomboy Mine hits a rich vein of gold.

Tellingly, when Mickey is conscripted into becoming a servant, she wears a cloth dress that resembles Minnie's and dons the beaded moccasins that Minnie had given her. Mickey's maid uniform consists of a shapeless muslin dress and Minnie's moccasins.

That she would wear the moccasins while cleaning the Drake home is indicative of her resistance to becoming an indentured servant. She taps into dominant representations of Native Americans as "wild" and "savage" when she refuses to do housework properly by sweeping dirt under a polar bear skin rug and by sliding down the banister to dust it. Her self-conscious choice to wear the moccasins may also serve as an acknowledgment of her biological/surrogate mother's condition as indentured servant and how she is following, literally, in her mother's footsteps because of the conflated oppressive conditions of race, gender, and class. Although her racial identity is not explicit in the intertitles, Mickey performs here as many twentieth-century Native American and working-class women were forced to in the dominant culture: she holds an inferior social position, even though she is related to the family by birth, and is subject to sexual violence.[81] She is not only the rustic and naïve country cousin: her unspoken, yet intimated mixed-race identity and class identity makes her existence in the metropolis as dangerous as it would be on the California "frontier." In fact Minnie and Herbert move to California after their marriage, perhaps because such a mixed-race union would be deemed less of a social death there than it would be on Long Island.

Minnie's unspoken roles as wife and mother challenge conventional cinematic images of Native American women as what Marubbio calls "Celluloid Princess" figures: light-skinned women who conform to European American ideals of beauty. Marubbio defines these roles as "innocent, attached to an exotic culture, and linked to ritual and the American landscape; she yearns for the white hero or western European culture; and she sacrifices herself to preserve Whiteness from racial contamination."[82] Minnie neither fulfills a white standard of beauty—she is dark-skinned and overweight—nor does she traffic in fetishized notions of culture. She has long braids but wears a simple cloth dress and no jewelry (not the standard Hollywood Indian regalia), a costume marked more by poverty and the conditions of colonialism than by white fantasies about Native American accoutrements. As well, her tribal affiliation is not identified, and she does not appear to have a relationship with any local Native American communities.[83]

Minnie's role points to the violence of colonialism rather than to an internalization of the dominant culture's stereotypical notions of Indigenous femininity. Her condition as "housekeeper" that intersects with and discursively overshadows the silenced roles of mother and wife reflects the violent history of the Americas, and particularly of California, where women and children were sold into chattel and sexual slavery under the Act for the Government and Protection of the Indians, and where many communities, referred to by the derogatory term "Digger Indians," faced rapid, drastic reductions in population due to the effects of genocide associated with the mission system under Spanish colonization and the subsequent Gold Rush: murder, poverty, disease, social injustice, vigilantism, and diaspora.[84] Minnie, as a disenfranchised Indigenous woman, may have been part of Mickey's father's will: property to be inherited, protected, and exploited within a paterno-racist system that afforded her few, if any, choices.[85]

By the film's end, despite Minnie's performance as a common-law wife, it becomes clear that miscegenation is a liability and is only permissible in rural, isolated geographies. Joe and Minnie return to California, as do the newly married Herbert and Mickey, "where Indian/white marriages were acceptable," according to Aleiss.[86] Although the film offers up a critique of anti-miscegenation laws in the case of Native American–European American alliances by focusing on a plot that features the ingenuity, courageousness, and intelligence of a mixed-race protagonist who has been raised by a Native American maternal figure, by the film's conclusion this critique is emptied of some of its political and cultural work by resigning the main protagonists to a site of relative unimportance.

"Molly Spotted Elk is a dancer . . . but she also knows how to punch a typewriter": Gender, Redfacing, and Performance

The film that catapulted Molly Spotted Elk to fame in North America, *The Silent Enemy* (1930), also features a romantic love subplot at its core but eschews the vexed subject of miscegenation by featuring an all-Native cast. *The Silent Enemy* is an epic tale loosely based on the seventeenth-century annual reports of Jesuit missionaries proselytizing in "New France" (Canada), popularly known as *The Jesuit Relations*. The film is set in pre-Columbian life in an Anishinabe community in what would become known as northern Ontario.[87] It narrates the struggle of a small band against starvation and features a romantic subplot between a handsome young hunter and a beautiful young woman who has been betrothed to an older, corrupt medicine man. The film attempts to present itself as footage of Anishinabe life prior to the arrival of Europeans, an act that would require spectators to imagine the impossible: that film technology was available prior to the twentieth century and that such footage would not indicate the *a priori* presence of Europeans. The film was directed by H. P. Carver; was written and produced by William Douglas Burden; and stars an all-Native cast, including Spotted Elk as Neewa, the love interest of Baluk (Chief Buffalo Child Long Lance). Burden intended the film to be an exercise in salvage anthropology and hastened to make it because he believed in the popular misconception that Native Americans were destined to vanish off the face of the earth in the near future. In his autobiographical work, *Look to the Wilderness*, Burden wrote: "It was all too obvious that the Indians were dying off so rapidly from white man's diseases that if the story of their endless struggle against starvation, their Silent Enemy, was ever to be captured on film, we had no time to lose."[88]

Although he eventually became critical of films dealing with Native American issues, the film opens with an appearance by Chauncey Yellow Robe, a Lakota actor who attended Carlisle and later became a member of the Society of American Indians, whose prologue to the film appears, on the surface, to support Burden's anxieties.[89] Yellow Robe wrote the prologue to the film himself and recited it in Lakota, although the audience is led to believe he is speaking Anishinabe.[90] Since the overwhelming majority of the film's audience would not know the difference between Lakota and Anishinabe, Yellow Robe's prologue speaks to his double-consciousness and the "trickster aesthetic."[91] He understood that the generic image of Indian speech that circulated in Hollywood would permit him to play on the myth of what David Murray calls "transparent intelligibility."[92] Describing the epistemic stakes of speaking and translating Indigenous languages in a public forum, Murray writes, "the penalty to the subordinate group for not adapting to the demands of the dominant group is to cease to exist."[93] Yellow Robe did not need to be ethnographically accurate in this scene because learning and speaking Anishinabe would be an act lost on his ignorant audience who would interpret his speech using the representational codes already available to them. As Jay Ruby argues, "The illusion of film realism works best if the audience knows little about the subject."[94] The translation Yellow Robe provides fortifies this "penalty" as his speech conforms to the vanishing Indian paradigm that imagines Native Americans out of existence.

Yet Yellow Robe also lets his smaller, in-group audience in on a little joke in the prologue by pointing to this double-consciousness. He pretends to speak a rival nation's language by reciting his own, a symbolic form of counting coup. Unlike the Indian pidgin that would define cinematic Native American speech in later periods, Yellow Robe's translation of his prologue into full sentences also indicates a strategy of resistance to stereotype. Cinematic Indian speech, particularly in the sound era, Barbara Meek notes, marks Indigenous characters as simultaneously "foreign" since their dialogue usually contains grammatically incorrect sentences and pidgin phrases and unsophisticated, even ignorant fabricated "baby talk" through the simple, toddler-like nature of their speech patterns.[95] By refusing to translate his prologue into Hollywood Indian speech, Yellow Robe refuses to mark his character as both alien and as an evolutionary immature figure new to human language. Yellow Robe subtly articulates a trickster aesthetic by at once performing an ethnographic act of disappearance through speech while at the same time signaling survival and resistance to the rhetoric of anthropological extinction through the very fact of his physical appearance and his participation in a linguistic sleight of hand.

Film, as an electronic medium, militates against the certificate of disappearance Burden had intended the film to embody. "The cinematic has something to do with life, with the accumulation—not the loss—of experience," Vivien Sobchack argues in defense of film "presence."[96] "Cinematic technology *animates* the photographic," she continues, "and reconstitutes its visibility and verisimilitude in a difference not of degree but of kind. The *moving picture* is a visible representation not of activity finished or past, but of activity coming-into-being."[97] Film asserts Yellow Robe as a body in present time and operates as a form of what Audra Simpson has called "ethnographic refusal" by speaking to and looking directly at his audience and by pointing to his role as an actor introducing and translating the forthcoming action of the film rather than as an ethnographic subject of the colonial gaze.

In the prologue Yellow Robe appears as Chetoga, the Ojibway

13. Chauncey Yellow Robe delivering his pro-logue in *The Silent Enemy* (1930).

chief and Spotted Elk's character's father, dressed in his fringed buckskin costume to give the audience a brief history of the Ojibway people. His appearance is both ghostly and intimate. He seems distilled in timeless space, wearing anachronistic dress, with no background to provide him any kind of historical or social context, and he speaks directly to the audience as a kind of interpreter for the film. Interestingly this opening scene features sound technology while the rest of the film is silent. His performance is unique because while many filmic portrayals of Indian characters feature silent, brooding figures, Yellow Robe directly addresses his audience, subverting the racial gaze. He states, "Soon we will be gone, but through our magic we will live forever." Employing "vanishing Indian" rhetoric, Yellow Robe claims that the film ("magic") will keep Native American images—if not people—alive on the virtual reservation of the film reel. If one follows the logic of Yellow Robe's statement, then the film is a kind of nightmarish version of the Ghost Dance religion, a tableau vivant in which Native Americans return to the prelapsarian, pre–European contact past, but a "usable past" captured entirely on film for the edification of non-Indian audiences. An alternative reading, however, informed by the off-screen lives and legacies of the actors, illustrates that the film performed a more complicated kind of symbolic Ghost Dance.

Such a reading suggests that while the film traffics in imagery that effectively traps Indigenous people in the past with no hope for a future, the film also engages in cultural off-screen work for the actors who participated in it and has also opened discursive spaces for contemporary Native American artists. The year 1928, the same year Burden was scouting for Native Americans to play roles in *The Silent Enemy*, was a difficult one for Anishinabe communities in northern Ontario. A new rail route permitted European Canadian hunters to travel easily to the region, decimating the population of fur-bearing animals, a key source of income for Indigenous families.[98] As a result, more than one hundred Anishinabe from all over the area expressed interest in acting in the film. Burden offered sixty dollars a month, which eased many families' fears of extreme poverty and malnutrition.[99]

But the film offered more than an economic opportunity. In 1928 the Canadian Department of Lands and Forests also passed a law prohibiting Native Canadians from participating in vital traditional activities such as hunting moose and cutting down trees to make birchbark canoes and other goods.[100] The Indian Acts of the late nineteenth and early twentieth centuries also outlawed social and religious ceremonies such as the potlatch and dancing, and enforced European Canadian gender norms on Aboriginal communities, often disenfranchising Native women and their children by providing membership to Native men and their wives (including women who were not of Aboriginal ancestry) but not to Native women who married non-Native men.[101] Because of these laws and enforced assimilation through compulsory residential school attendance, some of the actors hired for the film had to be taught by the crew how to do such things as paddle canoes and wear snowshoes. The stagings of cultural traditions in the film allowed the participants to take part in practices that were outlawed by the Canadian government. Inaccurate though some of these practices may be, such as the scene where Baluk is almost burned at the stake, Burden and director Carver appear to have solicited Native opinion on hunting and other practices depicted in the film. Burden wrote in 1930, "Every night we would gather with the leaders of the Indians and the older men of the company and talk over the events that were to be photographed the next day. Thus the story was essentially [re]written by the Indians themselves. . . . The picture grew out of the actual life experiences of our players, the Indians."[102]

For Spotted Elk, who had grown up on Indian Island in Maine, the film presented an opportunity to live closer to the land and engage in cultural practices she had not been exposed to as a child. She wrote in her diary in 1930 that she "was not acting, but merely living and feeling the part of an Indian girl of long ago. It was as if I had lived fifty years ago on my own reservation, where my people were hunters. . . . My interest in making an Indian film and the opportunity of being in the woods appealed to me more than anything."[103] Like the stars of the Wild West shows, actors on the set of *The Silent Enemy* actively engaged in the creation of representations of Native Americans and were

14. Neewa (Molly Spotted Elk) flees from a bear attack before being rescued in *The Silent Enemy* (1930).

able to, at least for the duration of the film shoot, participate in cultural activities that had been banned by the government.

Unfortunately, the lives of three of the film's most prominent stars—Chief Buffalo Child Long Lance, Molly Spotted Elk, and Yellow Robe—ended tragically. Long Lance committed suicide, and Spotted Elk spent time institutionalized in a mental hospital and died in poverty.[104] Yellow Robe died of pneumonia just six weeks before the film's debut.[105] Spotted Elk in particular has had a significant influence on a new generation of Indigenous artists, as Michelle

Olson and Muriel Miguel's dance performance *Evening in Paris* suggests.

Olson, a Tr'ondëk Hwëch'in (Hän) choreographer and dancer from Canada, and Miguel, a Kuna and Rappahanock choreographer and performance artist from the United States, employ the case of Spotted Elk to revise conventional understandings of Hollywood Indians, representations of mental illness, and traditional oral narrative through attention to Indigenous epistemologies. They do so through exploring the connection between bodily practice, autobiography, tribal memory, and the meager historical archival materials on early twentieth-century Native American performers. I consider how Olson and Miguel explore the tensions in Spotted Elk's life through the version of *Evening in Paris* I saw staged at Trent University in 2004 in order to imagine her as a figure attempting to assert visual and literary sovereignty under conditions of oppression and silence. Culling together their research on Spotted Elk from a published (auto) biography, Bunny McBride's *Molly Spotted Elk: A Penobscot in Paris*; from the Internet; and from Miguel's childhood reminisces of Spotted Elk, who was a family friend, Olson and Miguel employ the actor's life as a vehicle for talking about traditional oral narratives as living repositories of Indigenous knowledges and embodied practices.

As McBride reports, much of Spotted Elk's diaries were thrown away by her daughter, Jean Archambaud Moore, due to their potentially self-incriminating nature; however, what remains is a fascinating and rare glimpse, through textual fragments, into how a turn-of-the-twentieth-century Native American woman experienced her incredibly complicated and contradictory social context, enacted redfacing, and performed acts of visual sovereignty. In 1921 Spotted Elk reports growing weary of playing Indian for white audiences. While traveling with Milton Goodhue's Indian show in Rhode Island, Spotted Elk writes, "Poor crowd . . . Rode around. Had to ballyhoo in my costume. So tiresome I could leave the company. They're making a regular little monkey out of me."[106] Clearly when Spotted Elk possessed no agency over determining the content of Goodhue's Indian performances, the experience was demeaning and dehumanizing. She also reports on her ambivalence in working with other Native American performers. In the 1920s she toured with a musical troupe composed of Lucy Nicola, a Penobscot dancer and singer known by her stage name Princess Watawaso, an accompanist of unknown tribal affiliation identified as "Tommy Little Chief," and a Cherokee soprano known as Princess Wantura. She recorded in her journal, "Can't say I am overjoyed. Indians are such a changeable lot."[107] On the set of *The Silent Enemy*, her relationship to other Native actors was even more complicated. The white production crew was cautioned against associating socially with the Indigenous actors, and the lead actors were in turn segregated socially and spatially from the "rank-and-file Indians" hired as minor characters or extras.[108]

Spotted Elk's role as Neewa in *The Silent Enemy* complicates most stereotypical images of filmic Native American women. She neither enters into a romantic relationship with a white protagonist since all of the characters are Indigenous, nor do her actions necessitate her death towards the end of the film.[109] In a plotline similar to that of *Atanarjuat (The Fast Runner)*, produced more than seventy years later, Neewa eschews the arranged marriage her father has negotiated for her with the community's medicine man, Dagwan (Paul Benoit), in favor of a relationship with the film's hero, Baluk (Long Lance). This breaking of social taboos has negative repercussions—Dagwan is angered and blames the lack of game animals and near starvation of the community on Baluk, who is almost immolated as a result—but concludes with a favorable ending after Baluk finds a herd of caribou. This is not to say, however, that her character is free of stereotypes. She is sexualized through her revealing costume. In addition, Neewa adheres to sexist notions of women's roles predicated by the dominant culture in the form of the damsel in distress: while on a hunting expedition with a young girl, she is saved from a bear attack by Baluk.

Although the film won rave reviews from critics at its premiere, it was unsuccessful at the box office.[110] In fact the film was virtually forgotten until 1973 when the American Film Institute rescued the silver nitrate negative from disintegration. Perhaps one of the reasons for its failure was that the film did not provide a point of entry for its white spectators. Without a key European American character with whom the audience could identify, the film may have seemed too incommensurable to its non-Native audience. Also, released on the eve of the revolution in sound technology, its box-office failure could have been the popularity of new films using sound rather than intertitles and an orchestra. Perhaps the film was seen by audiences to be old-fashioned and outdated in terms of its subject matter, lack of point of entry, melodramatic acting style, and obsolete technology.

Evening in Paris: Remembering Molly Spotted Elk, Reconfiguring Redfacing

Despite the film's lack of commercial success, it provides one of the very few archived moving records of Spotted Elk's life and work. While there are no extant clips of Spotted Elk dancing, the film, McBride's text, and Spotted Elk's surviving journal provided Raven Spirit Dance Company, composed of Muriel Miguel and Michelle Olson, with the inspiration for their dance piece, *Evening in Paris*.[111] The title of the performance references Spotted Elk's tumultuous years in France, performing burlesque in Paris at the same time Josephine Baker was there and eventually escaping Nazi-occupied France by traveling "by foot, ambulance, and horse-drawn cart"[112] with her six-year-old daughter to Lisbon, Portugal. The dance piece celebrates Spotted Elk's glamorous celebrity life at the same time it delves into the more painful aspects of her experiences as an indigent house-keeper whose writing career was continually frustrated by the manual labor her circumstances forced her to perform, as well as her recurrent institutionalization in mental hospitals. Miguel notes Spotted Elk's ambivalent position as a celebrity within their New York City performing arts Native American community and as a partial social pariah whose behavior was unstable: "She used to stay at a cousin of mine's place in New York, and she was scary. We were nine . . . and she would scare the hell out of us. She wrote constantly and would glare at us when we ran into the room.[113] The title of the piece refers to Olson's grandmother, who wore Evening in Paris perfume and struggled with alcoholism, domestic abuse, and shattered dreams of a sophisticated, urban existence in her remote Yukon community.

Olson weaves her personal story into Spotted Elk's in order to foreground an Indigenous epistemology that interprets life events through a traditional, oral narrative. Jacqueline Shea Murphy has described this recuperative project as "becoming, rather than playing at," an argument that supports dance as a space of accessing different modalities of time and subjectivity.[114] The performance develops an alternative methodology for historical research at the same time it demonstrates how representations of Native Americans in film and the actors who participated in early cinema continue to influence and provide inspiration for contemporary artists. The dance piece decenters a tragic read-ing of both Spotted Elk and Olson's unnamed grandmother's story that would privilege colonization, trauma, and Western conceptions of mental illness by situating these two lives as part of a broader narrative of transformation. Spotted Elk, as read through her posthumously published collection of oral narrative, *Katahdin: Wigwam's Tales of the Abnaki Tribe*, becomes, in the performative space, a woman who turns into a bird in order to escape the strictures of her historical and social context. Likewise,

15. Michelle Olson as Molly Spotted Elk in *April in Paris*. Performed at the Red Rhythms: Contemporary Methodologies in American Indian Dance Conference at the University of California, Riverside, in 2004. Photograph by Matt Blais.

Olson's grandmother's story is filtered through a Tr'ondëk Hwëch'in tale of a swallow who turns herself into a woman and returns to her bird-state upon death.

Olson mines from Spotted Elk's biography, journals, and performances to flesh out a story that is intricately woven with that of her own grandmother. This is symbolized most dramatically in the change from the performance piece's title at the 2004 Red Rhythms: Contemporary Methodologies in American Indian Dance Conference, *April in Paris*—an allusion to Spotted Elk's expatriate life in Paris—to its incarnation two years later at the University of Trent as *Evening in Paris*—a reference to Olson's grandmother's favorite perfume (and the fact that given her

16. Michelle Olson as
Molly Spotted Elk in
Evening in Paris. Per-
formed at NOZEM: First
People's Performance
Space, Trent University,
Peterborough, Ontario,
Canada, in 2006.

limited economic circumstances, this is the clos-
est to Paris she ever came). Olson's use of the
Spotted Elk material to foreground her own
autobiographical information mirrors that of
her tribe's historical cultural practice of depos-
iting Tr'ondëk Hwëch'in songs and dances with
other communities in Alaska for safekeeping as
a result of rapid change and "in the face of colonization."[115] The communities that safeguarded
the songs and dances no doubt were influenced
by them, as Olson has also been influenced by
these repatriated cultural practices, her own
contemporary dance training, and Spotted Elk's
life and work.

Evening in Paris commences with footage of birds in flight, screened against the stage curtain. The stage consists of this curtain and a semicircle composed of white feathers cut from fabric. As Spotted Elk, Olson creeps slowly from under the curtain onto the stage, her back toward the audience. She opens her mouth to scream, but no sound comes out as her shadow projects and blends into that of the flying birds. This image of Spotted Elk, drawn from the tragic close of her life, is completed by Olson enacting and recomposing a traditional story of transformation that she narrates:

> Once upon a time there was a woman who tried to turn herself into a swallow. First, she locked her kitchen door. Second, she opened up the window just enough so she could fly away. She sat on the stove and wiggled and wiggled and wiggled and wiggled. Nothing happened. It's magic. She stood on the stove; covered her head with a dishtowel. She hopped three times on one foot, then three times on the other foot. Nothing happened. She took the dishtowel and put it in her back pocket. And did the hula. Then turned three times. And leapt from the stove. It's magic . . . Oh my God! I'm flying! She flew around and around the room. And got caught up in the curtains and fell to the floor. She made Jello for dessert.

Both humorous and tragic, this story of partial transformation is set in the domestic space of a kitchen, suggesting Spotted Elk's inability to escape the confines of gender as well as racialized notions of Native Americans predicated on non-Indigenous images.

Shifting seamlessly to a celebratory mood (marked by more upbeat jazz music), Olson's dance movements become more exuberant and include air-writing gestures to foreground Spotted Elk's intense, life-long passion for literature. The curtain is again employed as a screen for projected film footage in which Olson appears in a fringed, 1920s-style flapper dress with feathered headband.

This dance sequence is set to Red Norvo's 1938 "Wigwammin," written by his wife, Mildred Bailey, a Spokane and Coeur d'Alene vocalist.[116] The lyrics open with "Dancin' on the reservation / Join in, it's a celebration / Jammin' to a new creation / Wigwammin" suggesting both enactment of stereotype and the Indigenous-authored "new creation" that stage dance and film performances by artists such as Spotted Elk offered. Olson's movements are frenetic as she shakes her hips and grabs her crotch and then slows down to strike stereotypical Hollywood Indian poses drawn from Spotted Elk's photographic stills that capture her as an erotic and exotic "Other." While this footage plays, Olson crawls out crablike from under the curtain, shoes on her feet, suggesting both the silencing of her writing by the exigencies of dancing for economic survival as well as rebirth from the prison of mass-mediated images of the Indian into the stage semicircle that she reclaims as her own. She begins to dance within the semicircle in a more graceful, flowing style and then begins performing some of the moves of the Hollywood Indian alter ego figure, but more joyously and slowly, reclaiming the stereotypical images on her own terms. The scene ends with her sliding onto her stomach and lifting her arms and legs like a bird in flight.

In the next scene, Olson shouts "Grandma!" and enacts the parallel, yet very different story of her grandmother:

> Once upon a time, there was a swallow who turned herself into a woman. Her feathered wings turned into long, brown hands; her beak into a knowing smile; and her bird legs into curvy legs. She fell from her tree . . . one drop, two drops, three drops. The sky is open for flight. Her body, jagged, twisted, torn to pieces. Once she could fly. Now only her mind can fly.

She enjoys an uneasy existence as a human until her husband becomes jealous of her bird-spirit and physically abuses her. She suffers domestic abuse "until she had no other choice but to spill all of her blood upon the earth. And turned back into a swallow.

Dance as an act of visual sovereignty here allows for the recuperation of redfacing from tragic, traumatic series of performances within a non-Indigenous circuitry of meaning to a site of healing as Olson and Miguel imagine the lives of these women differently. If the lives of Spotted Elk and Olson's grandmother, as well as Minnie Ha Ha, are interpreted through Yellow Robe's seemingly prophetic words, then the "magic" of performance opens up a space in which Native American subjects can "live forever" and in regenerative dialogue with contemporary Indigenous artists who are in the process of attempting to heal from the past.

Ha Ha and Spotted Elk's film performances make visible a complicated history of redfacing where violent and unacknowledged collective histories of Native American women are marked and mediated. As a profession, acting permitted both women access to geographical and cultural spaces and representational fields unavailable to most Native Americans at the turn of the twentieth century. Their work as Indigenous actors performing roles scripted for them primarily by non-Natives references the long and traumatic visual emblematics of colonization and its attendant gendered violence. Yet through the example of Olsen and Miguel's creative retelling of Spotted Elk's career, the lives of early Native American actors also become the stage for contemporary scholars and artists to rethink collective subjectivity and communal memory in North American film histories.

3 Tears and Trash

Economies of Redfacing and the Ghostly Indian

On January 4, 1999, Iron Eyes Cody died in his modest Silver Lake bungalow in Los Angeles at the age of ninety-four. A Wild West show recruiter, motion picture actor, stuntman, production crew member, and cultural consultant for almost eight decades, Cody began his career at the age of twelve and starred in hundreds of films (often in uncredited roles) as wide-ranging as *Custer's Last Stand* (1936), *Union Pacific* (1939), *The Paleface* (1948), *Broken Arrow* (1950), *A Man Called Horse* (1970), and *Ernest Goes to Camp* (1987), and in television series such as *Rawhide, Gunsmoke, The Waltons,* and *Fantasy Island.* Best known for his role as the crying Indian in the televised 1971 Keep America Beautiful Inc. (KAB) public service announcement, Cody became, for many people throughout the world, the quintessential symbol of the American Indian. In the announcement he weeps bitter tears about the destruction of the environment; he appears as a stoic and silent wise elder; and he wears the mid-nineteenth-century Plains accoutrements—the beads, buckskins, and braids, long

17. Iron Eyes Cody from the Keep America Beautiful public service announcement. Image courtesy of Keep America Beautiful Inc. © 1971. All rights reserved.

associated with a popular mainstream vision of redfacing. Each night in thousands of suburban homes, Cody's anachronistic, ghostly Indian figure paddled swiftly across the screen against the backdrop of polluting factories, an image that foregrounds modern anxieties about autochthony and (im)migration, nature and technology, authenticity and imitation. Cody, in all his majesty and high seriousness, was a real Indian.

But these images belie a tension surrounding Cody's identity that members of Native American communities, particularly those involved in mass media, had long known or suspected: Iron Eyes Cody most likely was not an Indian after all. Although he claimed to be Cherokee and Cree in his 1982 collaborative autobiography, *Iron Eyes: My Life as a Hollywood Indian*, Angela Aleiss and others have argued that he was white, the Louisiana-born son of Italian immigrants, who broke into the movie business by masquerading as an Indian.[1] Rayna Green terms Cody a "staple 'Indian' actor" who starred in hundreds of western films, but adds that although he was "enormously supportive of many Indian causes, [he was] really of Mediterranean heritage."[2]

While many Native American actors were compelled to enact redface performances for Indian roles, most Indian characters in Hollywood films have been played by non-Indians. Cody was an anomaly because he performed as an Indian both on- and off-screen. I examine two economies of the Indian that are central to the practice of redfacing—impostors and the "ghosting" of Native Americans in popular culture modes—in order to demonstrate how these economies trouble conventional, often static notions of Indigenous identity, identifications, and representation. Rather than define racial impostor identities like Cody's or create a barometer against which we can gauge "wannabes" from "real" Indians, I interrogate how figures such as Cody have inhabited, tested, and stretched the seams of Native American identity. I analyze redfacing by non-Natives, which parallels blackface, yellowface, and brownface performances of the twentieth century. Yet the striking difference in Cody's case is that, unlike other actors such as Al Jolson, John Wayne, and Marlon Brando, Cody rarely appeared out of character.[3] He tried on the stereotypical "leathers and feathers" costume of the Hollywood Indian and found it fit him like a glove, both on camera and off, throughout his long and successful acting career.

This chapter's literary, journalistic, and pop cultural archive—an autobiography, newspaper accounts, and a televised public service announcement—reveals an economy of passing that is counterintuitive in a national culture that privileges whiteness. Passing has always been tricky business in North America and arose as a result of the inherent instability of racial categories and the desire to codify, legislate, and control racial purity. It has been a central motif in American literature and visual culture and has been interpreted alternately as a sociocultural threat and opportunity. Passing has been a threat to the dominant racial ideology of the United States and Canada, which seeks to maintain Eurocentric hierarchies and control through visually recognizable phenotypes. It has also provided very clear economic and social opportunities to light-skinned individuals who are able to pass for white and gain access to careers and positions of power that were otherwise forbidden to them by what W. E. B. DuBois called "the color-line" in *The Souls of Black Folk*. The history of passing in North America generally assumes a racially ambiguous or phenotypically European individual adopting a white subject position in order to escape violence, acquire a middle-class lifestyle, or pursue sexual relationships prohibited by anti-miscegenation laws. Yet Cody's story reverses the historical flow of the passing subject from colored to white as he assumed a Native American identity.

Cody, through his peculiar form of masculine redfacing, participated in a long-standing history of Indians as what I call the "ghost effect" through his on-screen and off-screen performances, an effect and affect that opens up a larger discourse on passing, visual representations of Native Americans, and the strategic deployments of spectral images of Indigenous peoples that have a long history in North American culture. This tradition of ghostly

Indians in literature and visual culture follows a trajectory from at least the eighteenth century to the present with the continued invisibility of Native American history in public discourse and attempts by Indigenous filmmakers such as Chris Eyre and Shelley Niro, whose films reconceptualize the figure of the ghost in the service of Native American communities.[4]

Rayna Green, Philip Deloria, and Shari M. Huhndorf, among others, have demonstrated the importance of "playing Indian" to the creation and maintenance of European American identities in opposition to those of Europe.[5] Green writes that "Almost from their very arrival in the Americas, Europeans found it useful, perhaps essential, to 'play Indian' in America, to demand that tribal peoples 'play Indian,' and to export the performances back to Europe. . . . This performance, or set of performances . . . has its deepest roots in the establishment of a distinctive American culture."[6] Playing Indian also expressed anxieties about cultural change with increasing numbers of immigrants arriving in the nineteenth century and the attendant perceived threat to social mores, particularly in the United States. Huhndorf contends, "Adopting some vision of Native life . . . is necessary to regenerate and to maintain European-American racial and national identities. Going native as a collective phenomenon . . . expressed a widespread ambivalence about modernity, and it is in relation to modernity's ills that these Native representations took shape."[7] I build upon this crucial work in order to demonstrate how redfacing in the form of racial passing and the ghost effect not only contribute to our understanding of the scaffolding upon which European American identities are constructed, but also how Native Americans themselves have alternately contributed to, resisted, and redrawn the boundaries of mass-mediated forms of playing Indian.

Both racial impostors and Indian ghosts provide useful spaces from which to interrogate and reconceptualize Native American

identity since both operate slightl|
resentational continuums and the
center from its messy, excessive
figures force us to confront th'
discrete, bounded, essential ca
ghosts, as I read the character
announcement and his man'
uncanny, destabilizing sparks that ...
vanishing Indian rhetoric and Indigenous resis...
representation. Native Americans are rendered harmless and
unimportant through dominant discourses that treat Indigenous
peoples as spectral entities, when they are treated at all. The irony
of these apparitional figures, invoked in the nineteenth century
through spiritual mediums and represented in the twentieth
century through anachronistic televisual and filmic appearances
of typically lone, elderly, male characters such as the character
Cody plays in the KAB announcement, is that the ghostly Indian
is a platform from which a rhetoric of protest can be simultaneously launched and contained. Cody's character in the public
service announcement can prompt environmental action on the
part of the viewer through an appeal to guilt precisely because
he is figured as ghostly (i.e., therefore not within the bounds of
contemporary discourses on race in North America) and not a
member of a vibrant, extant community.

The KAB announcement representing Native Americans as
ghostly and silent stands in sharp contrast with the profound
social, political, and cultural activism of Native Americans in
the late 1960s and early 1970s and the intense media coverage
of events organized by the American Indian Movement (AIM)
and other groups. Dissatisfied with the civil rights abuses, inadequate health care, extreme poverty, and treatment by the U.S.
government of Indigenous people living on- and off-reservation,
Native Americans occupied Alcatraz Island for nineteen months

ng in 1969 in order to draw attention to the condition of
mporary Native communities.[8] Although not the first act
Indigenous civil disobedience of the 1960s, Alcatraz inspired
other Native American activist organizations such as AIM, which
in 1970 protested on Thanksgiving at the three hundred and fif-
tieth anniversary of the Pilgrims' landing at Plymouth Rock and
demonstrated against the desecration of the Black Hills by the
Mount Rushmore monument; in 1972 occupied the BIA head-
quarters in Washington DC and organized the Trail of Broken
Treaties, a cross-country protest of unrecognized treaty rights;
and in 1973 occupied Wounded Knee, South Dakota with Oglala
Lakota tribal members, resulting in the deaths of two Native
American men and attack by an unprecedented military force.[9]
When the KAB announcement was released in 1971, Americans
received contradictory images of Native Americans as social
actors struggling for recognition and empowerment and as lone
ghostly figures at odds with modernity.

To imagine Native Americans as existing solely in the past
as historical figures and in the present only as spectral entities
participates in what Renato Rosaldo calls "imperialist nostalgia."
"Imperialist nostalgia," Rosaldo argues, "revolves around a paradox:
a person kills somebody, and then mourns the victim. In more
attenuated form, someone deliberately alters a form of life, and
then regrets that things have not remained as they were prior
to the intervention."[10] Yet because so many Indigenous scholars,
activists, and community members argue for an epistemology
that considers the role of the spiritual and spirits as a vital part
of human existence, films like Shelley Niro's *It Starts with a
Whisper* (1993) and Chris Eyre's *Imprint* (2007) intervene in
an important discourse that takes spirituality and its attendant
"ghosts" seriously, without falling prey to a nostalgic, past-tense
vision of Indigenous culture.[11]

Through a discussion of the economies of passing and effect, I

examine the issue of Native American identity and identifications
and how these have been positioned within North American
media almost wholly within a discourse of nostalgia for what is
irretrievably lost. I discuss the ways Native American identity
remains an evasive character within the popular sphere and problematizes how scholars discuss the figure of the racial impostor in
literature and visual culture. If Cody was in fact a clever mimic
of the Hollywood Indian stereotype and achieved international
status as the world's most loved Indian as a result, then what
does his "unmasking" as a Sicilian-American actor tell us about
the ways in which Native American identities can be performed
and represented and how North American mass publics express
a willfully ignorant desire to believe these performances and
representations?

The primary reason I became interested in the figure of Cody,
and in the more general phenomenon of the Native American
"wannabe" or impostor, is because Cody's self-styled image became
a pervasive metonym for "Indianness" and Native American concern for the environment in the late twentieth century. Regardless
of whether Cody was or was not a "real" Indian, Native American
individuals, particularly those involved in mass media, to a large
extent have had to confront, conform to, or rethink the ways
in which Cody fashioned his Indian image. Cody was savvy in
choosing the style of the Plains warrior to emulate since this has
signified 'Indianness' to non-Native Americans since the advent
of the Wild West shows in the mid- to late nineteenth century.
His performance in buckskin drag opens up dialogue on a series
of difficult yet vital issues in Native American Studies, from
"traditional" notions of adoption and belonging to the historical,
social, political, and cultural ramifications of individuals who
have been either disenrolled from their tribes, who come from
communities not recognized by state and federal governments,
or who have no archivally verifiable way to prove their Native

American identities. Yet the ways in which Native Americans whose phenotypes do not match the Hollywood one that Cody mimicked have negotiated this image is important in the field of Native American studies as the twinned issues of identity and representation remain at the forefront.

The intersections between race, identity, representation, and literature remain an important and unresolved (and perhaps unresolvable) feature of the field of Native American Studies—particularly literary studies—and center on issues of cultural patrimony.[12] The question of who controls Native American representation is central to the debate and depends on clear definitions of what exactly comprises Native American identity, a question that is tricky—if not impossible—to answer. Terry P. Wilson contends that "No more knotty issue preoccupies Indian America than that of identity," which is usually expressed through degrees of Indian ancestry or blood quanta and attendant tribal enrollment, although "many within and outside the Native American community decry this framework of analysis."[13] As Hilary N. Weaver notes, "Indigenous identity is a truly complex and somewhat controversial topic. There is little agreement on precisely what constitutes an indigenous identity, how to measure it, and who has it."[14] Elizabeth Archuleta adds, "One of the most provocative issues facing American Indians today concerns the competing definitions of Indian Identity."[15] She suggests paying more attention to the ways Native American writers and performance artists imagine identity, blood quantum, and authenticity as metaphor rather than "a colonial discourse that promotes internalized self-hatred, alienation, and fractionation."[16] Weaver likewise contends that "rather than detangling where someone fits on a continuum between two cultural identities or worlds, it may be more accurate to say that indigenous people live in one complex, conflictual world."[17] Other Native American scholars, such as Jace Weaver, have contended that a preoccupation with issues of identity and authenticity has precluded any sincere discussion of Native American literature by and for Native people, a concern borne out of a tendency on the part of many in the field to employ identity as the lens through which to view all discourses relating to Indigenous people.[18] Yet the question of identity is important since mainstream U.S. and Canadian culture still views Indigenous issues in terms of authenticity and imitation and thus forces Native scholars and writers to contend with the messy business of identity. While it would be beneficial to move beyond questioning a particular author's claims to his or her Indigenous heritage and attempting to define what it means to be Indian to an analysis of the work that is being produced, the field is still grappling with these issues precisely because they are so complex. As Anne Anlin Cheng insists, identity issues continue to remain central in scholarship on critical race discourse: "The next generation of race scholars has to address the fundamental paradox at the heart of minority discourse: how to proceed once we acknowledge, as we must, that 'identity' is the very ground upon which both progress and discrimination are made."[19] Native American identity is a proving ground for radically different conceptions of the self and community—from the multiple modes of expressing self- and community-hood from Indigenous nation to nation to race-based, Western juridical notions implicit and explicit in the U.S. and Canada's desire to measure blood quantum and other Western concepts as a legal marker of belonging. Identity is, alongside sovereignty and theories of decolonization, one of the simultaneously vexing and liberatory issues at the heart of Native American Studies.

Iron(eyes)ing Drag: The Politics of Buckskin

Cody's debut as an autobiographer came in 1982 when he and his ghost writer, Collin Perry, published *Iron Eyes: My Life as a Hollywood Indian*.[20] The autobiography is a conventional

18. Iron Eyes Cody as he appeared in 1984. Image courtesy and copyright of Gary
L. Friedman/www.FriedmanArchives.com.

one, intertwining personal and professional details, and follows a fairly chronological order. The reader learns about the actor through his childhood stories, visual artifacts such as film stills and family photographs, and the description of his long career as a Hollywood actor from the 1910s to the 1980s. The reader is also presented with the actor's commentary on his own complicity in the shaping of the image of the filmic Indian and the ways in which his on-screen identity was both affirmed and problematized throughout his career.

I contend that it is important to read the actor's collaborative autobiography alongside a reading of his visual culture career and the history of passing in North America in order to better understand the complex ways in which Cody circulated in the public eye and responded to his image in redface. While auto-biographies are not unadulterated reflections of an individual's life, Cody's autobiography is fascinating because of the ways in which he anticipates his reader's desire for an authentic Native American subject. One of the most compelling aspects of Cody's autobiography is that it foregrounds the tension between what it means to "be," and to pass for, Native American and the kinds of pressures Native American subjects face in performing both a personal and mass-mediated version of an Indigenous identity for a large audience.

The reader meets Cody at the door of his small bungalow in Los Angeles. Perry writes in the prologue:

> I am greeted at the aluminum storm door by a tall man wearing long, black braids, a loud shirt, and hand-beaded moccasins made from what looks like an old pair of Hush Puppies. His sad, dignified face, deeply etched with age-lines, is instantly recognizable as the haunting one with a single tear in those famous ads for the environment. I shake hands with Iron Eyes Cody, the lines in his face almost disappearing as he breaks

into a boyish grin. "I'm amazed you found this place. You must have an Indian's sense of direction."[21]

Perry recorded the actor's life story over the course of five and a half hours one day in May 1981 in the intimate, domestic space of Cody's home. From Perry's first assessment of Cody, the reader gets a sense of the actor as a has-been, a rather pathetic, elderly figure marked as lower-middle class (he answers his own aluminum storm door) and rather tasteless (he wears a "loud shirt" and a revamped pair of worn, mass-produced, loafer-style moccasins). The reader also understands from Perry's description the ways in which Cody's choice of career forces him to enact an Indian identity every day, whether on-screen or off. For example, his face is universally recognized as the one from the public service announcement and he interprets the amanuensis's navigating skills as specifically "Indian."

Perry's prologue highlights the trope of Native Americans as domestic exotics. Cody's small bungalow does not have a guest bedroom, so Perry sleeps in the living room. Cody pushes all the furniture back and spreads buffalo skins on the floor for Perry to sleep on. While Perry stares at the blank screen of the actor's large color television set, he listens to Cody chant in his bedroom. He writes, "Must be a prayer, I think, and drift off into boyhood dreams filled with adventures unknown to my conscious life."[22] It is ironic that Perry stares at a blank television set, filling the screen with his own fantasies of Native American life, especially since most Americans' knowledge of Native Americans comes from Hollywood western films shown as reruns on television and serial programs such as *The Lone Ranger*, *Gunsmoke*, *Little House on the Prairie*, and *Dr. Quinn, Medicine Woman*. Yet it is not unusual that he projects fantasies from his boyhood on the screen since Native Americans are typically associated with American childhoods. The Boy Scouts and Camp Fire Boys and

Girls, for example, encourage children to master skills that troop leaders believe are specifically Native American survival tools, as Deloria points out in *Playing Indian*.

Cody's redface act for Perry strengthens the ghost writer's belief that the actor is, in fact, the genuine article. "As long as Native Americans who are very much alive today do not look, live, and talk like the anachronistic inventions portrayed in novels and movies," Louis Owens contends, "they remain invisible and politically powerless. If they caricature their ancestors by dressing and acting as they are shown to do in film and fiction, they become instantly recognizable as cultural artifacts of significance, but only insofar as they serve to inseminate the dominant culture with an original value."[23] In order to make his act believable, Cody had to enact his performance in redface on a daily basis. This is particularly ironic since he laments later in his autobiography, "I think most people have the notion that Indians have trouble being anything other than, well, Indians."[24]

The photographs Cody includes in the autobiography from his private collection evoke a nostalgic, ghostlike image of an American past at odds with its technological future. Motion picture technology signaled a new era of visual entertainment but also effectively foreclosed any viable and sustained imaginative present and future for Native Americans. After the silent era, western films featured Native Americans as marauding figures haunting the fringes of civilization, eventually giving way to white expansion. Beyond the silent era, contemporary Native communities were rarely portrayed on film. In the photographs Cody includes in the autobiography, the Indian is an anachronism, appearing in buckskin drag at Boy Scout jamborees and at the White House to legitimate the kind of harmless, accidental colonial encounters essential to U.S. nation-formation fantasies.

Yet despite the work the photographs perform in the pages of the autobiography, the exchange between Perry and his subject that takes place on the opening pages of *Iron Eyes: My Life as a Hollywood Indian* differs from the mode of production of many of its nineteenth- and early twentieth-century predecessors. According to H. David Brumble III, non-Native amanuenses who sought to record Native American lives were typically driven by scientific curiosity or had developed a personal relationship with the subject in question. Brumble writes, "In many cases the collaborators developed warm friendships [with their Indian informants]. For an immediate sense of this, one has only to read through old issues of *The American Anthropologist*, where one occasionally finds obituaries of Indian informants written by the anthropologists. There is always a real collegial feeling in these and often a personal sense of loss."[25] One would be well served, of course, to be suspicious of reading too much "real collegial feeling" into obituaries published by anthropologists who earn part of their salary from the work of informants. Yet Perry does not display this kind of generous spirit towards his subject; instead he appears slightly condescending and stereotypical in his views of contemporary Native American communities.

Unlike most of the autobiographies Brumble describes, Cody's begins not with his birth, but with his career as an actor. In the opening scene Cody is in the process of physically becoming a Hollywood Indian. He describes being spray-painted with *bole armenia* in order to attain the pigmentation directors and producers believed Native Americans possessed. But Cody is also quick to point out that Native American actors themselves were also often painted and fitted with prostheses in order to look "Indian."

Throughout the text Cody vacillates between making bold, sweeping statements about his Native American identity to expressing his anxiety about being an inadequate or inauthentic actor and autobiographer. On the one hand he describes feeling a newfound sense of indigeneity when he shoots a scene in the Dakotas: "I was roaming the prairie again, like my forefathers! . . . I had my hair long and braided in the traditional manner of the Northern Plains Indians. . . . I dreamed of my forefathers racing across the plains after buffalo."[26] On the other hand, he reflects, "Looking back over it all I feel I didn't live so much the insider's life as one who spent his time looking at it from a particular point on the outside. I've lived this double life somewhere between white civilization and my Indian heritage. Never felt completely comfortable with one or the other, to be honest."[27] Like many Native American actors, raised either on- or off-reservation, Cody feels neither completely at home with the domestic life he created with his Seneca wife and the two sons they adopted together nor does he feel altogether at ease with the highly public and performative identity he created for the screen, an identity that bolstered stereotypical notions of what an Indian should look and act like. Cody undoubtedly felt uneasy about his identity if, as Aleiss argued in her well-known interview, he had no Native American ancestors.

In fact Cody contends that he and his wife, living far from the Native communities they claimed affiliation with, had to continually reinvent their Indigenous identity for the public lives they were living. Cody writes about himself and his wife Bertha "Birdie" Parker:

[We] rediscovered our Indian heritage. We weren't rejecting the white world; that, if nothing else, would be hypocritical on our part, having enjoyed so much wealth, success, and yes, happiness. But we were finding there was something missing in our lives: the crucial link to our past, our identity as Native Americans. And you've probably noticed something else missing too. This book is supposed to be about a Hollywood Indian, right? So what about the *Indian* part of my life?[28]

And this is a question the actor leaves open ended. This statement may have certainly been true for Cody's wife, an accomplished Abenaki and Seneca anthropologist, archaeologist, writer, and actor with whom he cowrote *Indian Legends* (1980) and appeared on radio shows together to discuss Native American oral legends. Bertha "Birdie" Parker's father was noted Seneca anthropologist and writer Arthur C. Parker. Her mother, Beulah Tahamont, was an Abenaki actor. Bertha's maternal grandfather was Elijah Tahamont (Chief Dark Cloud), an Abenaki silent film actor from Quebec who was part of the growing transnational Native American community in Southern California during the first decades of the twentieth century. Bertha's aunt, Edna L. Parker, was married to Mark Raymond (M. R.) Harrington, archaeology curator at the Southwest Museum from 1928 to 1964. Bertha lived and worked far from both her Abenaki and Seneca homelands and may have felt some level of disconnect from her Native American identity, despite Los Angeles's large Indian community. It is equally plausible that Cody mined her family history, connections, and culture for his own redface performance. Cody digresses several times in the text to express his anxiety that his readerly audience will not find his textual performance as convincing as his redface performance off the page. He argues:

> My story isn't really a reflection of Indians per se any more than the shenanigans of some white actors are a reflection of white America as a whole. Or, I don't know, maybe it is—you'll have to decide that one, depending on your politics or your view of America itself. I guess all I'm saying is that this is the story of *my* life and it's a story about Hollywood. The Indians who participated in acting out their role in the myth of the American West, including myself, *became* part of Hollywood.[29]

Cody attempts to resist the autoethnographic impulse, the impulse to divulge unmediated and detailed information about his racialized identity. Instead he intimates that once a Native American chooses to perform his or her identity for a mass-mediated audience, he or she inhabits a particularly Hollywoodesque identity that is removed from traditional tribal communities, and yet is not entirely scripted by the film industry. This would make Cody a prime candidate for admission into the DeMille Indians because of his heterodox identity and its collusion with Hollywood's perceptions of indigeneity. Yet in order to inhabit the body of the Hollywood Indian, the logic of identity politics surrounding Native American actors and actresses suggests, one must be Native American. Since Cody had no archivally verifiable claims to Native American ancestry, his performance in redface is called into question.

Cody and others before him beginning with the "Mohawk" participants in the Boston Tea Party create a collective identity through a particular kind of redface performance, one that doesn't question racist and sexist hierarchies of power but instead reinforces them. His performance mirrors colonial fantasies of Native Americans by his adoption of the stereotypical stoic and silent Indian and his pastiched costume of Plains Indian regalia. His autobiography demonstrates his complicity within a patriarchal, sexist, and racist culture.

Cody was able to access what Lakota actor and writer Luther Standing Bear believed was a privileged position in Hollywood because non-Native American "imitators" were often supported by the film industry at the expense of "real Indians." Dismayed by hiring practices that privileged non-Native actors, Standing Bear wrote, "As I look back to my early-day experiences in the making of pictures, I cannot help noting how we real Indians were held back, while white 'imitators' were pushed to the front."[30] A contemporary of Standing Bear and Cody, film critic Ernest Alfred

Dench argued against hiring Native Americans in favor of European Americans. He contended that European American actors make much better Indians because they are "past masters in such roles, for they have made a complete study of Indian life, and by clever makeup are hard to tell from real Redskins."[31] Preferring non-Native actors who are well versed in performing stereotypical representations of Indians, Dench implied that Native Americans were untrustworthy, unreliable, and lazy. Responding to writers like Dench, Standing Bear criticized Hollywood's practice of hiring actors to play Native American characters who embraced stereotypical notions of Indian identity rather than those who questioned the ways in which Native Americans had been portrayed historically on-screen, such as himself.

By assessing the economy of passing, it is also important to trace out an economy of affect whereby the mass-mediated Indian subject inhabits several important roles for a liberal audience—environmental steward, precolonial subject, and spiritual guardian—all as parts of a representational field that creates a ghost effect. These roles have been constructed by corporations, scriptwriters, and Native American performers alike to elicit sentimental and nostalgic feelings on the part of the audience, often without implicating the individual viewer-reader to be accountable to Native American communities. The images evoke a kind of ghostly Indian presence that simultaneously renders Indians highly visible by their easily recognizable and commercially saturated trappings—the beads, buckskins, and feathered costume of the Indian Everyman—and, in a well-rehearsed display of historical amnesia, effaces Native Americans from any kind of contemporaneous existence by situating them in a static nineteenth-century context. As Renée Bergland observes, "Indian ghosts are everywhere in the pages of American literature"; however, contemporary images of Native Americans are few and far between.[32] Many U.S. novels, films, and even towns have stories of Indian ghosts who—it is claimed—still haunt the characters and inhabitants, but few persons within the media industry acknowledge the continuing presence of Native Americans unless it is to make a case for the effectiveness of assimilation to the dominant culture or to critique Indian casinos.

Ghostly Indians and Affective Economies

Texts and images by and about impostors can be read to better understand contemporary Native American literature and identity. It is important to read these texts because they can inform discussions about the slippery subject of identity in general and the ways in which Native American identity in particular has been mass-mediated historically. Although scholarship on the subject is slowly changing perceived notions of indigeneity, Native American identity, if it is to be believable by a large audience, depends on stereotypes.

The KAB public service announcement symbolizes the context of popular representations of Native American identity. Its overt references to Hollywood Indian images structure its public pedagogy. Cody embraces the visual markers of Hollywood Indianness, dressing in regalia on a daily basis in ways that make him appear anachronistic, even ghostly, as most Native Americans by the 1940s wore, by force and by choice, mainstream American clothing in their quotidian lives. From 1971 to 1985, Keep America Beautiful Inc. sought to curb littering and urban blight by running televised public service announcements that linked an interest in Native American reverence for the natural environment with the desire to stop the rise of pollution in the world's most industrialized nation. The ad, entitled, "People Start Pollution, People Can Stop It," features a beaded and buckskinned figure with long braids paddling his aluminum canoe through a murky lake surrounded by factories billowing black smoke into the sky. As he reaches the shore and wades through the trash on the beach, the camera pans in to focus on the tears streaming down his haggard and careworn face.

Since the ad was enormously popular when it first aired, KAB released a new thirty-second version of the original entitled "Back by Popular Neglect" in 1998 in response to the continued problem of litter in major metropolitan cities. The new ad features the same well-known face, only this time the image is captured on a bus stop poster in "Anytown USA." Each time a commuter enters a bus and leaves trash behind on the sidewalk, a tear slides down the wrinkled face on the poster.

In both versions the Indian is silent on the screen, but his tears speak volumes to the estimated twenty four million Americans who have watched the public service announcements.[33] As many scholars have pointed out, images of Indians such as the one featured in the anti-litter campaign have been employed to relay mass-mediated messages of various types since the sixteenth century.[34] And despite the fact that these images have saturated the market and are used to sell everything from margarine to motorcycles, Indians have been rendered silent on screen, on stage, and in literature.[35]

Since authors from Thomas Jefferson to James Fenimore Cooper cultivated the trope of the vanishing Indian, Native Americans as subjects with a present and future were effectively exterminated in the American popular imagination.[36] According to Jacquelyn Kilpatrick, "It was Cooper himself who most thoroughly established in the realm of fiction the stereotypical extremes of the Indian—the noble savage and the bloodthirsty savage—and introduced a depiction of Native American behavior that book and film audiences would come to expect.[37] Images of long-dead historical leaders or generic Plains- and Southwestern-style Indians stuck in a static and tragic nineteenth-century context have been employed over time to reflect Indianness. These images function as an affective economy—in circulation they are recognized worldwide as markers of "the Indian" and are meant to register particular emotions in the viewer, specifically guilt and nostalgia for what has been lost. In the context of Iron Eyes Cody's image, the photograph is circulated not to call viewers to action on behalf of Native American treaty rights, sovereignty recognition, and decolonization struggles, but to simultaneously celebrate the romantic figure of the Native American as he (for the pop culture Indian is almost always male) appeared at contact and mourn his passing and the concomitant destruction of the environment.

As the KAB ad demonstrates, this generic image of Indians has been used to invoke a particularly modernist and nostalgic guilt about the destruction of the natural landscape through pollution. Especially since the 1970s, Native Americans have been figured as the stewards and conservators of precontact America and have been called upon to save the United States—at least symbolically—from further environmental degradation. Common are the environmental organizations that invoke Suquamish Chief Seattle's famous 1854 speech and employ his image (particularly the close-up photograph of him as an elderly man with face and eyes downcast) to sell Earth Day–related products.[38]

In keeping with this tradition KAB President G. Raymond Empson argues, "It is fitting that we use an image depicting a Native American of long ago to recall the special reverence those honored cultures held for the preservation of the natural beauty of our land."[39] Thus, KAB displays the image of a "long ago" Indian to invoke a specific type of action in the television viewer. Viewers are not called upon to stop pollution by multinational corporations and their factories, such as the one featured in the background of the 1971 ad, but to "think globally, act locally," as the slogan goes, to respond personally to the silent Indian man's gaze and remove litter from local streets and bus stops. The 1998 ad has an even more specific purpose than the original version.

It implores commuters, who ostensibly live in the suburbs and take public transportation to work, to keep urban streets clean. The use of Cody's image is even more ironic in this ad since Native American images are typically used by such organizations as the Sierra Club to promote concern for America's last refuges of wilderness, not the urban scene.

The two versions of the anti-litter announcement are significant because they represent two different ways of constructing American Indians within the economy of affect with the same ends: the evocation of Indian images in the service of erasure. In the first, the solitary Indian appears in the late nineteenth-century Plains Indian accoutrements viewers are familiar with, yet he is taken out of this context and placed in an industrial region in the late twentieth century. Thus he is figured within the trope of the "vanishing" or "last of his tribe" Indian. Viewers are not prompted to ameliorate the socioeconomic situation of contemporary Indians because, as the commercial suggests, Indians exist merely as premodern ghosts haunting the fringes of late capitalist urban overdevelopment. Rather, the viewer is expected to register sadness that the land spiritually granted to U.S. citizens by their predecessors has been despoiled. Although it is too late to save the Indian, the logic of the commercial suggests, it is not too late to save the environment.

The use of a ghostly apparition of the Indian, rather than a material representation, has been popular in North American literature since the seventeenth century when Puritans feared Satan's appearance in the form of Native Americans. Bergland notes, "For more than three hundred years, American literature has been haunted by ghostly Indians."[40] She argues, "First and foremost, the ghosting of Indians is a technique of removal. By writing about Indians as ghosts, white writers effectively remove them from American lands and place them, instead, within the American imagination."[41] In the nineteenth century, European

Americans found Indian ghosts utilitarian in their ability to bolster their own political and cultural views, providing a supernatural, and therefore authentic, voice that was forever removed from the realm of living peoples (and thereby rendered safe to the middle-class audiences who participated in these channeling events). Molly McGarry argues, "Legendary as well as unnamed Indians would deliver words from beyond the grave at séance circles, rendering the mythological manifest. Indian spirits began as guides to the afterworld, as healers, and as disembodied envoys of American historiography."[42]

In the context of the KAB ads, the Indian appears as a ghostly presence in nineteenth-century clothing to guilt suburban viewers into action. For Bergland, Americans both want to inhabit the body of the Indian and force him to disappear. "I believe that Americans are obsessed with Native Americans," she notes. "What I mean is that everyone, Czech to Chickasaw, who tries to imagine himself or herself as an American subject, must internalize both the colonization of Native Americans and the American stance against colonialism. He or she must simultaneously acknowledge the American horror and celebrate the American triumph." And this, she demonstrates, creates "an obsessional mindset, in which American subjects continually return to the Native American figures who haunt them."[43] Even Native Americans themselves must deal with the omnipresent apparition of the Indian. As the KAB public service announcements demonstrate, Native Americans must continue to confront an image of themselves that fulfills a certain romantic stereotype but which does not, for the most part, mirror contemporary experiences and concerns of Native communities.

In the second version of the public service announcement, the Indian as a material object has completely disappeared and has been replaced by an endlessly reproducible paper image. Rather than witnessing the spectacle of a "real" Indian responding to trash being thrown at his feet, we are now under the constant surveillance of a silent disembodied image posted on bus stops and on billboards. The lack of what Walter Benjamin would call the "aura" of the first public service announcement would be further reduced in the subsequent version, but for a counterpolitics that serves a colonial agenda.[44] Although viewers born in the late 1970s and later have no pop cultural context with which to read this commercial, the iconic face on the ad is still marked as "Indian" with its feather and braids since associations between concern for the environment and Native American lifeways are still a common stereotype. The fact that Cody is not a "real" Indian points even further to the complexity of the image. The allegedly fake Indian in generic dress relays a problematic version both of Indianness and Native American environmentalism. His on-screen and off-screen performances call attention to both the historical contradictions of American Indian identity and also the mainstream U.S. culture's ongoing obsession with that identity.

Passing Economies and the Politics of Buckskin

In his autobiography, Cody identifies his father as Thomas Long-plume Cody, a Cherokee trick rider employed by Buffalo Bill, and his mother as Frances Salpet, a "short, round-faced, always cheerful, and very strong—typical Cree" woman.[45] Yet this lineage was contradicted by Rayna Green in 1988 and nearly a decade later in 1996 when Angela Aleiss published an interview in the *New Orleans Times-Picayune* that exposed him as a racial fraud. According to May Abshire, Cody's then eighty-year-old half sister, the Louisiana-born actor desired a cultural identity that offered an escape from his dysfunctional family. "He always said he wanted to be an Indian," Abshire notes. "If he could find something that looked Indian, he'd put it on."[46] Later, Abshire claims, Cody changed his name from Espera DeCorti to Oscar

Corti to Iron Eyes Cody, and thus the legendary Hollywood
Indian was born.

Shortly before the interview went to print, Aleiss telephoned
Cody to confront him with the information about his identity that
she had uncovered. Through interviews with neighbors, local
librarians, and family members, Aleiss discovered that Cody's
parents were Francesca Salpietra, a recent immigrant from Sicily,
and Antonio DeCorti, an Italian immigrant who later changed his
surname to Corti.[47] During the conversation with Aleiss, Cody
disavowed this information and responded, "You can't prove it.
All I know is that I'm just another Indian."[48]

Tensions between authenticity and imitation have defined
European American encounters with the "Other" since 1492, so it
is not surprising that the question of Cody's ancestry hangs in the
air like an accusation. Cody's identity raises important questions
about what it means to be "just another Indian." Whether we
deplore the actions of racial impostors as engaging in a kind of
discursive violence against individuals whose phenotype, family
history, and experiences leave them no room for a choice in the
matter or find impostors playful at best and morally bankrupt
at worst, the kinds of cultural work they engage in—the autobiographies they write, the films they star in, and the kinds of
redface minstrelsy they perform in daily life on-screen and off-
screen—inform our understanding of the full range of Native
American identities and identifications. On the one hand, Cody
participated in and was complicit with a mode of passing and
playing Indian in the media that further entrenched Native
American representations within white-mediated discourses of
(in)visibility through stereotype and through the rhetoric of the
vanishing Indian. Even if this mode of passing can be considered
transgressive because it appears to operate under the guise of
eschewing white privilege, it nevertheless still operates within

an economy that has historically valorized non-Indians adopting Indigenous personas.

Redface performances by non-Indians enact what Katrin Sieg has called "acts of representational violence"[49] through film industry hiring practices that have historically privileged non-Indian actors and by seeking and accepting positions of representational power in mass media by speaking on behalf of Native Americans. At the same time these performances are both similar to and different from those of Native American performers and have been useful to both Native American actors and filmmakers interested in engaging in visual sovereignty by overturning stereotypes and creating self-generated representations of Native American identity. They also suggest the endurance, in a multitude of forms, of the ways that Native American forms of identifying, which are off the available grid of options offered up by European American culture, have survived.

Historically, Irish, Italian, African American, Asian American, and Jewish individuals who shed their ethnic and racial skins for Protestant white ones have done so to avoid the political and material implications of a racialized and ethnicized subjectivity. According to Elaine K. Ginsburg, passing "is about the boundaries established between identity categories and about the individual and cultural anxieties induced by boundary crossing."[50] Those who pass usually do so consciously and create "confessional" narratives that reveal the importance of keeping up the act both publicly and privately in order to maintain social cohesion. Passing has long been associated with the history of African Americans. As Juda Bennett underscores, "'Passing' is an inelegant term that most probably comes from the 'pass' given to slaves so that they might travel without being taken for runaways."[51] Yet in post-Reconstruction America, passing "refers more easily or logically to an 'act' than a person."[52] Passing, therefore, connotes motion; one must always keep up the act to make the pass believable.

Passing helped some slaves such as William and Ellen Craft, perhaps the most famous "passing" couple, escape slavery in the Antebellum South, and it also enabled light-skinned African Americans to avoid violence during Reconstruction, Jim Crow, and segregation. Likewise, though Native Americans were not held as chattel slaves on the scale that African Americans were in colonial North America and the early U.S. republic, Indigenous people, especially those with lighter skins or mixed parentage, often chose to pass for white for a variety of political and social reasons. Sometimes, as was the case during the early years of the U.S. census, there were only two racial categories—white/Caucasian and black/colored—and many Native Americans de facto chose the category "white." This did not indicate that these Native Americans assimilated smoothly into mainstream society. Rather, some families chose to hide their tribal identities by enacting a series of public strategies such as learning English, marrying non-Indians, and entering the wage labor force, but maintained their identities as Native Americans privately.

The question posed by Amy Robinson, "Is there a politics to passing?" lies beyond carving out an economically and socially beneficial life for those who engage in black-to-white passing.[53] What kinds of politics are inscribed on the body of the individual who reverses that logic? This question is particularly relevant for racial impostors who are almost universally condemned and whose work has, as a result, been underexamined by scholars. Robinson contends that although writers since Plato have deplored the simulacrum as an empty signifier of the real thing, she espouses the simulacrum for its ability to create what Sieg has called "epistemological havoc."[54] Robinson moves the discussion of the simulacrum from the site of the passing body to what she terms the "triangular theater of identity"—the passing figure, the "in-group witness" (an individual or group of individuals who recognize the "true" nature of the passing body), and the "dupe" (a white person who "misreads the passer's skin as a mimetic sign of racial identity").[55]

In Robinson's reading of the passing figure, agency and power rests in the hands of the "in-group witness" who recognizes the performance of the imposter, as well as the perception of the "dupe," and is therefore in a position to reveal or keep secret the desires of the passing figure. In the case of Cody, the "in-group witness" is Los Angeles's Indian community who, for the most part, understood or suspected Cody's identity as a Native American to be fraught at best, yet were not invested in "outing" Cody in print, a strategic collective choice I discuss later in this chapter. Like Nella Larsen's fictional protagonist in *Passing* (1929), the "in-group witness" in Cody's case responds to permanent and situational racial masquerade with a paradoxical emotional register of erotic frisson, desire, repulsion ("It excites our contempt and yet we admire it. We shy away from it with an odd kind of revulsion, but we protect it").[56] When Aleiss's interview was published, it was, therefore, the white audience who felt most betrayed by the actor's identification as a racial impostor, not the Native American community.

Drawing on Judith Butler's theories of gender performativity, Traise Yamamoto addresses the question of the politics of passing by discussing "racial drag" as a potentially subversive site from which to transgress normative representations of racialized bodies. She writes, "In one sense, racial drag implies the possibility of interrogating originary racial difference, but only to the extent that racial parody circulates in a social or discursive arena separate from a polarized racial economy in which difference is the necessary component of self-definition."[57] The danger, Yamamoto points out, is that "racial drag" and its attendant subversive promise ultimately relies on conventional notions of racial difference in order to prove its point, "Reconfirming race as an originary site of essential alterity."[58] The risk of "racial drag" is that it slides so easily from its transgressive potential to repression where all articulations of identity are contained and controlled by hegemonic European American discourses.

Cody's autobiography and on-screen and off-screen performances raise the question of whether racial impostors might be engaging in political work, or at least creating a politicized space for others, that deconstructs or at least troubles essentialism without decomposing the sometimes fragile boundaries of Native American identity as lived experience and the right of tribes to set membership requirements, thereby entrenching Indigenous identity further within the fields of stereotype and invisibility. Perhaps the white dupe's investment in Indian identifications such as Cody's also opens up a space for political work for Native Americans. If Native American identity can be so easily mimicked and believed by a white audience, then closer attention needs to be paid to interrogating and deconstructing the performative elements of this identity. Malinda Maynor, for example, in *Real Indian* (1996), a short, autobiographical documentary film that situates Lumbee history and identity in North Carolina against the larger representational field of Native American visual images, refuses to play a conventional "Indian" role on-screen. Dressed in generic buckskin clothing, she states, "War paint doesn't suit me" in order to highlight the Lumbee's lived experience as a markedly different one than the stereotypical images created in western films. Perhaps racial impostors shed light on the vexed relationship between U.S. and Canadian institutions of power, as manifested through popular culture, and Native American attempts to self-governance and control over the representation of Indigenous identity.

Before Aleiss published her article and Rayna Green had pointed to Cody's Mediterranean ancestry in a footnote of her essay on "wannabes," gossip had already begun circulating about his identity. Yet unlike contemporary entertainers for whom part of their fascination is the circulation of gossip and rumor, for Cody, gossip about his identity could only have damaging effects, and so he actively sought to efface his biological origins, to conceal from his extremely public life what his genealogy might betray. After his death those who protected Cody from the public eye revealed information that would have jeopardized his identity as a professional actor whose career was dependent on others' perception of him as an Indian. Cheryl Simon, a resident of Gueydan, Louisiana, where Cody was born, told Los Angeles–based journalist Ron Russell that the actor's identity "was always like an open secret" and that few in the area wanted to expose his Italian American identity.[59] Hollywood actors such as Jay Silverheels, the Mohawk actor who played Tonto on *The Lone Ranger* television series, also doubted Cody's identity but never publicly revealed him. According to Mary Silverheels, the actor's widow, "Jay knew from day one because when Iron wasn't around, [his brother Joe] would openly talk about being Italian and that the two of them were brothers. It was that simple."[60]

Others who felt that Cody was an impostor undeserving of the attention his career garnered voiced concerns about his identity during his lifetime, but either did not feel comfortable "outing" him or did not have access to widely read media. Ron Andrade, whose father acted alongside Cody, argues, "There were considerable discussions among the Indian community for many years beginning in the 1930s that Iron Eyes was not Indian, but he maintained his image because of his contacts within the movie industry. . . . While there were various stories during the many years about Iron Eyes, the image makers in Hollywood were able to dispel any criticism of him. Instead those Indians who criticized Iron Eyes soon left Hollywood."[61] Andrade's argument sheds light on Hollywood's perception of and control over Native American representation. If casting directors and others knew or suspected that Cody was not Native American, the stereotypical image he displayed was so important to the myth-making business that the origins of his identity were protected.

Another actor, Lois Red Elk, claimed that she knew Cody was an impostor because the actor's "hair and the way he wore his feather were all wrong. There were no experiences. He could only offer a façade,"[62] yet she did not publish her suspicions until after Cody's death. Red Elk's comments are particularly compelling for what they say about notions of authenticity. The logic of her commentary would suggest that if an actor or anyone else studied ethnographic documents and could mimic the positioning of feathers in one's hair, the performance of an Indian identity would be believable. Her pairing of an "authentic" hairstyle (presumably a Plains Indian hairstyle, although Cody claimed to be Cherokee and in his later years wore a braided wig) with correct "experiences" further suggests that for Native American actors there still exists an inflexible code of identity performance and that any deviations from stereotypical displays of identity are suspect.

Others involved in the film industry challenge the claims of Andrade and Red Elk and support Cody's identity performance. Running Deer—identified as a retired stuntman, actor, and longtime friend of Cody—replied in an interview with Russell, "Do I believe [the accusations]? Hell, no."[63] Another Native American actor acquaintance of Cody, Lee Thunderbear Tatu, also dismissed the rumors surrounding Cody's identity, saying, "I don't put any credence on that stuff."[64] Cody's surviving adopted son, Robert "Tree" Cody, who is of Dakota ancestry; is an enrolled member of the Salt River Pima Maricopa Tribe; and is a well-known musician, actor, educator, and dancer, argues that he learned his artistic and professional skills from his "step-father, the late

Iron Eyes Cody who taught 'Tree' the many different aspects of show business as well as the traditional red road of his people."[65] While not explicitly identifying Iron Eyes as Native American (it is unclear whether it is Iron Eyes or Robert's people who follow the "traditional red road"), Robert clearly credits his adoptive father with teaching him how to enact a Native American identity and to pursue the kinds of philanthropic ventures for which Iron Eyes was known.

Glenda Ahhaitty, a Cherokee mental health counselor whose family knew Cody for more than thirty years, has a more complex response to the question of the actor's identity. She argues that while many actors, writers, and artists have launched their careers by fabricating an Indian persona, Cody was different because he contributed much of his income to helping Native American individuals. She notes, "I can't tell you how many families, whose family member passed away in Los Angeles that Iron paid to have their body transported home for burial, or helped pay for the burial service here in LA."[66] She adds that while assuming a false identity is wrong, most Native American actors, in her opinion, do not contribute the same amount of time, finances, or energy to the Native American community: "I don't know of any of the past or current Indian media actors/personalities that I could say the same about."[67] From Ahhaitty's description, it seems that Cody was able to forge meaningful relationships with his colleagues in Los Angeles that recompensed for the dysfunctional relations he experienced with his birth family.

In one of his last film appearances, Cody played the role of an elderly Indian chief who donates land to a youth camp, Kamp Kikakee, in the B-grade comedy *Ernest Goes to Camp* (1987).[68] This role is similar to most of the roles he played on- and off-screen over the course of his career. Because of his limited English skills, Cody's character communicates with other characters in the film either through his granddaughter, a nurse at the camp, or through sign language. While the film's main protagonist, Ernest P. Worrell (Jim Varney), knows some sign language, he is easily confused and convinces the Indian chief to sign ownership of the camp over to a mining company. Perhaps unintentionally, the film posits theft of Native American land and dispossession as comedic material. And because intermediaries such as Worrell are portrayed as fumbling, but well intentioned and loveable, it becomes easy to view Native American dispossession as merely a series of honest mistakes. Like most screen Indians, Cody does not speak much, is easily fooled by white bureaucrats and land speculators, wears buckskin clothing and a headdress every day, and has a unique affinity with nature. Like many of the roles scripted by Hollywood, Cody's Indian characters rely on stereotypes to become believable.

Lauren Berlant has discussed the enabling fiction of the public sphere and argues, "The nation provides a kind of prophylaxis for the person, as it promises to protect his privileges and his local body in return for loyalty to the state."[69] Yet Cody, unlike Clare Kendry, one of the main protagonists in *Passing*, did not wish to surrender to the protective anonymity the dual shields of citizenship and whiteness provide, but rather created a fictive embodied identity while at the same time masking any discrepancies in that identity from the public gaze. Cody was an Indian on-screen and on the pages of his autobiography at the same time he lived in redface at home and in public. While Larsen's novel attempts to tell a national story through individual characters, the life of Cody—a nonfictional individual—also relates a national narrative about race through the figure of an individual.

Even though newspaper articles published exposés of the actor following his death, articles in smaller circulation Native American newspapers such as the *Navajo Times* and *News from Indian Country* praised Cody as an Indian actor who advocated for more positive representations of Indigenous people in the media and made significant social investments in Native communities.[70] In an interview with *The Navajo Times*, Robert "Tree" Cody insists that his adoptive father was Native American and notes that he did much to change the representation of Native Americans in film for the better.[71] Iron Eyes Cody was generous in sharing elements of material culture through his massive collections of Native American regalia. He operated the "Moosehead Museum" from his home in Los Angeles and donated historical objects and regalia that he collected during his lifetime to the Autry Museum of Western Heritage, the Roy Rogers Museum, the Turtle Museum, and the Southwest Museum.[72]

Cody's autobiographical redface act is a site of anxiety because it lays bare the ways in which representations of Native American identities have been fabricated out of sheer colonial fantasy. Cody's performance as an Indian was believable to so many because he did not challenge the ways in which Native American identity and images have been constructed by twentieth-century mass cultural institutions, even as he invested social capital in reservation visits and philanthropy. No longer perceived as a threat to westward expansion, Indians in the twentieth century became icons of an idyllic prelapsarian American past. Cody, in his Plains-style buckskin, beads, and feathers, addressing audiences ranging from the Boy Scouts to Pope John Paul II, was a believable Indian because he did not spur his audience to question preconceived notions about what constituted Indianness.

Cody's case also may have harmed Native American individuals whose identities do not necessarily fit the colonial mold or who are not enrolled members of their respective tribes. Gerald Vizenor writes that impostors may gain access to opportunities otherwise denied to them, but they also may "close . . . some doors on honest tribal people who have the moral courage to raise doubts about identities."[73] Because Native American identity in the United States and Canada has been complicated by a series of catastrophic historical events and governmental policies, nonstatus or nonenrolled individuals, whom A. T. Anderson has termed "the Uncounted," may feel more cautious about discussing their experiences for fear of being dismissed as an impostor, a "wannabe," or a fraud.[74]

Umberto Eco, in *Travels in Hyperreality*, claims, "The American imagination demands the real thing and, to attain it, must fabricate the absolute fake; where the boundaries between game and illusion are blurred."[75] "Hyperreality" is a useful way to think about representations of Native Americans such as Cody's because ever since Indigenous communities were first portrayed in literature and visual culture, Europeans and European-Americans have projected their fantasies on the "New World" canvas and created the "absolute fake" Indian who never existed off the page, sometimes compelling Native Americans to play these roles as well. This practice has been particularly evident in the nineteenth and twentieth centuries with the advent of new performative contexts such as Wild West Shows, world's fairs, and western films that situate Native Americans in a prelapsarian ("Noble Savage") or barbaric past, useful as icons only in museums or as foils to manifest destiny. To some extent, Native Americans have to conform to European and European American conceptions of Indianness in order to exist at all. As Owens argues, "Living descendents of original Americans, unless they impersonate the 'other,' have no place in the world. No other people are expected to dress and live as their ancestors did five hundred years ago. Imagine the reaction if a Frenchman walked into a social gathering dressed as his ancestor had dressed half a millennium earlier. Would he or she be recognized as a 'real' Frenchman, or might laughter be the result?"[76]

To many, Cody's act was a convincing simulacrum of an Indian because he conformed to his audience's expectations, and those who took him for such register anger at his decades-long ability to dupe them into believing that he was Indigenous. Instances of racial imposture such as Cody's are not a new phenomenon, but are instead part of the long tradition of playing Indian in America. Native Americans themselves have defined and redefined elements of Indigenous identity in a variety of performative spheres, from speeches recounting a community's or individual's history to contemporary intertribal powwows, academic conferences, and Indigenous theater groups.[77] According to Steven Leuthold, "Aesthetic expression and assumptions about the aesthetic help keep native communities together."[78] Rituals and performances are vital because they open spaces for communities to reflect on, contest, and imagine group- and self-identification and their place in the world.

In Native American communities, whether reservation-based, urban, suburban, or rural, ceremonies and celebrations are not static, are not performed as they were in the nineteenth century as many people expect, but are kinetic and fluid. As Betonie, the medicine man character in Leslie Marmon Silko's *Ceremony*, states, "The ceremonies have always been changing . . . things which don't shift and grow are dead things."[79] Native American academic conferences, for example, do not constitute a "traditional" form of communication, but in the late twentieth and early twenty-first centuries they provide an intellectual virtual reservation for academic and nonacademic communities that draws from precontact gathering traditions and forges new traditions as well. In addition, powwows are not "traditional" for many tribal communities, but have become a vital cultural, economic, political, and collective site throughout North America for practicing "survivance" and its attendant forms of knowledge production. In spaces as diverse as academic conferences and powwows, Native Americans enact, create, and rehearse identity and culture in often nonarchived virtual reservations off the indexed and official grid primarily for themselves in order to remember and reconstitute what Marita Sturken has called "cultural memories."[80]

On the other hand, in radically different ways, European Americans have developed specific forms of "playing Indian" that have been a crucial means for white Americans to distinguish themselves from Europeans, particularly their English counterparts.[81] By incorporating aspects of an imagined Indian identity into their own newly emerging national identity, European Americans have been able to demonstrate their uniqueness and separateness in public and semipublic spheres such as the theater, fraternal organizations, and pageants without fear of actually becoming Indian. With the removal of many nations west of the Mississippi River and increased urbanization in the early to mid-nineteenth century, the threat of contact with and assimilation into Native communities on the part of European Americans was diminished. In the United States's dominant discourse on race, heritage and identity became increasingly defined by blood kinship and lineage. Therefore, in the absence of miscegenation, non-Indians could "play Indian" with impunity. The threat that an individual could take on the "savage" traits of an Indian through performance and emulation was removed. Over time, performing in redface has allowed individuals to test out new and politically oppositional ideas and has helped to assuage white guilt about, among other things, the destruction of the environment. From the Boston Tea Party to New Age members of "rainbow tribes" to OutKast's Indian-themed 2004 Grammy extravaganza to Ke$ha's ridiculous appearance in full headress in 2010, these performances have served to bolster the popular misconception that it is acceptable, even admirable, to "play Indian" since few Indians exist to represent themselves.[82] When European Americans "play Indian," they project an edited version of their own colonial history on the body of the Indian.

Appropriating an Indian identity through dress and generic cultural rituals has been essential to the formation of a specifically American identity since the eighteenth century. "From the colonial period to the present," Deloria contends, "the Indian has skulked in and out of the most important stories various Americans have told about themselves."[83] And not surprisingly the phenomenon of playing Indian in fiction and more explicit appropriations such as public performances, he argues, reveal more about contemporary political and cultural currents in U.S. history than it does about Native American life.

Racial impostors have attempted to achieve the transformation from European American to "Other" through both psychological and material means. Unlike individuals who seek to hide their racial or ethnic identity and pass for white, impostors enact a morphologically similar, but also quite distinct and complex performance. The economy of passing in the United States arises from the inherent instability of racial categories and the desire to codify, legislate, and control racial purity. It has been a central motif in American literature by writers such as Nella Larsen, James Weldon Johnson, J. Hector St. John de Crèvecoeur, Mark Twain, Charles Chestnutt, Sinclair Lewis, James Fenimore Cooper, William Faulkner, Jessie Fauset, and Thomas Dixon and has been interpreted alternately as a sociocultural threat and opportunity. Passing continues to be a popular theme in American culture as evidenced by the controversies surrounding the racial and ethnic ambiguities of popular celebrities and politicians. For example, country music singer Shania Twain (Eileen Regina Edwards) has received a great deal of criticism for claiming to be Native American. Although her biological father was white, her adoptive father, Jerry Twain, was an Ojibwa from Canada, and she claims that because he raised her, she grew up in a bicultural household, an argument that harkens back to a long tradition of Native American adoption of nontribal members.[84] One of the many ironies of European American legal jurisdiction over Indigenous identities, however, is that while Louis Owens did not possess the requisite documents to become an enrolled member of either the Cherokee or Choctaw Nation with whom he claimed kinship, Twain does possess, through her adoptive father, membership in the Temagami Bear Island First Nation in Canada. According to Eva Marie Garroutte, "She is formally recognized as an Anishinabe (Ojibway) Indian with band membership" through her stepfather, whereas Owens was not legally recognized as Native American.[85]

Often Native Americans were faced with the decision of living in intolerable conditions on reservations or inhabiting areas bordering reservations where white resentment was high and Native lives were deemed worthless. Many families moved away from their homelands entirely to escape violence and persecution or passed for white in certain social situations in order to remain in areas from which others were removed. For many mixed-blood Native Americans, and even some who self-identify as full-blood, rich new identities on the margins of European, African American, and Native American communities were forged on reservations, in rural areas, and in cities.[86] Yet while these new identities challenged and enriched more static definitions of culture and community, they have also often been painful identities for those who inhabit them. As Joseph Roach notes:

> The marginal condition of life between powerful categories, the condition that postmodern ethnographers find so rich in cultural expressiveness, renders the persons actually trying to live between them extremely vulnerable to the punitive consequences of their undecidability. If they choose not to take the path of "straightline assimilation," leading ultimately perhaps to "symbolic ethnicity" at most, or if they are forbidden this path by some uncorrectable accident of their births, they live, for better or worse, in a double culture, invested in two worlds (at least), yet faced with powerful laws and customs favoring unitary identities.[87]

The lived experiences of those whose bodies and life histories are marked by mixed cultural, racial, and ethnic heritages often indicate a vexed relationship to communities formed through strategic allegiance to a single identity. Mixed-race individuals or those with ambiguous cultural identities do not always seek to pass for a single cultural, racial, or ethnic identity, yet it is often also difficult for them to identify consistently with all of their biological and adopted relations.

While figures like the Mardi Gras Indians to whom Roach refers are not interpreted as threatening by the dominant culture since they are contained by the parade audience and perform during a socially sanctioned time and space in New Orleans, other figures, like Cody, who performed in redface outside of a ritualized, mass cultural space are much more dangerous for those who seek to police the boundaries of identification. "Ethnic transvestites," to use Werner Sollors's term, borrowed from queer studies to describe transgressive figures who conceal their racial and ethnic identities by creating new ones in literature, have been profoundly disturbing to audiences who embrace fixed notions of gender, racial, and ethnic identity.[88]

The racial transvestite remains a figure of deep distrust at the same time this figure opens up debate on the still-untested issues surrounding Native American identity, particularly as it relates to Hollywood Indians. Sylvester Long (Chief Buffalo Child Long Lance), for example, who acted in *The Silent Enemy* and whose Winston Salem, North Carolina family was identified in local archives as "Negro," although they most likely were of Lumbee, Cherokee, African American, and European American ancestry, escaped the Jim Crow South by enrolling as a Cherokee at Carlisle Indian School and later claimed in his autobiography, *Long Lance*, to be a full-blood Blackfeet chief who spent his childhood roaming the Plains.[89] Unable to carve out a public identity that relied on an acknowledgement of his mixed heritages, Long created a stable persona complicit with popular notions of a buckskin-bedecked Plains warrior. Haunted throughout his career by actors and colleagues who did not find his pass entirely believable, Long committed suicide in 1932. His story is the tragic outcome of fixed and inflexible definitions of identity. Southern writer Forrest Carter, author of the immensely popular *The Education of Little Tree* (1976), was also posthumously revealed to be a racial impostor. Forrest Carter was the pseudonym of Asa Carter, ghost writer of George Wallace's hateful 1963 pro-segregation speech and a Ku Klux Klan sympathizer. Although he claimed to be Cherokee, his widow denied this assertion.[90]

To rephrase Amy Robinson's question, is there a politics of redfacing by non-Native Americans? Of course there is. Economic issues, certainly, are a key factor. Historically, Native American actors were paid less, were rarely credited, and struggled to survive in Hollywood while other non-Indian actors in redface were compensated more fairly. Impostors also pander to audiences' expectations and desires for a neatly packaged, accessible, and stereotypical form of Native American identity performance removed from any sense of social or community obligation or responsibility.

The politics of this form of redfacing, then, revolve around the fact that Native American writers, actors, filmmakers, and artists enter a representational field that has already been defined by the dominant culture and often does not reflect the lived experiences of people who have lived most of their lives in Native American communities. Native Americans whose phenotype, education, aesthetic style, sexual orientation, politics, or personal affect does not align with Hollywood representations may find it much more difficult to secure a publisher, find an agent, or exhibit their work than an individual like Cody who so seamlessly mimics a familiar and comforting vision of Indianness. Cody's performance ultimately fixes Native Americans in the distant past and relegates this site as a space of mourning, refusing to consider the complex, often fraught and sometimes humorous engagements with the present and future that Native American writers and filmmakers have enacted both in response to and outside of the performances of imposters.

4 Prophesizing on the Virtual Reservation

Imprint and *It Starts with a Whisper*

The Keep America Beautiful Inc. public service announcement featuring Iron Eyes Cody and other visual artifacts circulate the image of the ghostly Indian as a figment of an American imagination invested in Native Americans as spectral entities of a tragic and mostly elided past within a broader field of historical amnesia. Drawing from Donald Pease's assertion that scholars of American studies, including postcolonial critics, "have fallen into the ideological trap of American exceptionalism by concluding 'that colonialism had little or nothing to do with the formation of the U.S. national identity,'" Ali Behdad argues that European American "anamnestic disavowal" of U.S. national origins and history of genocide against Indigenous peoples is both intentional and is "a crucial component of its national culture."[1] Native Americans become apparitional excesses in the dominant culture's repressed imagination, which seems perpetually unable to confront the violence of its founding. "The ghost makes itself known to us through haunting and pulls us affectively into the structure of feeling of a reality we come to experience as recognition," Avery Gordon writes. "Haunting recognition is a special way of knowing what has happened or is happening."[2] Native American ghosts haunt the North American literary and visual cultural imagination to remind settler nations of the unspeakable, horrific past.

Native American ghostly images remind the nation of its brutal past, but ironically also give lie to the concerted national effort to render Native American communities extinct. Speaking against these silences instituted by historical uses of the ghostly effect, Native American writers and filmmakers often employ the figure of the ghost as a means to draw attention to the embodied present and future. Two recent Native American films in particular perform this double function, at the same time they provide a way to represent Native American spirituality on tribally specific terms. In Chris Eyre's *Imprint* (2007) and Shelley Niro's *It Starts with a Whisper* (1993), gendered ghostly images invoke a violent past in order to trouble conventional readings of historical events but also to reconfigure temporality. *Imprint* offers a reading of the horrors of events at Wounded Knee in South Dakota in 1890 as an allegory for a vibrant Lakota future rather than only as a melancholic elegy of an unsettled and unsettling past. Likewise, *It Starts with a Whisper* evokes spectral Tupelo tribal members as a means to engage with Mohawk aesthetics in the past, present, and future. As Bliss Cua Lim asserts, "The hauntings recounted by ghost narratives are not merely instances of the past reasserting itself in a stable present, as is usually assumed; on the contrary, the ghostly return of traumatic events precisely troubles the boundaries of the past, present, and future, and cannot be written back to the complacency of a homogeneous empty time."[3] Images of Native American ghosts in dominant culture representations can compel audiences to an emotional economy of guilt and remorse, but this does not serve contemporary Indigenous communities invested in visual technologies that reflect the creative, robust vitality of living people. I discuss the work of contemporary Native American filmmakers whose projects stimulate discourses that take the figure of the ghost and its attendant evocation of spirituality seriously, attempting not to fall prey to the kind of nostalgic, past-tense vision of Indigenous culture that bolsters the myth of the vanishing Indian. I do so by welding a discussion of Indigenous mass-mediated ghosts to discourses of prophecy in order to argue that film and other forms of new media operate as a space of the virtual reservation, a space where Native American filmmakers put the long, vexed history of Indigenous representations into dialogue with epistemic Indigenous knowledges.

After contextualizing how the virtual reservation signifies in film and then how Indigenous prophecy works as an embodied discourse in visual culture, I examine two films that foreground the importance of spirituality as an enabling tool for combating colonialism and reengaging Indigenous epistemologies without attempting to explain particular aspects of specific tribal practices or inviting spectators to partake of Indigenous spirituality through commodification and consumption. *Imprint* and *It Starts with a Whisper* are two key films that create and intervene into discourses surrounding the supernatural. These films overturn the image of the static ghostly Indian through Indigenous manifestations of the spirit and conflations of time that challenge hegemonic Western understandings of human relationships to the metaphysical and prophetical.[4] As Lim argues, "The ghost narrative opens the possibility of a radicalized concept of noncontemporaneity; haunting as ghostly return precisely refuses the idea that things are just 'left behind,' that the past is inert and the present uniform."[5] The past and historical time in both films is animate, kinetic, and sometimes illegible, an imagined territory that shapes but does not prefigure the present and future.

In this chapter I do not extract "authentic" spiritual traditions of particular Indigenous communities. Rather, I emphasize how contemporary Native American filmmakers produce narratives about spirituality that contest national discourses of Native people as primarily concerned and vested with spiritual matters. Additionally, these filmmakers create narratives of Native relationships to spirituality that attempt to represent core principles of the spiritual, in this case, Lakota and Mohawk, in a way that does not offer these representations up to a colonial gaze, but rather invites the spectator to rethink both Native American spirituality on its own terms and the viewer's relationship to it.

I suggest a reading of contemporary Native American cinematic practices through the lens of a particular Indigenous epistemic knowledge—prophecy—on the virtual reservation. Discursive prophecy is intertwined with the broader notion that twentieth-century mass-mediated images of Native Americans, as inaccurate and offensive as they sometimes are, create the possibility of a virtual reservation where Indigenous people can creatively reterritorialize physical and imagined sites that have been lost, that are in the process of renegotiation, or that have been retained.

Because spirituality and the figure of the ghost have been employed to filmically equate absence and alterity, an examination of Indigenous filmmakers' use of these images serves as a way to reinhabit and reimagine colonized terrain. I interrogate how Native American filmmakers represent the spiritual realm without either absenting contemporary Native American bodies within the paradigm of the vanishing Indian or invoking stereotypes of the mystical Indian that offer a spiritual supplement to a non-Native audience at odds with spiritual belief systems practiced by Native Americans. Indigenous filmmakers instead demonstrate that seemingly discordant discourses of spirituality and prophecy can be put in conversation with each other, promising access to a fetishistic world of hidden, "authentic," mystical Native American epistemologies.

At Home on the Virtual Reservation

The virtual reservation is as complex and paradoxical as its geographical counterpart. It is a site that displays Indigenous knowledges and practices in sharp relief against competing colonial discourses. By doing so, it opens up multiple narratives for dialogue within and outside the community on a site that is less invested in the traffic in authenticity and fixed definitions of indigeneity imposed by outsiders than in reconsidering the relationship between the visual image and larger cultural and political contexts. Indigenous people at the same time recuperate, regenerate, and begin to heal on the virtual reservation directly under the gaze of the national spectator.

The virtual reservation is an imagined space, in this instance, for the film industry, but has also been transformed by Indigenous people into something of value, a decolonizing space. Lorna Roth describes "media reservations" as negative sites of segregation, isolation, and the televisual equivalent of the stereotypes structuring representations of reservation and reserve life in North America.[6] For Roth, Native Americans have been consigned to an Indigenous form of what amounts to a ghetto. They compete for small pools of funding and their self-generated images generally appear only on programs broadcast by the Public Broadcasting Service (PBS) and the APTN. The virtual reservations this chapter describes acknowledge the colonial histories of reservations and reserves, but also the crucial cultural, aesthetic, and political work produced by Native American filmmakers and media artists.

Gerald McMaster observes that the historical role of the real-life territorial reserve in Canada has been more nuanced than conventional scholarship has supposed. The reserve is, according

gotiated space set aside for Indian people by
governments to isolate them, to extricate them
abits, and to save them from the vices of the
oxically, isolation helped maintain aboriginal
other traditional practices. The reserve
ffirming presence despite being plagued
____orical uncertainties."[7] Following McMaster's lead,
I suggest that the virtual reservation is a more creative, kinetic,
open space where Indigenous artists collectively and individually
employ technologies and knowledges to rethink the relationship
between media and Indigenous communities.

Edward W. Soja's "critical strategy of thirding-as-Othering," a
historicized and radical site for the dispossessed and marginalized, is also key to understanding how the virtual reservation
intervenes in the real and imagined, the metropolis and the
reservation.[8] Soja draws from what he calls Henri Lefebvre's
"trialectics of space" in order to think about the productive sites
interwoven with and in between three social spaces ("perceived
space," "conceived space," and "lived space").[9] This "trialectics"
disrupts binary thinking about the real and imagined by creating "a limitless composition of lifeworlds that are radically open
and radicalizable."[10] I find Soja's liberatory theories of social,
historical, cultural, and political space productive in thinking
about the virtual reservation as a recombinant, fluid re-reading
of space that exists within and in between geographical territory;
the past, present, and future; the Internet; film; everyday lived
experience; the possible; and other such sites of Indigenous
production and practice.

For Indigenous people, the reservation is a complicated and
often vexed marker of the enabling conditions of collective and
personal homeland and a site of cultural retention and renewal,
seemingly far from the intervening pressures of the dominant
culture. Often conceived of as bounded, sovereign physical space,

Native American sites also include urban and rural enclaves where more than half of the Indigenous peoples of North America live. These on- and off-reservation locations serve as places of cultural, physical, and spiritual continuity, improvisation, and survival where "traditional" practices can be protected and revised.

The reservation, often created under punitive conditions that represented a small fraction of traditional tribal homelands or a space to which Native Americans were relocated, is also in some cases akin to what some have called North America's version of "concentration camps"—loci of limited mobility, disproportionate rates of alcoholism, drug abuse, violence, unemployment, suicide, and poverty.[11] Spanning a historical period of over two hundred years, the reservation has structural and metaphysical similarities to the state of being Giorgio Agamben describes for the European concentration camp inmate of World War II. Agamben contends:

> Precisely because they were lacking almost all the rights and expectations that we characteristically attribute to human existence, and yet were still biologically alive, they came to be situated at a limit zone between life and death, inside and outside, in which they were no longer anything but bare life. Those who are sentenced to death and those who dwelt in camps are thus in some way unconsciously assimilated to *homines sacres*, to a life that may be killed without the commission of homicide.[12]

Isolated from the outside world and created as an inherently unequal simulacrum of European American institutions, the reservation, particularly in its nineteenth-century manifestation signified the condition of "bare life" as Native Americans were disciplined through state-sanctioned violence to assimilate, with the intention of social death and attendant genocide.

As geographically isolated metaphor and physical and imagined space, the reservation exists for the dominant culture somewhere out there, beyond the limits of national and popular memory, a repository of the repressed and spectral, a homeland for America's ghosts. Gordon argues that ghosts act as an indexical critique of still unresolved historical violence and trauma. As such, ghosts have demands, and they push us to reckon with such demands "not as cold knowledge, but as a transformative recognition."[13] She contends, "If the ghost is a crucible for political mediation and historical memory . . . the purpose of an alternative diagnostics is to link the politics of accounting, in all its intricate political-economic, institutional, and affective dimensions, to a potent imagination of what has been done and what is to be done otherwise."[14] Referencing Native Americans in particular, Susan Scheckel posits that the nation's haunting by Indian ghosts "marks the limits of that forgetfulness out of which the nation arises."[15] The reservation (and its northern cousin, the Canadian reserve) is imagined in popular culture to be a space of dysfunction and disappearance. It is a place the nation needs to continually invoke as a metaphor of its own imagined triumph and Native American defeat and subsequently forget about in order to maintain its originary fantasies. The "ghosts" that are produced in these memory gaps by Native American media makers are markers of a powerful resistance to colonization and disappearance at the same time they enable the creation of knowledges that draw attention to vibrant Native subjects as figures within a contemporary context.

While the virtual reservation still contains within its permeable boundaries the violent and violating representations that exist on territorial reservations, it also provides a creative, imagined space with critical ties to physical places that have protected what might be called "traditional" practices and permitted the maintenance of some Indigenous languages and knowledges, such as prophecy. Marie-Laure Ryan suggests three modes of interpreting the virtual: "an optical one (the virtual as illusion), a scholastic one (the virtual as potentiality), and an informal one (the virtual as the computer-mediated)."[16] The virtual reservation can be considered to occupy these three modes: the realm of the filmic as a field onto which an alternative vision of the world can be projected; as a meeting space for tribal intellectuals and scholars to workshop, debate, and define new projects for sustaining Indigenous knowledges; and as a network of computer-assisted transnational Indigenous communities who exchange and create information. Unlike Jean Baudrillard's notion of the virtual as simulacra, fake, and substitute for the "real," the virtual reservation is a supplemental arena of the possible that initiates and maintains a dialectical relationship between the multiple layers of Indigenous knowledge systems—from the dream world to the topography of real and imagined landscapes. The virtual reservation does not stand in opposition to or as substitute for the material world, but creates a dialogue with it. It helps us see things in the material world in a different dimensionality, thus enhancing our understanding of online and virtual as well as off-line and off-screen communities.

On the virtual reservation, which can be located in a multitude of different discourses—from the Internet where Native Americans meet as disembodied, often anonymous voices and personas to engage in profound and profane dialogue, to films that stage alternate "communitarian"[17] scenarios—Indigenous people workshop on sites where they can recuperate, regenerate, contest, and begin to heal, under the radar of the direct gaze of the national spectator. The virtual reservation in its ability to transcend time and space has also been transformed by Indigenous people into a utopian geography of possibility and renewal, as films like *Smoke Signals* (1998), the humorous, heterodox sculptures of Santa Clara Pueblo artist Nora Naranjo-Morse, and the exuberant, life-affirming work of Mohawk dancer and choreographer Santee Smith demonstrate.

19. Characters from James Luna's *Petroglyphs in Motion* (2001). Image courtesy of the artist.

But beyond their potential to reframe, reappropriate, and reimagine the tribal world joyously with hope and healing, Native American media-makers on the virtual reservation also challenge and complicate representations of Indigenous people by voicing dissent, offering counternarratives that reveal the often dismal and depressing aspect of inhabiting homelands that are still colonized in an otherwise seemingly postcolonial world. James Luna's performance art, for example, is a scathing indictment of a dominant culture that renders Native American aesthetic production a safe, exotic, and quaint cog in the wheel of multiculturalism as well as of Indigenous people who surrender to mass-mediated representations of themselves. Luna's *Petroglyphs in Motion* (2001) is a performance piece that animates several different, often discomfiting characters—a lascivious coyote-trickster, an ailing emphysematic pulling an oxygen tank, and a drunken *cholo* panhandler who solicits money from the audience on the catwalk-like stage, among others.

The virtual reservation Luna creates here is self-conscious and ritualized. Luna enters the theater in each character's costume, touches a wall to begin the transformation into character (against the wall a spotlight creates an ephemeral shadow petroglyph), and then ends the character's performance with a similar ritual that creates and closes the virtual space of change, possibility, and play with stereotype. Jennifer A. González suggests that Luna's "resignifying practice is an exaggeration of already-present, though more subtle, resignifying practices that have been performed by Indigenous cultures in contact with colonizing populations for centuries."[18] Other experimental works likewise create agonistic and antagonistic virtual reservations that compel spectators to undergo a radical rethinking of what constitutes community, nation, family, gender, and self. These include films such as Arlene Bowman's *Navajo Talking Picture* (1986), a documentary about the filmmaker's grandmother that is a painful turn on Mary Louise

Pratt's notion of the "autoethnography";[19] Clint Alberta's *Deep Inside Clint Star* (1999), a study of the lives of six urban Indians from Canada that purports to be pornography because of the kinds of looking relations it structures; and Thirza Cuthand's *Helpless Maiden Makes an "I" Statement* (2000), a short experimental film that employs clips of Disney female villains to underscore and trouble issues of queer and raced identity, as well as colonial histories, through the discourses of sadism and masochism.

Perhaps the first extant experimental films by Native American artists were those created by anthropologists John Adair and Sol Worth and their Navajo students in 1966. Adair and Worth later published an analysis of the project as *Through Navajo Eyes: An Exploration in Film Communication and Anthropology* (1972). Faye Ginsburg notes that the project "attempted to teach film technology to Navajos without the conventions of Western production and editing, to see if their films would be based on a different 'grammar' based on a Navajo worldview."[20] The films, according to Beverly Singer, "were intended to serve as an anthropological case study and not as films to be publicly distributed,"[21] yet did feature a Navajo aesthetics of long shots of the landscape, few close ups of individuals, and topics of interest to Navajos. Native American experimental cinema that has operated outside the auspices of visual anthropologists includes work by Victor Masayesva Jr., a Hopi filmmaker who has been creating experimental film since 1980.[22] His film *Imagining Indians* (1992) made connections between what Singer calls "visual genocide"[23] and the history of representations of Native Americans in film through interviews with Native American actors and clips from Hollywood westerns.[24] The film is framed by a narrative of a young Indigenous woman visiting a white dentist, which further underlines the connection between the various forms of violence endured by Native people, especially during the Columbus Quincentennial year.[25]

Prior to the inception of motion picture technologies, non-

Indians satisfied their visual and experiential curiosity about the Indigenous "Other" through photography and other methods of travel to Indigenous communities. While these remain popular means of representing American Indians, film became the mode through which most people in the world encountered Native North American communities (and mostly still do). And, subsequently, film has also become a technology of the self through which Native Americans themselves have structured their identities. Part of the work of contemporary Indigenous filmmakers is to contend with the legacy of mainstream images of Native people from the silent era (including the work of early Native filmmakers James Young Deer and Edwin Carewe) to the present. Yet many recent Native American films refuse to trade in outright corrections or critiques of genres such as the western, which privileges colonial discourses. Due to the discursive space film as virtual reservation leaves in its wake, Indigenous filmmakers are now able to present fresh representations of Native America. These representations reconnect and refigure Indigenous epistemes such as gender complementarity, the role of the spirit, and alternate conceptions of time in contrast to the dominant culture's misunderstandings about atemporal Native "wisdom." Significantly, these epistemes are not stuck in time but have changed and transformed just as Native communities themselves have. Some of these self-representations include Beverly Singer's *Hózhó of Native Women* (1997), a documentary about the cultural, spiritual, and physical health of Native women; Mary Kunuk and Arnait Video Productions' *Anaana* (2001), a celebration of the life of Inuit hunter, storyteller, and mother of filmmakers Mary Kunuk and Zacharias Kunuk, Vivi Kunuk, and her contemporary Inuit community's complex relationship to the land; and Dorothy Christian's *a spiritual land claim* (2006), an experimental short that thematizes trauma, loss, and renewal through reinvigorated connections to a tribally specific landscape.

Prophecy and Native American Discourses

Native American expressions of prophecy have recently been taken up by contemporary cultural critics as representative of how Indigenous epistemes have changed, transformed, and resisted devaluation at the hands of colonial powers over the years. Many contemporary Indigenous scholars, activists, and community members argue for an epistemology that considers the role of spirits and the spiritual as a vibrant and integral part of human existence. Dale Turner argues, "Indigenous spirituality is central to Indigenous philosophical thinking, which European cultures cannot and will not respect on its own terms. In a sense, this is *the* most significant difference between Indigenous and European world views."[26] Indigenous spirituality has been elided and suppressed by Europeans in the so-called "New World" because it poses a threat to Judeo-Christian understandings of gender, the primacy of written narrative, and hierarchical genealogies of meaning and power. But it also, importantly, challenges Western conceptions of temporality, something European American governments and cultures have not tolerated.[27] Turner further describes Indigenous spirituality as a kind of personal and collective minefield wherein one of the most crucial elements of Indigenous ontologies must also not risk explanation in the field of Native American Studies because of the legacies of colonialism. "As Indigenous people," Turner contends, "many of us believe that we can explain our understandings of the 'spiritual' and that the dominant culture will some day 'get it.' But history has shown us that at least at this time in the relationship, we must keep to ourselves our sacred knowledge as we articulate and understand it from within our own cultures, for it is this knowledge that defines us as Indigenous peoples."[28] Turner points to the difficulty of making commensurable a key component of epistemic Indigenous knowledges and cultures while at the same time acknowledging that misunderstandings pose a risk to tribal communities. Citing the nineteenth-century Lakota war leader, Crazy Horse, who resisted having his photograph taken because of a suspicion of the way images circulate in the dominant culture and refused to discuss Lakota spirituality with non-Natives: "This 'Crazy Horse' approach to protecting Indigenous philosophies is necessary for our survival as Indigenous peoples. Yet at the same time, we must continue to assert and protect our rights, sovereignty, and nationhood within an ongoing colonial relationship."[29] Native American visual culture, I argue, provides a field on which the tension between representing the importance of spirituality (without either divulging sacred information that could be weaponized by the colonizer or stressing its alterity and disengagement with political and cultural movements) and the desire to conceive of Indigenous philosophies unhitched from or critically engaged with the West can be played out.

Ironically, the same kinds of environmental concerns that propelled the KAB campaign also inspire many Native American filmmakers—from the Arctic to Tierra del Fuego—to employ ideas about prophecy as a didactic tool in this time of acute global climate crisis. Because vast indices of knowledge ranging from the ethnobotanical to the philosophical are housed in Indigenous communities of the Americas (specifically geographical sites typically thought of as resource-rich in the West but devoid of human habitation), it is critical that filmmakers "people" sites under environmental siege in order to preserve these knowledges for future generations. Films such as Arnait Video Productions' *Ninguira/My Grandmother* (1999) and *Before Tomorrow* (2008) not only teach Inuit youth in Nunavut, Canada's newest territory, about traditional relationships to the spiritual world, grieving, attitudes toward the land, and the importance of women's roles in the community, they also populate an area many consider *terra nullius*, demonstrating how settler colonialism and even the most minute increase in global warming adversely affects complex networks of human, plant, and animal communities. Creating films that engage the spiritual realm without defaulting to the ghost effect and romantic notions of Native American spirituality provides Indigenous filmmakers with a vehicle not only to overturn the representational history of the vanishing Indian but to engage environmental consciousness through visual sovereignty by offering up alternate ways of thinking about and living on the land.

Scholarship on Native American filmic representations has historically presented a reading of Indigenous peoples as victims of Hollywood interests and a national rhetoric of invisibility and disappearance. This is the familiar register along which Native Americans inhabit stereotypical roles first scripted during the early colonial period in visual and print culture and continue along a trajectory through the creation of the western film genre to the present. Yet this, of course, is not the whole picture. As a supplement and antidote to these images, important recent work on Indigenous film demonstrates how contemporary Indigenous filmmakers have resisted Hollywood by employing culturally specific representational practices of visual sovereignty and by sometimes ignoring or eliding dominant representational conventions and other forms of colonization.

Imprint: The Spectral Indian on the Virtual Reservation

Cheyenne and Arapaho filmmaker Chris Eyre employs the ghost effect and representations of prophecy to different purposes than the conventional image of the spectral Indian in his most recent narrative film, *Imprint*. *Imprint* is an ultra–low budget film produced by Eyre and directed by Michael Linn. Eyre, the most well-known contemporary Native American filmmaker and producer, directed *Smoke Signals* (1998), as well as *Tenacity* (1995), *Skins* (2002), *Skinwalkers* (2002), *Edge of America* (2003), *Thief of Time* (2004), and *A Thousand Roads* (2005), a film produced by the National Museum of the American Indian. He also directed the first three films in the PBS *We Shall Remain* (2009) series. He worked on *Imprint* in collaboration with Linn Productions, a small, family-owned, non-Native production company based in Rapid City, South Dakota.[30] The film was originally set on a rural white family's haunted farm in South Dakota, but conversations between Eyre, Native American actors, and Michael Linn, who directed *Imprint*, resulted in a film that is set and shot primarily on the Pine Ridge Reservation and employs local, as well as nationally recognized, Native American actors. According to Carolyn Linn, executive producer of *Imprint*, Eyre; Larry Pourier, a Lakota coproducer of the film; and Native American actors in the film, including Dave Bald Eagle and Charlie White Buffalo, made significant contributions to the film's plot and served as Lakota language consultants.[31] The film features a plot driven by Indigenous epistemes of prophecy and the role of the spirit created in consultation with Eyre, the film's actors, and local tribal members.[32] It is particularly significant that the film is set and filmed on the Pine Ridge Reservation since this site figures so prominently in Native American history. Pine Ridge not only signifies authentic "Indianness" in the dominant film imaginary (warriors in full headdress riding on horseback, wide horizons dotted with tipis, herds of thundering buffalo, etc.), but it is also the site of the Wounded Knee Massacre of December 1890 (and the Wounded Knee cemetery where victims of the carnage perpetrated by the United States Seventh Cavalry are buried) and what came to be known as Wounded Knee II, the violent seventy-one day standoff in 1973 between AIM members and U.S. marshals, state police, and supporters of Richard A. "Dick" Wilson's government.[33]

Carole Quattro Levine details the crucial contribution the film makes as a narrative that focuses on the independent, strong-willed protagonist and her relationship with her equally independent, strong-willed mother.[34] The film's point of entry through an intelligent, articulate, well-educated female lead protagonist overturns Hollywood film conventions of the western, in particular, in which Indigenous women are either absent or abject. Both *Imprint* and *It Starts with a Whisper* complicate Native American film history by featuring powerful female characters, as does both films' use of a supernatural plot. In the service of visual sovereignty, *Imprint* overturns the image of the ghostly Indian as a spectral artifact of the past through its use of Indigenous manifestations of the spirit and conflations of time. Termed a "thrilling Native American supernatural ghost story," and a "shrewdly moody attempt at an old-fashioned ghost story with a Native American twist,"[35] *Imprint* plays on audience expectations of both the horror film genre and conventional images of the Native American ghost in terms of its use of suspense, setting, diegesis, and technical considerations.

The film's plot centers on Shayla Stonefeather (Tonantzin Carmelo), a Denver-based Lakota attorney from the Pine Ridge Reservation. In the opening scene she successfully prosecutes Robbie Whiteshirt (Joseph Medicine Blanket), a Lakota teenager, also from Pine Ridge, who has been, as is later revealed, unjustly accused and convicted of killing a senator's wife. After the trial, Shayla returns to her parents' buffalo ranch to celebrate the birthday of her father, Sam (Charlie White Buffalo), an artist who appears to be suffering from a catastrophic disease and attendant mental illness.[36]

While she is home, Shayla begins to notice that her parents' ranch appears to be haunted by some kind of unresolved past event that is linked to her father's illness. At night she glimpses a ghostly figure (a wispy shimmer achieved by low-tech special effects that is nevertheless spooky) accompanied by aural intimations of violence and a spectral handprint on a wall that quickly disappears. The ghost does not appear to threaten Shayla but

20. Tonantzin Carmelo as Shayla Stonefeather in *Imprint* (2007). Photograph courtesy of Linn Productions.

rather to suggest that these violent acts have taken place recently on the Stonefeather property. The spectral figure does not scare Shayla as much as it activates her need to investigate its cause and purpose.

Shayla concludes that the specter may have one of four origins: it may be the ghost of Robbie Whiteshirt, who committed suicide immediately following his conviction; his brother Frank (Russell Chewey), who follows Shayla back to the reservation and seems to be stalking her; the troubled spirits of Lakota people murdered during the Wounded Knee Massacre, whose bodies have been interred in a nearby cemetery (there is a temporal plausibility to this argument in the text as the film is set in late December, the same time of year the massacre occurred); or the ghost of her brother, Nathaniel Stonefeather (Gerald Tokala Clifford), who has been missing for two years and is presumed to be deceased because Shayla's father, Sam, found Nathaniel and his friend Allen using drugs in the house.

Shayla intuits the fourth theory to be the most plausible and begins to suspect that her father murdered Nathaniel and Allen. The imagined reenactments of the "murder" scene and the ghostly appearances, which both originate in Nathaniel's bedroom closet, intimate that the two were not only using drugs in the house but that they were lovers and that her father killed them both out of homophobic rage. This theory is corroborated towards the end of the film when Shayla finds Nathaniel's and Allen's motorcycles buried beneath the family's barn, and Sam—in one of his few lucid moments—draws a violent image of an individual hanged in that same barn.

In order to rid the house of its haunted presence, Shayla's mother, Rebecca (Carla-Rae Holland), asks an unnamed medicine man (Dave Bald Eagle) to smudge the house with sage and locate the source of the restless spirit. He later speaks to Shayla at the cemetery. The representation of the medicine man in the film overturns conventional Hollywood images of Native American medicine people and shamans. Rather than trafficking in alterity, extreme costumes, and incommensurability, as most Hollywood images of medicine people do, *Imprint*'s medicine man sports a cowboy hat, fleece vest, and dress pants. No one in the film refers to him as a medicine man, and the only marker of his profession is his sage bundle. He speaks both Lakota and English to Shayla, is humble in his approach to spiritual affairs, and possesses a wry sense of humor. He has no particular insights into the haunting, except to note that the spirit has a special message for Shayla. Appearing ghostly through the wisps of sage smoke that encircle his face, he tells her that the "past, present, and future all touch each other. Time doesn't exist. For spirits, time doesn't exist."

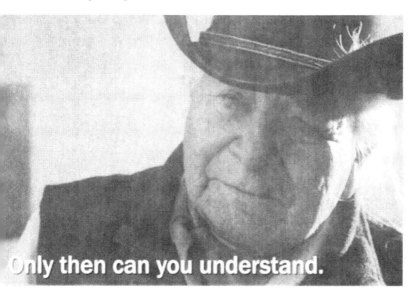

Only then can you understand.

21. Dave Bald Eagle plays a medicine man in *Imprint* (2007).

This welding of Shayla's individual experience with those of the women, men, and children murdered at nearby Wounded Knee revivifies an ongoing relationship and responsibility to the past and future by drawing connections between seemingly disparate events. The title image of the film refers to the ghostly handprint that appears in the house as well as to the story of Wounded Knee victims, whose memory is "forever imprinted on this land," as the medicine man relates. According to Lim, "Ghost films that are also historical allegories make incongruous use of the vocabulary of the supernatural to articulate historical injustice, referring to 'social reality' by recourse to the undead. Such ghost narratives productively explore the dissonance between modernity's disenchanted time and the spectral temporality of haunting in which the presumed boundaries between past, present, and future are shown to be shockingly permeable."[37] The medicine man draws attention to a historical event that remains painful because of the scope of the violence committed, the trauma left in its wake, and its illegibility in the national consciousness. At the same time, this character provides a language for healing to the other figures in the film, drawing from the specific context of Wounded Knee.

The medicine man comes to the Stonefeather house to assuage the restless spirits abiding there and locates the source of the supernatural presence in Nathaniel's closet. Shayla's suspicions about her father are thus (wrongly, as is revealed later) confirmed. She subsequently confronts Sam with this evidence, and while he is paralyzed from his illness and cannot speak, he communicates by crying, which Shayla reads as an admission to the crime. He dies shortly thereafter, released, as Shayla confers, from the guilt of his crimes.

Perhaps unintentionally, the figure of a speechless Native American elder, able to communicate only through tears, invokes Cody's performance as the crying Indian in the KAB campaign. In *Imprint*, however, the cause of silence is medical, and Sam prophesizes about the future through his tears not to activate guilt on the part of non-Indian spectators but to save his family and, by extension, his community from further violence. The tears also signify his frustration at being misunderstood and unable to communicate sufficiently through either language or an artistic medium, a frustration that metaphorizes the historical condition of Native Americans whose speech has often been either unheard or misconstrued.

Imprint draws from a long cinematic, literary, and popular culture tradition of locating Native Americans in the past, as ghosts whose political power resides in their function as disembodied reminders of historical violence and injustice. Taken in psychoanalytic terms, Indian ghosts such as Cody's character in the KAB campaign haunt the national imaginary and serve to suggest that guilt can be ameliorated through appeasing spirits who are perceived as easier to placate than contemporary Indigenous survivors, whose presence challenges the very foundations of the United States and Canada. At this point in the film, *Imprint* likewise leads the spectator to believe that the haunting of the ranch is the result of the unsettled spirit of a Native American for whom a crime needs to be (re)solved in order to be released from the ties that bind it to earthly existence.

The film's conclusion, however, reveals a surprising plot twist: the ghost who has haunted the plot is Shayla's future self, who will be the victim of an attempted murder by her European American boyfriend, attorney and aspiring politician Jonathan Freeman (Cory Brusseau). Freeman follows Shayla to South Dakota ostensibly to celebrate her father's birthday but also to demonstrate to her how hopeless and dysfunctional the situation on the reservation is, a move intended to lure her permanently to the city with him. At Sam's funeral Jonathan becomes enraged when Shayla confronts him with evidence that their law firm fabricated the case against Robbie Whiteshirt. His political career in jeopardy, Jonathan storms away from the funeral.

Later, in her parent's empty house, Shayla and her childhood sweetheart, Tom Grey Horse (Michael Spears), a tribal policeman who accompanies Shayla home after her father's funeral, sit in Nathaniel's room and discuss a ghostly apparition Shayla believes she saw near the cemetery. She glimpsed what she thought was a spectral image of Nathaniel, which would lend credence to her belief that her father had killed him and that his spirit would now be released from its earthly moorings. Near midnight, at the exact time the figure that haunted the house would appear, Jonathan emerges from the closet with a knife and attempts to kill both

Tom and Shayla. The medicine man's prophecies were therefore directed at that time rather than rooted in the past.

The events prophesized by Shayla's spectral future self conclude in the barn where Shayla saves herself by becoming entangled with a hook while Jonathan plunges to his death. The image of Shayla dangling from the hook was prophesized by her father's artistic rendering of the same scene, meant to visually warn Shayla about the danger that her father could not verbally articulate. In a chance meeting at the Wounded Knee cemetery earlier in the film, the medicine man encourages Shayla to "listen." "You have closed many doors in your life. Very little light can shine in," he notes. "Only when you open these doors can you begin to listen. Only then can you understand. There are messages all around us, but few are listening, few understand." The attack serves as pedagogy for Shayla to learn to reimagine spectral temporality and its possible futures. As historical pedagogy, it serves to teach the spectator about the ongoing lessons of the historical past and spectral futures.

Both Tom and Shayla survive the attack, and Shayla's brother, Nathaniel, returns to Pine Ridge, absolving her father of her brother's supposed murder. By the film's conclusion, Shayla resolves to resume her relationship with Tom and reconnect to her Lakota community. A wolf that had appeared earlier in the film to present Shayla with a cryptic message rematerializes to lead her to a vista of the village of Pine Ridge. The film concludes with an image of her standing, palms forward, to receive what her future might hold, a future that is informed by the past but not tethered to it. Shayla leaves her family at the film's conclusion to return to Denver, where she will devote her career to serving the Native American community there or perhaps eventually return to Pine Ridge Reservation to perform legal advocacy work. By representing the spectral as an intervention into Indigenous notions of time and space, *Imprint* provides a

22. Concluding scene
from *Imprint* (2007).

critical rereading of the Native American ghost figure on a virtual reservation that permits an engagement with alternative conceptions of the past and future not generally represented in more conventional films.

Matriarchal Time/Space Machines: Film as Virtual Healing

Like *Imprint*, Mohawk artist Shelley Niro's experimental short, *It Starts with a Whisper*, provides a critical reframing of Indian ghosts through Indigenous-inspired representations of spirituality. The film narrates a day in the life of Shanna Sabbath (Elizabeth Burning), a young Haudenosaunee woman from the Six Nations Reserve in Ontario, Canada.[38] The film simultaneously critiques and elides colonization by supplying humorous Haudenosaunee-generated images that develop what Larry Abbott has called Iroquois "alter egos,"[39] images that do something beyond overturning negative stereotypes with "traditional" representations. The film opens midway through Shanna's performance of a kind of vision quest that unfolds over the course of the film. As in a traditional vision quest, in which an individual undergoes a liminal experience in isolation from other people in order to receive knowledge from the spiritual realm in the service of a broader community, Shanna spends the film in dialogue with spirit beings in human form that console, challenge, and encourage her. The prophetic message she receives from the spirits about healing from the discursive and physical violences of ongoing colonization is intended to benefit not only Shanna but also members of the larger imagined community on the virtual reservation each time the film is screened. The film both recognizes the settler colonialism of the Canadian nation-state and makes the case that the Haudenosaunee are not a colonized people.

One of the spirit voices urges Shanna to draw on "voices of the past, voices of the present" in order to guide her path out of trauma, what the voice describes as "sorrow inside and beyond you." These nondiegetic voices do not give Shanna explicit directives for healing from colonialism but provide her with support, through communal memory, to negotiate her way towards a new status as a healthy Haudenosaunee woman. The film works to provide encouragement and support to Haudenosaunee spectators through Shanna's example, but also to validate, revive and reconfigure Haudenosaunee knowledges, particularly gender and prophecy and its attendant relationship to the spiritual world on the virtual reservation. The opening scene sets the stage for the recovery of a Haudenosaunee worldview that values the balance of equal opposites as a formula for intellectual, spiritual, physical, and cultural health and well-being that the film enacts.

The film commences with an extreme close up of the distinctive style of Haudenosaunee beadwork displayed against a crackling fire. A female voiceover lists sets of opposites—"whispering waters / raging torrents; earth of bounty / parched and starving land"—followed by a male speaking untranslated Mohawk. These whispered opposites set the stage for a recuperation of Haudenosaunee intellectual knowledge practices in the service of contemporary communities—the "It" to which the title refers. According to the Haudenosaunee, the universe is divided into equal halves that achieve their optimum state in balance. This balance is not predicated on the Judeo-Christian binary of "good" versus "evil" as the Haudenosaunee dichotomy operates ideally not in conflict, but in harmony. In addition, the gendered binary, part of a broader set of opposites, is not grounded in a belief that men and the products of their labor are superior to women, but that the two are valued entities in a universe where their intellectual and physical production is respected equally.[40]

The Haudenosaunee origin story is instructive as a theorization of this notion of balance, as well as a relationship to temporality that is, in Michel Serres's words, "polychromic, multitemporal, and reveals a time that is gathered together with multiple pleats."[41] In one of the many versions of this story, a woman from the Sky World falls through a hole created by an uprooted tree and on her way into the abyss grabs corn, beans, and squash seed (known as the "Three Sisters"). As she tumbles through seemingly endless darkness, Canada geese take pity on her and carry her until they become tired and call on a giant, primordial turtle below to assist them. She lands safely on his or her shell, and with the assistance of other animals, creates the world on the turtle's back. Her daughter later gives birth to two male twins, Sapling and Flint, who are responsible for creating the earth's topography. Sapling facilitates geographies that ease human existence such as rivers, lakes, hills, and forests, while Flint engenders challenges such as mountains, inhospitable climates, and rocky surfaces.[42]

While this originary event occurred in time immemorial, it can also be imagined to recur every time a child is born as it moves from the space prior to its earthly existence ("Sky World"), travels through the birth canal (the abyss through which the Woman Who Fell from the Sky moves), and brings its own special gifts in the form of metaphoric seeds to this world. In Haudenosaunee prophecy, this will continue to happen until the turtle becomes weary, flips over, and dives back under the water to end life as we know it and begin anew. Some scholars insist that we are currently in the process of experiencing this prophecy. Mohawk scholar Deborah Doxtater posits that Haudenosaunee women "grapple with the uneasy questions of how to think about a world where another culture's mind has superimposed its own intellectual constructs on the landscape and drastically altered how that land looks to us; of how our cultural metaphors and the way in which we connect to land have become reinterpreted and entangled for us by a 'dominant' Euro–North American ideology grounded in scientific rationalism, new age spirituality, and ecological liberalism."[43] She asks if "there can be a healthy act of creation emanating out of our own way of thinking even if we picture and envision the world as fragmented, distorted, and in distress."[44] Niro's film, I argue, responds emphatically to this question and embodies this sense of prophetic renewal as a moving image that can be replayed endlessly. "The *moving picture*," as Vivien Sobchack argues, "is a visible representation not of activity finished or past but of activity coming-into-being."[45] Film, particularly the conventions of experimental film, permit a staging of the temporal that aligns more closely with Indigenous notions of time.

The nighttime opening scene in the film gives way to its opposite, daytime. Unlike the opening scene, with its warm fire glow and lush, detailed beadwork shots, the day scene is less animated. A pair of disembodied arms throws dirt on the fire, and the ensuing smoke clears to reveal intertitles that relate the story of the Tutelo, an Indigenous nation that found shelter on the Grand River among the Haudenosaunee in the 1840s and whose survivors were adopted by the Cayuga, a nation whose members currently live on the Six Nations Reserve.[46] The intertitles narrate the story of the Tutelo in the past tense, suggesting a sense of melancholy and loss. The intrusion of the documentary film style text also signals and critiques the ways Native Americans have been conventionally represented on screen. The text both offers up historical evidence as inscribed, archived "fact," but also contests the privileging of the textual by juxtaposing the past tense description of the Tutelos with their extant connection to and influence on contemporary Haudenosaunee people. This text creates what Bill Nichols has called a "discourse . . . of sobriety" that opens up the filmic image to the possibility that "what we say and decide can affect the course of real events and entail real consequences. These are ways of seeing and speaking that are also ways of doing and acting."[47]

The emotional effect of the intertitles is heightened by the appearance of a woman wearing traditional Haudenosaunee clothing who is revealed in obscured, brief shots of parts of her body—her feet, her head and torso from afar, her face in profile—and the sound of rustling through the forest. The appearance of this woman, viewed only in fragments, following the story of the Tutelo visually suggests the ghostly metaphors of the vanishing Indian. Is it Shanna or the ghost of a Tutelo woman from long ago? Alternately, could this figure be Shy Woman, revisiting earth in the shape of the film's main character?

The film offers a counternarrative for exploring the thematics of history, loss, and the spiritual by overturning nostalgic discourses

23. Shanna (Elizabeth Burning) in *It Starts with a Whisper* (1993).

of the vanishing Indian. Shanna is not trapped outside of time as a lone ghostly figure haunting the frames of the film, but returns from her vision quest to her life in metropolitan Canada. She links the present and future to the traumatic past of the Tutelo, much as *Imprint* involves Wounded Knee as a site of violence and healing. The film slowly pans the sky and cuts to an image of skyscrapers in Toronto. The call of birds and lapping water are replaced by their opposites: a cacophony of urban sounds (jackhammers, sirens, and car horns). Wearing a business suit, Shanna negotiates this landscape as deftly as she does the banks of the Grand River. The female voiceover spirit returns to speak to Shanna again, connecting the politics of geography and removal to the experiences of contemporary Native Americans rather than severing the past from the present as do conventional representations of the ghostly Indian. The voice instructs Shanna:

> Don't be afraid. The voices of the past are calling you. The voices of the present urge you on. The voices of the dead tell you their sorrow. The sorrow inside you and beyond you. You're so young, Shanna. Where are your years across the centuries? What can you do? Reading, writing, thinking. Too much thinking. Tears that won't come. Peace that won't come. . . . How do you go forward? Who knows what else has been forgotten? Who knows where to look? . . . Listen to the voices, Shanna. Sing your own song. Play your own drum.

In the film Shanna is not a ghost but a young Indigenous woman grappling with issues of alienation, identity, and the violence of encounters with Europeans and white settlers. The voiceover spirits have no visual representation but make manifest an unbroken connection across time and space. This strategic use of representations of the spirit not only opens up the possibility for a visual sovereignty that imaginatively performs epistemes that do not easily conform to linear plottings of time and Western juridical notions of property, but also permits creative virtual spaces of community.

The film does not dictate that Shanna make the proverbial choice between the "Indian" and "white" worlds. To be a contemporary Haudenosaunee person, the film suggests, is to interact with an imaged and territorial landscape inhabited by historical and spiritual ancestors. As Darrell Varga writes, "In Niro's films . . . the grim stereotype image of the disenfranchised native typically found on Canadian television is replaced by characters who have a sophisticated historical consciousness and desire to navigate the flux of identity formed out of tradition, everyday reality, dominant media culture, and the creative process of change."[48] The film suggests that imagining this connection with the ancestors is a way of countervailing against the legacy of colonialism.

Shanna leaves this city scene for a weekend road trip to Niagara Falls with her tricksteresque "Matriarchal Aunts/Clowns" (as they are identified in the credits), one of whom has won a romantic getaway to the site popularly recognized as the Honeymoon Capital of the World. The aunts, Emily (Debra Doxtator), Pauline (Beverley Miller), and Molly (Elizabeth Doxtater), each named for a prominent Mohawk historical figure (Emily General, Pauline Johnson, and Molly Brant), gently tease Shanna about her life off the reservation and her passion for reading throughout the journey.[49] Once they arrive in Niagara Falls the aunts disappear, leaving Shanna to inhabit what Gilles Deleuze calls an "any-space-whatevers"—a dysfunctional, fragmented, and anonymous filmic site.[50] Shanna confronts a hallucinogenic, intimidating, and terrifying space of whirling neon signs, carnival music, and the ping of a shooting gallery where Indians are the targets. These tourist trappings do not draw Shanna in but make her feel alienated and alone until the voiceover female spirit intones: "Shanna, don't be sad. We made it through another year. A short five hundred years. Next year will be better. There are so many people who care about you. Look around you. You can see the circle grow."

The scene jump cuts from a space that signals a suturing of "reading, writing, thinking . . . too much thinking" to a place where she can acknowledge her emotional circuitry during her virtual reservation meeting with Cree political leader Elijah Harper (played by Harper himself who, ironically, is wearing a Hollywoodesque full headdress).[51] This scene deflates again the stereotype of the ghostly Indian because Harper is a living person, not a specter.

24. Shanna meets Elijah Harper in *It Starts with a Whisper* (1993).

The space where he and Shanna meet is both deterritorialized and outside the bounds of space as it is neither part of a dream nor "reality." As a break from the chaos of Niagara Falls, Shanna and Harper meet in a quiet, peaceful, decontextualized space, surrounded by a blank background. This space, which could be read as "heaven" because of its likeness to filmic representations of the Christian afterworld, brings the religion of the European colonizers into dialogue with Native American notions of prophecy. Shanna's last name is Sabbath—the day of rest and completion in the Bible (signaling a representation of both the beginning and the end). Harper's first name, Elijah, refers to a prophet from the

Hebrew, Christian, and Islamic traditions who performed miracles, such as raising the dead, and ascended to Heaven without first dying. This scene lends itself to a reading of Harper as a prophet bringing wisdom not to a male novitiate but to a young woman who holds the promise of enacting a rebirth among her people (and reviving the "dead" Tutelos), bringing the world back into balance on Haudenosaunee terms, but through metaphors commensurable to Christians as well.

This time/space marked within the film is what Robert Stam has called "chronotopic multiplicity."[52] The simultaneous rendering of time wherein Harper can occupy his place in chronological time both outside and inside the frame mirrors Indigenous oral narrative and the conduciveness of cinema as a technology for expressing Indigenous knowledges, a technology Stam has posited "is ideally equipped to express cultural and temporal hybridity."[53] Harper recognizes Shanna and acknowledges the violence conventional film images have inflicted on Native Americans: "I know all the influence the mass media has had on us. We must fight these negative stereotypes. We must be aware and not let them upset us so that we doubt our self-worth." Yet "fighting" stereotypes within the scope of *It Starts with a Whisper* means being receptive to the spirit realm and the promises of prophecy.

After meeting with Harper, Shanna is magically transported to a hotel room to perform a musical interlude with the aunts, all of whom wear fancy gowns and sing what at first appears to be a dreamy girl-power, self-esteem song whose lyrics begin with "I'm pretty," in front of a kitschy Niagara Falls honeymoon suite vanity. But the concluding part of the verse punctures this image of a surface reading. The verse ends with the phrase "mad at you." The women go on to critique the Canadian colonizer's policies of the residential school, institutionalizing aboriginal people in mental hospitals for "acting otherwise," and for normative sexual policies that undermine both the matrilineal nature of Haudenosaunee culture as well as the homoerotics of the musical scene itself (the four women are in a honeymoon suite, lie down on a heart-shaped bed together, and perform seductive, synchronized dances whose climax occurs off-stage). The sassy song ends with the verse, "I'm survivin'. I'm thrivin'. I'm doin' fine without you," suggesting that colonization has been but a blip on the Indigenous radar screen. As Rob Shields has noted, Niagara Falls "was consecrated as a place betwixt and between one social status and another, passing over all the taboos separating the lives of the respectable single and the married," a "place for transitions and *rites de passage* in the life cycle."[54] Niagara Falls itself constitutes a virtual reservation, as it is both sacred territory to Native Americans and a dominant culture constructed tourist space, both a location of transformation and the shedding of old selves.

In the concluding scene, Shanna presides over a tea party overlooking Niagara Falls on December 31, 1992, at 11:55 p.m., the very end of the Columbus Quincentennial year. One of the aunts reads a poem by nineteenth-century Mohawk writer Pauline Johnson as Shanna cuts an earth-shaped cake (symbolizing the destruction of this "world" in favor of a new one and prophesizing similar transformations for other tribal members coping with the trauma of history). As the cake is cleaved in half, fireworks in the background constellate to form an image of a tree sitting atop a turtle—the Haudenosaunee visual icon for the female-centered origin of the world.

This image at the end of the film signifies one world coming to an end (both in terms of its temporal date concluding the Quincentennial and its symbolic temporality that privileges Indigenous time and space) and a new one beginning in the broadest sense of cataclysmic and metaphoric change. It simultaneously signals a more personal tectonic shift in the young protagonist from traumatized subject to Haudenosaunee woman—a shift that the film suggests can be replicated for any spectator. In this scene, the film acknowledges an alternate sense of time, wherein "history" is taken to mean the entire scope of Haudenosaunee experiences within which European invasion is a small blip on this longer space/timeline—the "short five hundred years" invoked by the female spirit voice who condoles the past at the same time that she offers hope for the future.

The film makes manifest what Jonathan Lear calls "radical hope."[55] Lear discusses the Crow Nation as a people who "ran out of time" as a result of the devastating nineteenth century. Yet under the visionary leadership of Plenty Coups, the Crow exist today as a vital, strong community in the process of revitalizing their traditions. *It Starts with a Whisper* also engages in what might more usefully be called "prophetic hope" by hinging not on an individual leader but by demonstrating the work of prophecy from the ground up. Rather than relying on a messianic figure or divine intervention, as do millennial and eschatological belief systems, the film reads the Indigenous body itself as a prophetic text. The film prophesizes an omnitemporal new beginning that takes place simultaneously in several different time/space continuums.

The experimental *It Starts with a Whisper* participates in the Indigenous-led aesthetic and cultural efforts to rethink the Columbus Quincentennial. These efforts mobilized along a register that both contemplated and condoled five hundred years of oppression while at the same time it commemorated and celebrated Native American "survivance." As a result, *It Starts with a Whisper* critiques Canadian colonial representative practices that have rendered aboriginal communities either invisible through discursive genocide and the myth of the vanishing Indian or hypervisible through mass-mediated images of Native peoples unrecognizable and of little or no value to tribal communities.

While Niro privileges Haudenosaunee systems, she does so by dispensing with the fraught notion of authenticity. Her film is built on scaffolding that understands cultural identity to be fluid and that a confederacy such as the Haudenosaunee survived and thrived not only its tumultuous birth, but over four hundred years of invasion and colonization through a complex series of diplomatic, philosophical, and epistemological negotiations that relied on the kinetic force of transformation. "Haudenosaunee life began," Niro states in her more recent *Suite: Indian* (2005), "and has remained alive through the need to express one's life and creativity." The creation of the Great Law of Peace at least five centuries before contact with Europeans sets the groundwork for framing what was to come and how Haudenosaunee communities might cope with the resultant changes.

The themes addressed in *It Starts with a Whisper* are also invoked in Niro's co-created exhibit at the 2007 Venice Biennale, "The Requickening Project."[56] This project, according to Nancy Marie Mithlo, is a "reference to the Iroquois condolence ceremony that rectifies states of fragility, and ensures life continues to flourish."[57] Niro's exhibit features an experimental black-and-white short entitled *Tree* (2006), produced with Lena Recollet (an Anishinabe actress and writer who plays the protagonist in the film), which according to Mithlo "pays homage to the 'Keep America Beautiful' campaign from the early 1970s where actor Iron Eyes Cody gazes at the environment and sees it no longer being cared for or respected. Niro replaces Cody, the perpetual Indian stereotype, with a matriarchal figure who witnesses the same environmental degradation, some thirty years later."[58] One of the main differences between the two moving images, however, is that while Cody's address calls for curbing litter, Niro's silent young woman wears contemporary clothing and appeals for a more active emotional, political, and psychic investment in the environment as her image is mapped onto that of a bare tree, a

25. Image from Shelley Niro's *Tree* (2006).

signal, according to Onondaga Chief Leon Shenandoah, for the imminent end of the world.[59] *Tree* features a postapocalyptic world in which Sky Woman appears on Earth again to either heal the wounded environment or enact its final destruction.

Present Predictions: Native American Discursive Prophecy

Native American media artists Chris Eyre and Shelley Niro employ film as a virtual reservation to foreground, contest, and reinvigorate such key concepts as prophecy, chronology, spirituality, and gender. The logic underpinning recent scholarship on prophecy and its relationship to Native American science and some of the climatological, philosophical, and cultural changes witnessed in the past few years critiques the stereotypical notion of Indigenous time as a metaphorical circle that loops back to and proceeds from some originary point, as opposed to European conceptions of chronological time that originate somewhere in the past and stretch forward linearly to a future along a single trajectory.[60] Instead, recent work by scholars such as Beverly Sourjohn Patchell suggests a conception of time that conflates these two ways of thinking about chronology.[61]

For Patchell and many Native American writers and media makers, what is conceived of as the past is endlessly available through cultural modes such as one's relationship to the land, language, dance, song, and stories that have rested in dormancy, despite over five hundred years of colonialism and attempted genocide. These modes have changed but are nevertheless accessible through embodied memory, dreams, the process of writing, imagination, and, most significantly for my work, film.

An example of a text that exemplifies Native American relationships to prophecy is Leslie Marmon Silko's *Almanac of the Dead* (1991), an encyclopedic, apocalyptic novel that constitutes itself as a prophetic text, and underscores this critical tradition of pre-1492 conceptions of time and space. *Almanac of the Dead* memorializes the Indigenous genocide from the turn of the fifteenth century to the present as well as prophesizes the "death" of Western culture and its attachment to linear time and hierarchical binary oppositions, capitalism, and neoliberalism. In her work on Silko, Yvonne Reineke draws on the work of Jonathan Boyarin, Enrique Dussel, Gordon Brotherston, and Georg Wilhelm Friedrich Hegel to suggest that "despite new directions that physics has posed for our sense of time/space, such as the challenges of quantum mechanics and the theory of relativity, many of us in the West generally operate in the daily world and in our social and political lives as if 'Cartesian space' inhered. That is, we tend to separate out time and space."[62] She contends that, conversely, Silko's sense of the prophetic and its relationship to history, geography, and chronology "insists on time and space as living, and hence, as moving time through space"; therefore, "The novel's insistent message is clear: the passage of time does not diminish Indigenous people's call for justice through the return of their homelands."[63] This sense of the prophecy's connection to ongoing struggles for sovereignty is foregrounded at the inception of the novel with a hand-drawn map of the border between what is now known as Arizona, Texas, and California and the northern states of Mexico. The map resembles a womb, concretizing the relationship between women and the land, not as a site to be conquered through sexual and territorial violence, but as a space of generation and recognition of female power through the novel's strong female protagonists.[64]

A key on the map marked "Prophecy" states, "When Europeans arrived, the Maya, Azteca, and Inca cultures had already built great cities and vast networks of roads. Ancient prophecies foretold the arrival of Europeans in the Americas. The ancient prophecies also foretell the disappearance of all things European."[65] As tribal historians and scholars have noted, most Native American communities have an oral tradition that foretells the invasion of their homelands by strangers from Europe. These gifts from the past not only warn descendants about the cataclysmic change, death, and destruction that are impending, but also assure them of their survival.

Recent scholarship indicates that Indigenous people have historically presented sophisticated reading strategies of prophecy.[66] Indigenous readings of prophetic narratives reassert agency into the historical record and demonstrate the importance of a cosmology that conceives of time, space, and humanity's relationship to the universe in a profoundly different way than European colonizers. In *Storyteller* (1981), Silko narrates one such prophetic text. In an origin story that appears on the page as an untitled free-verse poem occupying the centerfold of the book, Silko describes a convention of "witches" from all over the world who compete in a contest "in dark things."[67] The conventional witches boil gruesome concoctions in cauldrons, but an unassuming, gender-ambiguous witch steps forward to create a monster using only words—"What I have is a story"[68]—a monster whose genesis appears to be in Europe ("white skin people / like the belly of a fish / covered with hair"[69]) and whose violent history parallels that of European colonizers ("When they look / they see only objects. . . . The wind will blow them across the ocean / thousands of them in giant boats. . . . Entire villages will be wiped out / They will slaughter whole tribes."[70]). When asked to recant this ritual, the witch replies, "It's already turned loose. / It's already coming. / It can't be called back,"[71] indicating the power of language to both create and destroy the world, a theme that recurs in Native American literature. In this narrative, not only is the colonizer's arrival predicted but colonial powers are created by Indigenous people. Silko ironically reverses the representational flow in which Native Americans are "discovered" and "civilized" by Europeans.

Indigenous interpretations of prophecy enact ideological work by militating against the dominant culture's reading of Native American prophetic texts. These texts have been employed in dominant culture against Indigenous people to argue for recognition of their inferiority within the confines of their own discursive traditions. For example, Europeans are often interpreted to be gods or Christ-like in the prophetic narratives, thereby viewed to be light-bearers to pagans living in the darkness of Christianity.[72] In this view, Indigenous peoples, fatalistically aware of what the future would hold, are passive victims, awaiting slaughter without protest.

Another danger of interpreting translated and transcribed narratives of prophecy is that these documents always already exist in a world where Native American spirituality and Christianity have met on the discursive battleground, and it is challenging to parse the two out. For example, the *Popul Vuh*, a codex that contains the Quiché Maya origin story and prophecies, was most likely destroyed by the Spanish in their book-burning frenzy at Utatlán in the sixteenth century. An Indigenous survivor of the Spanish invasion transcribed the text from memory in order that the knowledge contained in it would be remembered, yet he acknowledges that he is also writing within a new cultural context where Christianity has been imposed. The transcribed text elides the role of female divinities in the creation of the world and has parallels with the biblical book of Genesis. But at the same time, it narrates an origin story that departs from Christianity with its stress on creation as a collaborative act.

While text-based interpretations of prophecy do provide the means of strategically constructing or reconstructing temporal circumstances, the realm of prophecy incorporates more than text-based traditions, which are necessarily filtered through particular individuals. Prophecy, broadly conceived, constitutes a belief system and/or a way of understanding and interpreting history and events where the past, present, and future converge. The most well-known Indigenous prophecies in popular histories are those that have been filtered through prominent male historical figures such as Moctezuma, Handsome Lake, Plenty Coups, John Slocum, Wovoka, Smohalla, Tenskwatawa, and Tecumseh.[73] But the types of prophecy that are more compelling for the purposes of this project, because they are unmoored from the personalities of individual historical figures, are those that have multiple interpretations and divergent origins. In his single-nation study of prophecy, Tom Mould locates prophetic discourse in individual memory—"a third kind of time"—rather than in books and oral narrative.[74] Mould argues, "As a philosophical contemplation, [prophecy] is the verbal genre devoted to the discussion of change, its focus as much on the past and present as the future. . . . It is a tradition that fundamentally challenges the way historians, anthropologists, and theologians have constructed our understanding of American Indian prophecy."[75] The prophetic tradition in both *It Starts with a Whisper* and *Imprint* follows this more fluid tradition that posits prophecy and transformative power as inherent within individuals rather than without in sacred texts and spiritual leaders.

Michael G. Doxtater contends, "Indigenous scholarship argues against the homogenizing European master narrative that seeks to colonize Indigenous knowledge."[76] But Indigenous scholarship not only argues against Western paradigms, it also supersedes them. In his comparative study of American origin stories, Andrew Wiget writes that Native American methods of conceiving time and experience create alternative narratives of power vis-à-vis colonialism, the lens through which Native American history is most often contemplated. He employs the Zuni as his case study:

> Their genres of oral narrative and their collective memory distinguish important moments in the past, such as the coming of Coronado and the first Europeans in the sixteenth century; the Pueblo Revolt in the seventeenth; bad relations with the Spanish, Navajos, and American soldiers in the eighteenth and nineteenth; and the building of Blackrock Dam at the beginning of the twentieth. But all of these past moments, however important from a European American perspective, did not fundamentally shape or alter the Zunis' view of themselves and of the world, which was brought to completion when they found the center of the world in ages past. Ordained by the Sun Father, their emergence and migration were foundational. That was history; everything else is commentary.[77]

The liberatory politics of prophecy displayed here as Indigenous ways of conceiving language, origin, and history are positioned as foundational rather than marginal. This strategy not only interprets the Zuni as having agency, but decenters Eurocentric historiography, a useful strategy employed by Indigenous film-makers as well.

By visually representing Indigenous knowledge production through cultural epistemes such as prophecy, filmmakers like Niro and Eyre demonstrate that film itself, as a virtual reservation, is an expressive site that evokes and enacts Indigenous knowl-edges. The filmic virtual reservation both critiques conventional representations of Native Americans and demonstrates how the privileging of Indigenous ways of understanding, seeing, and rep-resenting the world operate outside Western paradigms, thereby diminishing the hegemonic influence of colonialism on Native communities. This view of Indigenous film presents a world in and of itself, neither a representative window on the "real" world nor the Lacanian mirror reflecting back an image that spectators either identify with or become autonomous through.

The work of contemporary Indigenous media makers does more than resist colonization, as this chapter demonstrates. Both Niro and Eyre narrativize not only Indigenous struggles against the dominant culture but how Native American ways of understand-ing the world continue to give meaning to communities, even in the face of seemingly overwhelming odds. Niro, for example, privileges Haudenosaunee epistemes of complementary gender systems (the dual spirit voices, the balanced guidance of the Matriarchal Aunts and Harper) and strategically deploys humor and prophecy in order to demonstrate how Native American communities have remained intact for more than five hundred years. The film as virtual reservation thereby stages a space where aboriginal knowledges are unhitched from colonial discourses, intervening in what Linda Tuhiwai Smith calls "decolonizing methodologies" through staging Haudenosaunee ways of interpreting the world as primary.[78] Niro and Eyre suggest ways of decolonizing knowledge and methods of interpretation through putting seemingly discordant discourses in conversation with each other, not by promising access to hidden, "authentic," and mystical epistemologies. Both create works in collaboration with non-Native filmmakers, contemplate the relationship between historical archive and oral community wellspring, and reinvigorate ancient knowledges regarding prophecy with a fresh, contemporary idiom.

5 Visual Sovereignty, Indigenous Revisions of Ethnography, and *Atanarjuat (The Fast Runner)*

In an early scene from Robert Flaherty's *Nanook of the North* (1922), Allakariallak, the Inuit actor who portrays the titular hunter in the film, is introduced to a gramophone by a white trader who, according to the intertitles, "attempts to explain the principle of the gramophone" to him.[1] Having never before seen such a device, the putatively naïve Nanook inspects all sides of the machine, touches it, laughs at it, seems to ask the trader about its operation, and subsequently bites the record in a haptic effort to understand this new technology. In this well-known scene, the viewer takes these on-screen actions as a cue that Nanook is both unfamiliar with Western technology (and therefore oblivious to the camera's gaze in recording his actions) and primitive (only a culturally simple person would respond to advances in sound technology—especially in the silent era—with levity). Yet while a non-Inuit audience might register Nanook's smile as a marker of his alterity and childlike nature, Fatimah Tobing Rony asserts, "Recent research has shown that the Inuit found Flaherty and the filmmaking a source of great amusement . . . from the Inuit point of view he may be seen as laughing at the camera."[2]

Not only is he laughing at the camera, his laughter performs public pedagogy for a viewing practice that reads cinematic Indigeneity as primitivism and innocence. The film invites the spectator to laugh at Nanook's expense in this scene, as the spectator is assumed to already understand the pretense of the gramophone, but William Rothman suggests an alternative orientation to the smile: "If we laugh at Nanook at this moment, as Flaherty's titles invite us to do, if we assume that this gesture reveals Nanook to be more of a child, or more of an animal than we are, that is a mark of our naïveté, not his. . . . When Nanook first hears the 'canned' voice, he breaks into a grin, amused that the 'canned' voice is not a profound mystery but only a special effect, as it were."[3] The trader purports, according to the intertitles, to teach Nanook "how the white man 'cans' his voice," suggesting the artifice of European American culture. The scene aligns the gramophone with the inexpensive trinkets of the trading post, the "beads and bright colored candy," that the trader will barter for the animal pelts, essential for survival in the Arctic, which he procured through "hand-to-hand combat," suggesting that while Native American cultural goods are objects of practical survival, European American culture offers artifacts of entertainment and frivolity.

It is tempting to read resistance into films like *Nanook*, which was created by an amateur white filmmaker formally trained as a mining specialist, that do not seem to permit much, if any, Indigenous agency, especially if the critical apparatuses necessary to "read" humor as a playful and powerful way of deconstructing audience expectations and the vast matrix of Native American (mis)representations have yet to be fully articulated or understood within their unique cultural contexts. And, since resistance as a

26. Nanook (Allakarial-lak) (*left*) at the trading post in *Nanook of the North* (1922). Courtesy of the Robert and Frances Flaherty Study Center, Claremont CA.

category deployed by various colonized peoples is not created equal in all situations but is located along a spectrum of political and social efficacy, Nanook's response might register one thing to his non-Inuit audience and quite another to members of an Inuit community who recognize the cultural code of his smile. While Nanook is portrayed as heroic and master of his physical environment in scenes that situate him outside Western notions of time and history, when he is compared with the world of the trader he is depicted as awkward and as lacking intelligence—an anachronistic and irrelevant, if quaint, figure in the early twentieth-century context of his non-Inuit audience.[4]

In this chapter, I explore what it means for Indigenous people "to laugh at the camera" as a tactic of visual sovereignty on the virtual reservation. Laughing at the camera confronts the spectator with the often-absurd assumptions that circulate around visual representations of Native Americans, while also flagging their involvement and complicity in these often disempowering structures of cinematic dominance and stereotype. I examine *Atanarjuat* (*The Fast Runner*) (2000), the first full-length feature film directed by an Inuit (Zacharias Kunuk) and produced by Igloolik Isuma Productions Inc., a collaborative, majority Inuit production company, as my primary context for analysis to examine the ways this film is embedded within discourses about Arctic peoples that cannot be severed from the larger web of hegemonic discourses of ethnography. I do this first by discussing the pervasive images of Native Americans in ethnographic films and then by theorizing the ways that *Atanarjuat* intervenes into visual sovereignty as a film that successfully addresses a dual Inuit and non-Inuit audience for two different aims. I consider how the *Atanarjuat* filmmakers strategically adjust and reframe the registers on which Inuit epistemes are considered with the twin, but not necessarily conflicting, aims of operating in the service of their home communities and forcing viewers to reconsider mass-mediated images of the Arctic.

I suggest a reading practice for thinking about the space between resistance and compliance wherein Indigenous filmmakers and actors revisit, contribute to, borrow from, critique, and reconfigure ethnographic film conventions, while at the same time operating within and stretching the boundaries created by these conventions. Terming this approach visual "sovereignty," I demonstrate how this strategy offers up not only the possibility of engaging and deconstructing white-generated representations of Indigenous people, but more broadly and importantly how it intervenes in larger discussions of Native American sovereignty by locating and advocating for Indigenous cultural and political power both within and outside of Western legal jurisprudence. My understanding of visual sovereignty is rooted in and expands upon three important discussions of sovereignty that think outside the perimeters of legal discourse: Jolene Rickard's call for expanding the boundaries of discourse around sovereignty to the arts, Beverly R. Singer's notion of "cultural sovereignty" as "trusting in the older ways and adapting them to our lives in the present," and Robert Allen Warrior's term "intellectual sovereignty," which in turn draws from Vine Deloria Jr.'s understanding of sovereignty "as an open-ended process" that involves critical and kinetic contemplations of what sovereignty means at different historical and paradigmatic junctures.[5]

The visual—particularly film, video, and new media—is a germinal and exciting site for exploring how sovereignty can be a creative act of self-representation that has the potential to both undermine stereotypes of Indigenous peoples and to strengthen what Robert Allen Warrior terms the "intellectual health" of communities in the wake of genocide and colonialism.[6] Visual sovereignty is a strategy that Indigenous filmmakers have engaged in since at least the 1960s—when North American Indigenous filmmakers began producing televisual, film, and video projects—and that has continued to the present with the explosion of hundreds of exciting films by Indigenous filmmakers whose work runs the gamut from short experimental videos to activist documentaries to full-length feature films.[7] Visual sovereignty is a practice that takes a holistic approach to the process of creating moving images and that locates Indigenous cinema in a particular historical and social context while privileging tribal specificity.

In the case of the Inuit of Canada, visual sovereignty has an earlier history as a result of their involvement in filmmaking projects such as the one that produced *Nanook*. While I find Rony's incisive critique of *Nanook* as "cinematic taxidermy" instructive, I am hesitant to disregard the complicated collaborative nature of the film's production. While Flaherty suffered from the ethnocentric biases and racism of his contemporaries, it is important to foreground the ways in which the Inuit instructed him on how to work collaboratively, according to their views of social and cultural interaction, as a form of aesthetic and technical diplomacy. This tradition would be carried forward to the present as the collaborative filmmaking projects of artists such as Eyre and Niro suggest. Faye Ginsburg has determined that Allakariallak and other Inuit community members worked with Flaherty "as technicians, camera operators, film developers, and production consultants."[8] Jay Ruby has argued that not only did the Inuit serve as production staff but that they also challenged Flaherty to work collaboratively on the project. "The Inuit performed for the camera, reviewed and criticized their performance, and were able to offer suggestions for additional scenes in the film—a way of making films that, when tried today," Ruby argues, "is thought to be 'innovative and original.'"[9] Furthermore, the film and its off-screen stories have had a lasting positive impact on Inuit communities, most likely because of the depth of their participation in its creation. Peter Pitseolak, an Inuit photographer from Cape Dorset and a contemporary of Allakariallak, met Flaherty in 1912 and was inspired to learn photography as a result. His stunning, intimate photographs of community members in the 1930s and 1940s militate against images of Arctic people that framed them as archaic, primitive, and doomed peoples.[10]

Even into the 1970s *Nanook* was employed to empower Inuit communities. At a training workshop in 1979, the Inuit Tapirisat of Canada—a language preservation, land rights, and cultural advocacy organization that later formed the Inuit Broadcasting Corporation (IBC)—screened the film for an Inuit community.[11] According to Lyndsay Green, operations manager of

Inuit Tapirisat, "The film excited great pride in the strength and dignity of their ancestors, and they want to share this with their elders and children."[12] Inuit audiences, like those in other communities, have utilized film as a mode of cultural continuity and preservation. This focus on the aspects of the film that reflect their relatives' contributions to the creation of *Nanook* demonstrates how visual sovereignty can involve a revision of older films featuring Native American plots in order to reframe a narrative that privileges Indigenous participation and perhaps points to sites of Indigenous knowledge production in films otherwise understood as purely Western products, as *Nanook* and Edward Curtis's *In the Land of the Headhunters* (1914) have been.[13] Moreover, by recognizing the imprint of Indigenous people working in various capacities as intellectual and cultural advisors and technical assistants, contemporary Indigenous filmmakers draw from this early motion picture material to frame their own projects that engage with notions of the traditional in order to think about how the past informs the present. Visual sovereignty, then, promotes intellectual health on at least two critical registers. By appealing to a mass, intergenerational, and transnational Indigenous audience, visual sovereignty permits the flow of Indigenous knowledge about such key issues as land rights, language acquisition, and preservation, which narrativizes local and international struggles. Visual sovereignty, as expressed by Indigenous filmmakers, also involves the employment of editing technologies that permit filmmakers to stage performances of oral narrative and Indigenous notions of time and space that are not possible through print alone.

Visualizing Sovereignty in Indigenous Films

Sovereignty in its manifold manifestations sets Native American studies apart from other critical race discourses. Native Americans have no single shared culture, event, or series of events necessary to imagine a collective group experience. Even the Wounded Knee Massacre, which resulted in the murders of more than three hundred Lakota tribal members, is not an event to which all Native Americans can cathect communal memories, although the fact remains that it is a significant visual register because the bodies of the victims were photographed and because these images were widely disseminated as commercial postcards.[14] Sovereignty is an ontological and philosophical concept with very real practical, political, and cultural ramifications that unites the experiences of Native Americans, but it is a difficult idea to define because it is always in motion and is inherently contradictory. As David E. Wilkins and K. Tsianina Lomawaima note, "The political realities of relations with the federal government, relations with state and local governments, competing jurisdictions, complicated local histories, circumscribed land bases, and overlapping citizenships all constrain" contemporary notions of sovereignty.[15]

As a result, sovereignty is perhaps the most important, overused, and often-misunderstood term employed in late twentieth and early twenty-first-century Native American circles.[16] While legal and social science discourses have used the term to describe a peculiar, problematic, and particular relationship between the Anglophone colonies of the United States and Canada and the Indigenous nations of North America, I would like to suggest a discussion of visual sovereignty as a way of reimagining Native-centered articulations of self-representation and autonomy that engage the powerful ideologies of mass media but do not rely solely on the texts and contexts of Western jurisprudence.

Sovereignty is a key term in the lexicon of Native American Studies because it demonstrates how Indigenous peoples are different from immigrant communities in the Americas (as well as other Indigenous nations) in terms of political structure, epistemology, and relationships to specific geographical spaces. In Scott Richard Lyon's formulation, sovereignty is "nothing less than our attempt to survive and flourish as a people."[17] Yet while he locates sovereignty within the history of the colonization of the Americas, considerations of the concept of sovereignty should also take into account expressions of sovereignty within traditional Native American aesthetic production prior to European incursion.

Prior to European contact, Native nations theorized about the concept of sovereignty in order to discursively distinguish themselves from the other human, spirit, animal, and inanimate communities surrounding them through performance, songs, stories, dreams, and visual texts such as wampum, pictographs, and tipi drawings. In a Native American context, the term predates European notions of nation-to-nation political sovereignty even as the Indigenous conceptions have now incorporated these non-Native articulations of the term into their definition. The English word "sovereignty," then, becomes a placeholder for a multitude of Indigenous designations employed to describe the concept that also takes into account the European origins of the idea. The contradictions of sovereignty are numerous. Its applications vary from Indigenous nation to nation, and it often maintains ties to older, Indigenous concepts of self-governance, which are remembered and constructed through oral narrative and a given community's consensus on what constitutes precontact forms and theories of government and social structure. It incorporates as well European notions of recognizing political autonomy and jurisprudence. In other words, sovereignty in a Native American context incorporates the paradox of multiple definitions into its genealogy. And the fact that sovereignty is paradoxical—located within and without Indigenous discourse—does not make it any less powerful or valid a statement of political, individual, or cultural autonomy.[18]

Visual sovereignty can be likened to the Haudenosaunee (Iroquois) Two Row Wampum Belt Treaty. This treaty, both a material artifact composed of strung quahog shells and a symbol of Indigenous diplomacy on tribally specific terms, is a visual representation of a pact based on mutual respect made between the Haudenosaunee and Europeans, stipulating that the communities would be allowed to coexist and recognize each other's sovereignty, nation to nation. It was first created in the seventeenth century as a pact between the Haudenosaunee and the Dutch. Haudenosaunee individuals interpret it as a visual manifestation of their inherent right to retain their geographic, cultural, political, linguistic, and economic sovereignty.

According to G. Peter Jemison, Seneca Faithkeeper, "The purple lines represent the Haudenosaunee traveling in their canoe. Parallel to them, but not touching, is the path of the boat of the Europeans that came here. In our canoe is our way of life, our language, our law, and our customs and traditions."[19] He continues, "And in the boat, likewise, are the European language, customs, traditions, and law. We have said, 'Please don't get out of your boat and try to steer our canoe. And we won't get out of our canoe and try to steer your boat.' We're going to accept each other as sovereign—we're going to travel down the river of life together, side by side." While European powers, Canada, and the United States have yet to fully honor this covenant, the Iroquois Confederacy continues to abide by the philosophy behind the belt—recognizing European forms of sovereignty, the continuing importance of oral narrative in maintaining a collective identity (the belt depends on "readers" who can decipher and interpret its meaning), and visual artifact as a mnemonic device. It is significant that one of the first treaties made between Indians and whites was recorded using an Indigenous form.

Visual sovereignty opens up a practice for reading Native American visual culture that incorporates both Indigenous traditions of community representation and non-Indigenous filmmaking practices. As the Two Row Wampum Belt Treaty demonstrates, visual sovereignty recognizes the complexities of creating media for multiple audiences, critiquing filmic representations of Native Americans, at the same time that it participates in some of the conventions that have produced these representations.

Sovereignty, because of this diversity of Indigenous relationships to it, has become a kind of collective placeholder term similar to "strategic essentialism."[20] In this sense, sovereignty indicates a powerful way to mobilize social and political action through situational—sometimes temporary—solidarity with the understanding that this solidarity is predicated on consensus that recognizes individual dissent. Likewise, visual sovereignty intervenes in larger discourses on Indigenous sovereignty but employs a slightly different set of tactics. Because visual sovereignty arbitrates in the broader world of Indigenous sovereignty and is not always directly involved in political debates that determine Native American survival and livelihood—as legal sovereignty in the U.S. and Canadian justice systems is—there is more room for narrative play. Under visual sovereignty, filmmakers can deploy individual and community assertions of what sovereignty and self-representation mean and, through new media technologies, frame more imaginative renderings of Native American intellectual and cultural paradigms, such as the presentation of the spiritual and dream world, than are often possible in official political contexts. Visual sovereignty is not outside of or disinterested in political activism and debate. While the film *Atanarjuat* makes no overt reference to local environmental concerns in the Arctic, it "peoples" this particular endangered space. Recent news reports detail how this global catastrophe is adversely affecting all forms of plant and animal life in the Arctic, and *Atanarjuat* intimates how human populations on the front line of global warming will also be devastated.

Igloolik Isuma is based in Nunavut, Canada's newest territory, established in 1999. With a population of roughly thirteen hundred, 93 percent of whom are Inuit, and a consensual government system that blends Inuit principles (*qaujimajatuqangit* in Inuktitut) with Canadian parliamentary democracy, Nunavut is the site of a unique and exciting Indigenous political economy and a practicing form of political and cultural sovereignty that provides an ideal site to host a production company that works in the service of visual sovereignty.[21] Moreover, Igloolik Isuma Productions Inc. employs ethnographic film conventions to serve didactic purposes within the Inuit communities of Canada: forging much-needed economic opportunities in depressed markets; educating younger generations alienated from community elders and tribal epistemologies through diasporic conditions; and addressing the lingering effects of colonization, natural environments in immediate peril, and high mortality, substance abuse, and incarceration rates.

Ginsburg notes that as a result of Igloolik Isuma's economic presence in Igloolik, "More than 100 Igloolik Inuit, from the young to the elderly, were employed as actors, hairdressers, and technicians, as well as costume makers, language experts, and hunters who provided food, bringing more than $1.5 million into a local economy that suffers from a 60 percent unemployment rate."[22] According to Zacharias Kunuk, one of Igloolik Isuma's four founding members, "We create traditional artifacts, digital media, and desperately needed jobs in the same activity."[23] His statement, coupled with Ginsburg's statistics, points to the important political work of visual sovereignty: making a commercially successful film that foregrounds Inuit epistemes and simultaneously accomplishes collective social justice off-screen by providing job training and a livelihood for Inuit communities. Most recently, Isuma engaged in its latest form of visual sovereignty by creating Isuma TV, "an independent interactive network of Inuit and Indigenous multimedia" broadcast free on the Internet.[24] In its mission statement, Isuma TV notes, "Our tools enable Indigenous people to express reality in their own voices: views of the past, anxieties about the present, and hopes for a more decent and honorable future. Our sincere goal is to assist people to listen to one another, to recognize and respect diverse ways of experiencing our world, and honor those differences as a human strength."[25] To this end, Isuma TV broadcasts in over four languages, most importantly, Inuktitut; offers testimony by residential school survivors of sexual, cultural, physical, linguistic, and psychological abuse; premieres new work by Indigenous video artists; covers arts festivals; features interviews by scientists and community members about climate change and the impact of mining on the Arctic; and links to over thirty channels that include blogs, news reports, and language lessons from all over the Indigenous world.

Isuma means "to think" in Inuktitut, and the members of both Igloolik and its sister company, Arnait Video Productions (Women's Video Collective of Igloolik), which focuses on issues of relevance to Inuit women, are dedicated to a production style that revolves around Inuit worldviews, such as collaborative conceptualizing of the film's diegesis and its incorporation of a subplot based on Inuit spiritual traditions rather than those borrowed from the West (or, in the Inuit's case, the South).[26] The filmmaking process, as a result, is much slower than that of Hollywood because members attempt to reach consensus on the details of the film (the director, for example, serves more as a contact person than as the director in the conventional sense of the term), and the film is screened before an audience of elders and community members and is edited accordingly prior to release.

The work of Igloolik Isuma and Arnait Video Productions aligns with and has, in some cases, inspired the kinds of work that have been produced recently by Indigenous filmmakers in sites such as Latin America, Africa, Europe, Asia, and Oceania.[27] This international project is part of a broader historical move from cinema produced by European settler and colonial nations to what Fernando Solanas and Octavio Gettino term "Third Cinema" to a variety of Indigenous cinemas that incorporate local epistemes and cultural critiques with new visual technologies.[28] While Third Cinema is a postcolonial movement that grew out of cultural and political changes in the 1960s in formerly colonized parts of the world to denounce Hollywood-style entertainment in favor of a national, popular, and activist vernacular, Indigenous Cinema has its roots in specific Indigenous aesthetics with their attendant focus on a particular geographical space, discrete cultural practices, social activist texts, spiritual traditions, and notions of temporality that do not delink the past from the present or future.

Igloolik Isuma's oeuvre similarly is not solely a vehicle aimed at either an internal or an external audience. *Atanarjuat* compels non-Inuit spectators to think differently about what constitutes Indigenous content in films and more conventional representations of Native Americans in cinematic history and also about Indigenous visual aesthetics. As Michael Leigh argues, Indigenous communities "are ensuring the continuity of their languages and cultures and representations of their views. By making their own films and videos, they speak for themselves, no longer aliens in an industry which for a century has used them for its own ends."[29] Inuit filmmakers do not only employ what have come to be envisioned as Western visual culture technologies to create activist-resistance texts that retell oral narratives in local languages for future generations, however. Rather, they also engage in dialogue with media communities outside the far North, reconsidering and transforming filmic genres and audience expectations.[30] Arnait's *Anaana (Mother)* (2001), directed by Zacharias's sister, Mary Kunuk, and Marie-Hélène Cousineau, for example, is an hour-long documentary about Vivi Kunuk, Zacharias and Mary's mother. Through lyrical, humorous, and poignant vignettes about Vivi and other members of her family, the spectator is presented with a portrait of an Inuit community that retains traditional elements of culture and embraces modernity, but on its own terms. The matriarch, Vivi, for example, hunts seal with a modified hockey stick, a scene that might make some audiences uncomfortable as the entire hunt is filmed. This scene has a dual purpose. On the one hand it provides a kind of visual how-to manual through which acculturated community members can learn how to hunt seal and other Arctic mammals. On the other hand it reminds spectators in the "South" that being carnivorous requires sacrifice and recognition of the mode of production of harvesting animals for meat. For the Inuit in the film, there is a respectful and intimate relationship between the hunters and the hunted.

Cultural difference, particularly as it relates to a shamanistic plotline, is deployed in *Atanarjuat* to trouble a history of discursive representations of Arctic peoples as simultaneously commensurable and alien. The film re-inscribes these scenes of cultural difference as regenerative sites of cultural preservation within a community that understands culture as a locus of fluidity, historical change, and adaptation. Igloolik Isuma filmmakers invert what non-Inuit might consider "aberrant" cultural practices—interacting with supernatural powers, eating raw meat, and engaging in a polygamous and sometimes violent trade in women—through humor and the strategic use of ethnographic film conventions.[31] By doing so they open up a more subtle, nuanced reading of these practices as a means of entering the debate on sovereignty and rupturing mainstream notions of feminism and aboriginal representation by mocking universalism and its untenable utopianism.

The film employs cinematic technology to retell the ancient oral story of Atanarjuat, a folk hero who rids his community of negative forces by violating cultural taboos. Born into a family of low social class due to the machinations of a malevolent visiting shaman, Atanarjuat (Natar Ungalaaq) defeats a rival, Oki (Peter-

Henry Arnatsiaq), for the attentions of Atuat (Sylvia Ivalu), who has already been promised by her family to Oki. This upsets the delicate balance of this close-knit community, and Oki quietly plots his revenge against Atanarjuat. When Atanarjuat takes Oki's sister, Puja (Lucy Tulugarjuk), as his second wife, Oki attempts to kill Atanarjuat for a perceived slight to his sister, murdering instead Atanarjuat's brother. Atanarjuat escapes by running naked for miles over ice and frozen land until he is harbored by an exiled community member, Qulitalik (Pauloosie Qulitalik), who lives out on the tundra alone with his wife and daughter. Atanarjuat apprentices under Qulitalik until he is ready to return to his camp, reunite with Atuat (who has been raped by Oki and his friends in the interim and lives an abject life with her son and Qulitalik's sister, Panikpak, played by Madeline Ivalu, on the fringes of camp), and reverse the damage initiated by the visiting shaman. The film ends with Atanarjuat acting nonviolently and Oki and his family being driven out of the community to purge it of negativity. Igloolik Isuma thus situates the traditional oral narrative of Atanarjuat on a virtual reservation opening up the narrative for dialogue within and outside the community on a site that is less invested in the traffic in authenticity than in reconsidering the relationship between the visual image, technologies, and larger cultural and political contexts.

"Here Come the Anthros": Sa(l)vages and Ethnographic Representation

In his biting musical indictment of cultural anthropology's intrusion into Indian country, Floyd Red Crow Westerman sings, "Here come the anthros, better hide your past away."[32] Inspired by Vine Deloria Jr.'s groundbreaking work, *Custer Died for Your Sins*, Westerman's song punctures the notion that amateur and professional anthropologists engaging in research projects in Native American communities are universally benevolent and objective.

Both Westerman's and Deloria's work responds to statements that assert the primacy for Native Americans of the putatively "lower order" functions such as attention to the body, to action over thought, and to doing rather than feeling. For example, Flaherty asserted in a BBC interview that "I don't think you can make a good film of the love affair of the Eskimo . . . because they never show much feeling in their faces, but you can make a very good film of Eskimos spearing a walrus."[33]

Deloria questioned the motives of anthropologists who conducted fieldwork in Native American communities in the late 1960s and produced "essentially self-confirming, self-referential, and self-reproducing closed systems of arcane 'pure knowledge'—systems with little, if any, empirical relationship to, or practical value for, real Indian people."[34] Although both anthropologists and ethnographers have adopted more self-reflective and sensitive research methodologies in response to critiques launched by Indigenous peoples, Native Americans are still positioned between complicity with and resistance to anthropological standards, definitions, and representations of Indigenous peoples.[35] An enduring oral tradition continues within many Indigenous communities, at the same time it is impossible to ignore the important cultural, linguistic, genealogical, and philosophical material in the ethnographic and historical record, especially as this material constructs a mass-mediated view of the Indigenous world and in some cases represents the full cultural patrimony of Native American nations.

The commercial motion picture industry in North America has been fascinated with the image of the American Indian, and hundreds of actualities featuring Indians engaging in "traditional" and quotidian practices were shown in nickelodeons from 1894 through 1908. These actualities and early documentary and ethnographic films simultaneously contributed to the myth of the vanishing Indian—the actors were clothed in anachronistic dress performing prereservation-era tasks—and helped to create a form of American spectatorship that coheres around the dichotomous relationship between Indian and white figures. The idea of the American spectator emerged at the turn of the twentieth century according to Miriam Hansen with the perhaps unintended effect of incorporating "outside" social groups, such as European American women and recent immigrants from Europe, into the national body politic as consumers of forms of knowledge, culture, and history through an alternative public sphere "not necessarily anticipated in the context of production."[36] While Native Americans and their relationship to specific geographical spaces provided the backdrop for a national origin myth around which immigrant identities could coalesce, Indigenous people represented in the films were erased through both the reenactment of the physical violence of the frontier and the discursive violence that notions of salvage anthropology propagated.[37]

Salvage anthropology inflicted a particularly damaging form of violence on Native American communities as these communities faced pressure from the government to assimilate while simultaneously receiving the message from anthropologists and ethnographers that their cultures were becoming increasingly inauthentic, impure, and irrelevant. Salvage anthropology would draw upon older forms of stereotyping found in early colonial texts, captivity narratives, and turn-of-the-century dime novels as well as scientific discourses on race to create the "sa(l)vage"—a doomed, "leftover" figure who, like Flaherty's description of "the Eskimo" exists only as a static, flat, proto-human type.

The stagings of "traditional" cultures in actualities and early films provided the kinds of artifacts that salvage anthropology hoped to rescue from oblivion. The actualities of the turn of the century are the cinematic source from which both representations of Native Americans in the western and in amateur and professional ethnographic films would take shape. Despite the sense of ethnography as a kind of inescapable frame through which Indigenous lives are screened, Indigenous filmmakers have deployed ethnographic film conventions to assert and revise a sense of visual sovereignty. Critically engaging this seeming paradox—questioning ethnography's tendencies by using the tools and conventions available to the filmmaker—is not entirely new. Jerry White states, "Ethnographic filmmaking has undergone a complete transformation in the last two decades. Once the safe vocation of earnest scientists seeking imagery for exotic cultures, ethnographic filmmaking has become fertile ground for revision by Third World and avant-garde filmmakers."[38] However, articulations of this paradox and how it complicates notions of sovereignty on the virtual reservation are unique to Indigenous filmmaking practices in a number of different settler colonialism contexts throughout the world.

With few exceptions, contemporary work by Indigenous filmmakers in the United States and Canada is set in the present as a response to films—particularly westerns and ethnographic films—that situate Native Americans in the nineteenth-century past with no viable future. While images of Hollywood Indians have saturated the market since the inception of films, the work of Native American filmmakers and issues of relevance to tribal peoples have been markedly absent from mass-market films, cinema scholarship, and the historical archive.[39] Native Americans in mass media have occupied a twilight-zone existence in which they are both hypervisible in ways overdetermined by popular and nostalgic representations and completely invisible because Native American actors are often uncredited; underpaid; and cast in ancillary, sometimes demeaning roles in support of a white protagonist who provides the point of entry for the spectator.[40] As a result, work by Indigenous filmmakers often creates narrative films that strive to overturn stereotypes of Indigenous people by featuring characters experiencing seemingly universal events. For example the title of Chris Eyre and Sherman Alexie's landmark film, *Smoke Signals* (1998), conjures up images from the western film imaginary, but the action is set on a present-day reservation in the Northwest and centers on a narrative about the complex range of emotions between father and son.

"I can only sing this song to someone who understands it": Multiple Modes of Address in *Atanarjuat* (*The Fast Runner*)

In the wake of the success generated by *Smoke Signals*, *Atanarjuat* (*The Fast Runner*) subverts the conventional paradigm by refusing a white point of entry for the spectator. Shot entirely on location in and around Igloolik, *Atanarjuat* is the first Inuit feature-length film. According to an article published in the Nunavut-based *Nunatsiaq News*, the film is drawn from a didactic "legend of power, intrigue, love, jealousy, murder, and revenge" more than a thousand years old.[41] It is a visual recreation of an oral narrative important to the Inuit community and centers on the taboo-breaking romantic relationship between the main protagonist, Atanarjuat (played by one of a handful of professional actors employed by the production company), and Atuat, who has been promised in marriage by her family to Oki. As in most Native American oral stories, there are no absolute binaries in the story or the film. Neither the main protagonist Atanarjuat nor his antagonist, Oki, are wholly good or evil, a narrative decision that undermines the expectations of spectators familiar with Hollywood film formulas. Both break cultural taboos whose stakes are very high (Oki kills Atanarjuat's brother as well as his own father, and as a result is banished by his grandmother, Panikpak, at the film's conclusion), but despite the fact that Atanarjuat performs an act that is socially unacceptable, his actions permit the community to heal from the devastation wrought years ago by the mysterious and ambivalent shaman figure, Tuurngarjuaq (Abraham Ulayuruluk). Yet unlike *Smoke Signals*, which features

English dialogue and familiar, contemporary references, *Atanar-juat* includes an all-Inuit cast speaking Inuktitut (with English subtitles), wearing costumes made of animal skins, performing ostensibly traditional acts such as hunting walrus and seal with harpoons, and eating raw meat. Additionally, *Atanarjuat* is situated within a shamanistic narrative framework and it captures pre–European invasion time.[42]

At first glance the film appears to be an ethnographic spectacle that seems, like its predecessor *Nanook*, to reinforce Flaherty's contention that Arctic people produce a cinema of the Indigenous body and its interaction with the land, but little else. *Atanarjuat*, with its good-natured main protagonist, amateur actors, teams of sled dogs, and long, slow shots of the frozen land and seascape (which lyrically operate as uncredited protagonists in the film because of the intense attention paid to them by the often hand-held camerawork), appears to share much in common with Flaherty's classic ethnographic documentary. Innupiat writer Joseph E. Senungetuk suggests Arctic communities in North America are depicted as "a people without technology, without a culture, lacking intelligence, living in igloos, and at best, a sort of simplistic 'native boy' type of subhuman arctic being."[43] Ann Fienup-Riordan terms these representations "Eskimo orientalism." She argues that "like the representations of the Orient, the representation of the Eskimo is about origins—in this case the origin of society in the 'pure primitive': peaceful, happy, childlike, noble, independent, and free. The Eskimo of the movies is 'essential man,' stripped of social constraint and High Culture. . . . Their position at the geographic and historical fringe of Western Civilization made them the perfect foils for an 'Eskimo orientalism' as potent as its namesake."[44] The filmmakers tap into this "Eskimo orientalist" representational history in the supplementary materials produced alongside the film. The companion book to the film opens with a quote by Claude Lévi-Strauss who writes, "I was . . . captivated by many ethnographic details."[45] Even *Isuma: Inuit Studies Reader* (2004), which was produced by Isuma Publishing, a division of Igloolik Isuma Productions, features ethnographic texts by writers such as Knud Rasmussen and Franz Boas, and the companion book demonstrates that the ethnographic verisimilitude of the film, particularly in terms of costuming, is based on drawings by Captain G. F. Lyon, who accompanied explorer William Edward Parry to the Arctic from 1821–23.

An examination of the bookends of the film—its opening scene and non-diegetic production shots shown while the credits roll—demonstrate that the filmmakers self-consciously deploy hallmarks of ethnographic cinematography without interpretive interventions such as the expert talking head. This is done in the service of drawing attention to the film as a film, as opposed to an "authentic" visual record of a vanished past, as part of a larger project of visual sovereignty. Igloolik Isuma Productions Inc., whose team of filmmakers created *Atanarjuat*, declines to narrate the legendary story of Atanarjuat in a contemporary Inuit context, focusing instead on an earlier period that permits the film to forgo representing the white-Inuit colonial equation and the types of nostalgia that often arise out of attempts to portray an unadulterated Indigenous past. Kunuk, the film's primary director, presents his audience with an intact Inuit world, one that does not rely on a binary opposition between Inuit and "southern" communities.[46]

The opening scene and cultural references of the film can be confusing and opaque to a non-Inuit spectator, so perhaps the filmmakers used the marketing materials—the companion book and *Inuit Studies Reader*—to provide the interpretive lens lacking in the film.[47] The film opens with a lone man standing on the snow-packed tundra with his howling dogs. This image is one of isolation and loneliness that hearkens back to what Rony calls Flaherty's "Primitive Everyman," a snapshot of the self-made man in conflict with a desolate and harsh landscape.[48] This image, evocative of *Nanook*, is undercut by the next scene, a tactic that the filmmakers repeatedly employ to challenge audience expectations. The following scene takes place inside a spacious *qaggiq* (large igloo), where a dozen or so adults and children are contemplating a visitor, referred to as an "up North stranger," who has arrived alone in the small community wearing a shaman's necklace made of polar bear claws (which designates him as a powerful person), a white fur coat, and white polar bear pants similar to the ones worn by Allakariallak in *Nanook of the North*.[49] We learn later that the events in the opening scene take place approximately twenty years before most of the film's action. The visiting shaman, Tuurngarjuaq, greets the local community leader and shaman, Kumaglak (Apayata Kotierk), who wears a shaman's walrus teeth necklace and coat decorated with raven feathers to designate his individuality and personal powers. Tuurngarjuaq sings a song in the *qaggiq*, which he prefaces by claiming, "I can only sing this song to someone who understands it. When you sing, you laugh at the same time. It must be because you're winning too! It's fun to sing and play a game at the same time."

The opening subtitled lines of the film are a cue to the non-Inuit spectator (including non-Inuit Native Americans) that the film's narrative and details may remain incommensurable since a non-Inuktitut speaking person wouldn't understand his song. Tuurngarjuaq's statement makes evident the multiple audiences the film is addressing: Inuits who understand scenes such as the opening one because they are already familiar with the narrative, non-Inuit Native Americans who may read some of the cues from the film and place them in dialogue with their own tribally specific oral narratives and discursive contexts, and non-Inuits who do not understand Inuktitut or the cultural practices represented in the film but who may be aware of the economy of stereotypes surrounding the Inuit in literature and film. Tuurngarjuaq's lines underscoring the link between humor and play are telling here as they point to how the filmmakers and characters "laugh at the audience," to return to Rony's phrase. Not only does the non-Inuit audience not fully understand the film, but the audience is also, unwittingly perhaps, engaged in a game with the filmmakers, one in which the filmmakers obviously have the upper hand.

This idea of narrative play is at work when Tuurngarjuaq and Kumaglak engage in a practice termed *illuriik* (opponents/partners) in the opening scene of the film, a public custom, according to the *Atanarjuat* companion book, that tests visiting strangers, particularly shamans, "physically and psychologically" by tying them together and letting their helping spirits (*tuurngait*), often associated with powerful animals such as the walrus and polar bear, encounter each other in the spirit world.[50] Often, if the stranger passes the test, he and the host shaman become friends and exchange their possessions; however, in this case Tuurngarjuaq's helping spirit, which takes the form of a polar bear, kills Kumaglak's spirit, which manifests itself as a walrus, and Kumaglak dies as a result. The two men are tied together, and one slumps over, apparently and inexplicably dead.

Although this *illuriik* has a disastrous ending, the scene is not devoid of humor. When Tuurngarjuaq first stands up to display his shaman's parka, he teases Kumaglak, "Since your clothes are different, take a look at mine. If you show me yours . . ." and the joke trails off here. Kumaglak retorts, "No, I don't want any lessons from some up North stranger." Throughout the film, a more theoretical understanding of *illuriik* is offered as social and political negotiations and confrontations vacillate between violence and humor. As an expression of a tribally specific episteme, *illuriik* in the film is a form of visual sovereignty that both places this practice within a local context in the services of linguistic and cultural revitalization and simultaneously makes a broader argument for self-representation and self-determination by involving the spectator in the process of decolonization. This is accomplished by presenting Inuit cultural practices and sensibilities on Inuit terms, without the kinds of explanatory apparatuses that typically accompany ethnographic films. To decipher exactly what is happening in this scene in its cultural context, the non-Inuit audience has to turn to the texts of ethnography, including Igloolik Isuma's own companion book. Because the *illuriik* is not a cultural practice that is universally familiar, even among Native North Americans, its decoding points to how Indigenous filmmaking is poised on a grid of representational practices: ethnography, aboriginal narrative, and the lexicon and technology of film.

Upon his death, Kumaglak's wife, Panikpak, provides voice-over narration in the opening of the film: "We never knew what he was or why it happened. Evil came to us like Death. It just happened, and we had to live with it." It becomes clear that Tuurngarjuaq occupies an ambivalent position as metaphorical tester of the audience in a kind of extranarrative *illuriik*, but he also serves as a precursor to the incursion of Europeans on Inuit land, leaving death and destruction in his wake. Read metaphorically as a seductive, enduring, foreign presence, the visiting shaman can be seen to represent both an individualized, spiritual, destructive power and the destructive power of European Canadian colonialism. Settler colonialism is read here through the lens of an ongoing, Inuit process of coping with and sometimes purging detrimental outside elements. The community struggles over the course of the next two-and-a-half hours to purge itself of the damage caused by the introduction of malevolent forces and begins to heal using community-based elements and strategies. This is instructive for the contemporary community at Igloolik and its environs who can take these lessons about negotiating the potentially dangerous terrain of the "Other" to apply to the present colonial and environmental context in their homelands.

27. Panikpak (Madeline Ivalu) and Qulitalik (Pauloosie Qulitalik) drive evil away from the community at the close of *Atanarjuat* (2001).

In the end, an elderly Panikpak is reunited with her brother, Qulitalik (played by one of the founding members of Igloolik Isuma who also cowrote the screenplay), who had been banished from the community immediately after Kumaglak's death. When Tuurngarjuaq returns years after his initial arrival, this time as a more ghostly presence marked by smoke and his eerie laughter, brother and sister work in tandem as complementary forces to force the shaman away permanently. Thereafter, Panikpak banishes her grandchildren (Oki and his followers) from the village:

> We are not finished here! Before we can go on we have to forgive some of our family who have done things no one should ever do. For many winters now we have been ruled and frightened just like that evil Tuurngarjuaq was

still with us! My own son Sauri's children have led an evil life to others day after day! This has to stop so our future generations can have better lives. Mistreating others, committing murders, telling lies. This has to stop now!

Panikpak's chastisement and call to collective healing reinforces the strength of Inuit women in the community, who hold positions of power that are equal to those of men.[51] This representation of the power of women within Inuit communities is an example of visual sovereignty, a subtle way of demonstrating gender complementarity.

Another means through which visual sovereignty is exhibited is the film's pacing and attention to landscape. The film has a running time of approximately 160 minutes, much of which is taken up with slow pans of the landscape, the quotidian actions of the characters as they find and prepare food, and shots of things such as feet crunching through the snow that would have been edited out of a conventional Hollywood film. In other words, the film is full of what Jennifer Doyle has called "boring parts," that if skipped over would mean missing the way in which the film constructs a specifically Inuit epistemology.[52] More careful attention to the film, however, demonstrates that what the filmmakers do is take the non-Inuit audience hostage, successfully forcing us to alter our consumption of visual images to an Inuit pace, one that is slower and more attentive to the play of light on a grouping of rocks or the place where the snow meets the ocean. The slowness of the sequencing matches the patience one must have to hunt on the ice, wait for hours at a seal hole, traverse long distances on foot or in a dog sled—or contend with over five hundred years of colonialism.

The filmmakers' refusal to edit the film to a more conventional length and willingness to "subject" the audience to seemingly interminable, long shots of people walking or running on the snow and ice marks a visually sovereign practice. Working against Hollywood film conventions, Isuma creates an Inuit aesthetic in *Atanarjuat* that requires a spectator to enter the virtual reservation of the film on Inuit terms and, in the case of a non-Inuit spectator, as an outsider. In a geographical site represented as *terra nullius*, the filmmakers' insistence upon peopling the land and demonstrating the Inuit's dependence on it is a means of asserting political and representational sovereignty at a time of crisis in terms of the United States and Canada's history of resource extraction and environmental degradation in the Arctic. As Steven Leuthold attests, "Group identities, especially before the advent of electronic media, were linked, as they still are, to shared but special access to physical locations, a main reason for the continued emphasis on place in Native American documentaries."[53] The land is not something that the characters of the film are in conflict with and attempt to overcome, but rather is a varied and essential backdrop against which the particularities of the narrative are played out. This is especially key to understanding the film since communities in the Arctic continue to rely on the land and its plant and animal population for survival.

The film closes with the expulsion of negative forces and healing in the form of the community singing Kumaglak's *ajaja* (personal) song in the presence of Atanarjuat and Atuat's son Kumaglak (Bernice Ivalu), a reincarnation of the original Kumaglak, making the narrative frame one that is circular rather than linear. The narrative follows the traditional story's plot by expelling the influence of a shaman who caused the community harm, but makes a larger, contemporary claim for repudiating the negative influences of the Western world brought on by colonialism. The cultural and political work of the film within the Igloolik community is to instill a sense of pride in young people through the success of award-winning projects such as *Atanarjuat* and to provide jobs and experience to its members who live in poverty, face substance abuse, and suffer from high suicide rates. Kathleen Fleming notes that both Igloolik Isuma and Arnait Video Productions continue to operate as community-based production companies, helping to stem the tide of violence that began with the advent of colonialism in Arctic villages.[54] She writes that the companies have provided "direct professional experience shooting and editing video, preparing story lines and scripts, and fundraising."[55]

The representation of the film's shamanistic storyline, coupled with the cultural and political work it has accomplished off-screen, are examples of visual sovereignty, as are the film's production shots included at the end of the film. In these scenes, the audience gets a glimpse into the filmmaking process and the context of the making of the film. As the credits roll and Kumaglak's *ajaja* song is still heard, camera sleds pulled by actors and the crew film a naked Atanarjuat running on the ice, the actor who plays Oki walks along the beach in hip waders and a motorcycle jacket listening to headphones, and actors out of costume wave to the camera from a modern boat. These shots, like Nanook's smile, poke fun at the spectator, forcing the viewer (who has the patience to sit through to the film's end) to imagine *Atanarjuat* as a narrative film produced by a vibrant contemporary Inuit community rather than a documentary on the mythic past or footage from a bygone era.

These final images lay bare and interrogate the project of ethnographic film. As Alison Griffiths asserts, "As a discursive category, ethnographic film refers less to a set of unified significatory practices or to the anthropological method of intensive fieldwork than to the looking relations between the initiator of the gaze and the recipient."[56] As a camera person sitting on the prow of a boat turns to film another crew member holding a camera, the audience realizes that while the film offers a glimpse into Inuit community life, it also reminds the audience that ethnographic

young qulitalik
Charlie Qulitalik

sauri's wife
Atuat Akkitiq

28. Cast and crew wave from boat while credits roll in *Atanarjuat* (2001).

film is often merely a mirror reflecting the gaze of the Western viewer. While Kunuk claims that "the goal of *Atanarjuat* is to make the viewer feel *inside* the action, looking out rather than outside looking in," the production shots bring the audience back to the present and situate the viewer outside the community, back in the space of the darkened cinema.[57]

Kunuk and the Igloolik Isuma team operate as technological brokers and autoethnographers of sorts, moving between the community from which they hail and the Western world and its overdetermined images of Indigenous people. James C. Faris has argued that Indigenous filmmakers "do not join the global village as equal participants, as just more folks with video cameras. They enter it already situated by the West, which gives them little room to be anything more

West will allow" because of the hegemonic effects
d consumerism.[58] Igloolik Isuma Productions con-
tatement by creating a film that incorporates and
raphic elements to offer up a corrective cultural
bat a century of anthropological monographs
documentaries. The filmmakers present an Inuit oral narrative through a visual register in the service of their community,
while at the same time stretching the boundaries of Indigenous
representation through the deployment of visual sovereignty.
Igloolik Isuma enters the "global village" of media production on
its own terms, engaging in a new, metaphorical form of *illuriik*
that retains a sense of humor—laughing, perhaps, like Allakariallak, about the paradoxical nature of the project.

6 Epilogue

Redfacing Redux

One week after I submitted the revisions of this manuscript to the press editor, I became intimately aware of the persistent, sometimes violent afterlife of redfacing and the importance of drawing attention to and critically engaging racist imagery. In November 2008 I learned that the public elementary school my daughter attended engages in a noncontinuous, forty-year tradition of dressing kindergarteners up in "Pilgrim" and "Indian" costumes with another school in the district as a way to teach American history and the significance of the U.S. Thanksgiving holiday.[1] Given that so many schools and elementary school systems have relinquished this racist practice, it was dismaying to learn that it still persists in some schools. In response I consulted with other parents whose children were in the same school district, with local Tongva tribal members, with colleagues who teach Native American Studies, with the Title 7 Indian Education Organization in the Los Angeles Unified School District, with members of a national association dedicated to Native American education, and with students at my campus's Native American student program, all of whom opposed the costuming aspect of the school's holiday celebration.

As a result of these conversations, a group of parents—myself included—sent a private email to my daughter's kindergarten teacher expressing our surprise at this practice, which perpetuates misleading mythologies of "reconciliation" and U.S. history. In the email we explained why our children would not be attending school on the day the spectacle of racial stereotyping took place and suggested some age-appropriate alternatives to this practice in order to commemorate the holiday and more sensitively teach the children about values of friendship and expressing gratitude.

Stereotypical images of Native Americans are predicated on a persistent ignorance about the richness and diversity of Native American communities. While Native American community members have tried to amend and correct them, these stereotypes still inform popular culture and curricula. The Thanksgiving costumes children typically don are historically inaccurate, and there are specific cultural mores governing such aspects of Native American regalia as eagle feathers, headdresses, etc. The school's website featured photographs of children dressed up from past years in Indian simulacra: war-painted faces, generic brown construction paper–fringed vests, pasta shell necklaces, and feathered headdresses. The rituals of the U.S. Thanksgiving holiday code Native Americans as always already part of the discourse of the settler nation and as figures that mysteriously disappear from the historical record. It is puzzling and disconcerting that children do not learn instead to examine a more complete and complex history of settler colonialism as well as Native American history on its own terms. For example, children could learn that the Haudenosaunee form of democracy, which many scholars argue provided an influence on the U.S. constitution, is as old as the Icelandic Althing, or learn about the richness and sophistication of many Native American origin narratives in order to improve the educational approach of the school curriculum. Jonathan Walton has likened the practice of purposefully teaching children partial truths and historical inaccuracies to "intellectual child abuse."[2] In a state whose public education system regularly ranks as one of the lowest, a curriculum founded on myth and fantasy seems particularly egregious.

I neither wanted my daughter to masquerade as a Pilgrim (an image that masks a violent, rigid, religious fundamentalist sect responsible for acts of attempted genocide) nor did I want her exposed to an educational "tradition" that constructs Native Americans as cartoonish figures from the past who sat around singing "Ten Little Indians," a song featured on the kindergarten program that glorifies the trope of the vanishing Indian. When children learn to caricature people through costuming or—worse yet—to do so with the assumption that a living group of people is extinct, it becomes much easier for them to commit acts of violence, however unintentional, against the stereotyped groups once they become adults.

My daughter's school found many imaginative and accurate ways of teaching Martin Luther King Jr.'s contributions and experiences of racism without resorting to dressing children in blackface. Surely there are equally creative and educational ways of helping young students understand colonialism, Indigenous history, and Native American perspectives. Thus, I found it curious that there is such a discrepancy in terms of how the genocidal history and stereotyping of "Indians" is rendered as an acceptable part of contemporary U.S. education compared with the histories of other people of color.

Dressing children up in stereotypical costumes rehearses traumatic histories and underwrites models of colonial power and white supremacy. In his study of numerous historical moments of "playing Indian" including the Boston Tea Party, Philip Deloria writes, "From the very beginning, Indian–white relations and

Indian play itself have modeled a characteristically American kind of domination in which the exercise of power was hidden, denied, qualified, or mourned. Not surprisingly, Indian play proved a fitting way to negotiate social struggles within white society that required an equally opaque vision of power."[3] Equally unsurprising, then, is the insidious way elementary school Thanksgiving costume pageants stage colonization as accidental—and even welcomed—through the emphasis on cordial relations and elision of the specific history of the Wampanoag and other Indigenous communities throughout the Americas in the wake of European invasion.[4] Native American communities practice rituals of thanksgiving for Earth's bounty and have done so for millennia; however, the national U.S. holiday perverts these traditions as a celebration of settler nationalism at the expense of Indigenous peoples.

Given the vast amount of information easily available in print and on the web that discusses the myth of Thanksgiving and suggests alternatives to racist costuming, it was disconcerting that a small college town in Southern California that prides itself on being open-minded and liberal would uncritically continue to perpetuate stereotypes in such a visible and egregious manner.[5] Mohawk scholar Barbara Gray underscores the insidiousness and long-lasting negative effects of Thanksgiving costumes:

> As a child, in kindergarten the class was asked to participate in projects that were supposed to teach us about Indians. Some of the projects included cutting out of paper eagle feathers and then pasting them into an Indian headdress, which was a western style war bonnet. The class was also asked to learn Indian songs and dances. I was asked to pump my hand over my mouth in a mocking war whoop, to dance around like I had ants in my pants, and to sing the song "Ten Little Indians." I remember feeling badly. . . . I felt like the teacher and the students were making fun of my Indian people and our ways.[6]

In a study of the psychological effects of stereotypes of Native Americans, Stephanie A. Fryberg et al. note that the limited range of images of Indigenous peoples, including sports mascots and Hollywood film representations, promotes "disengagement, lower self-esteem, and decreased aspirations for careers and leadership" among Native American individuals.[7] Moreover, "although pro-mascot advocates suggest that American Indian mascots are complimentary and honorific and should enhance well-being," this study demonstrates that "the current American Indian representations function as inordinately powerful communicators, to natives and non-Natives alike, of how American Indians should look and behave. American Indian mascots thus remind American Indians of the limited ways in which others see them."[8] With these concerns in mind, I did not want to ingrain these types of one-dimensional, long-lasting, negative images in my daughter's understanding of Native Americans.

Without our knowledge or consent, my child's teacher forwarded the email, with the names of children and parents attached, to the principal, who subsequently brought the unredacted email before a meeting of kindergarten teachers and parents. Following this meeting, the email message was leaked to and read on the *John & Ken Show*, an incendiary, conservative talk show program that spun the story into a narrative about "elitism" (a code word for critical thinking) and fears about the loss of white privilege in the aftermath of Obama's election, while also ridiculing Native American victims of epidemics such as smallpox.[9] The radio show transformed the collective actions of a group of community members who wanted to protect their children from racist images in an attempt to diffuse the power and scope of the concerns. Nationally syndicated newspapers and television news agencies such as the *Los Angeles Times*, FOX, and CNN, as well as Internet blogs and local news outlets as far ranging as *Native America Calling* and the *Drudge Report* also covered the story, with varying levels of veracity.

The *Los Angeles Times* printed an editorial on November 26 that both acknowledged the genocidal violence of the Pilgrims toward Wampanoags in the wake of the so-called "first Thanksgiving," while also inexplicably advocating the spectacle of stereotypical costumes, noting that "making Pilgrim hats and Indian headbands out of construction paper is a lot of fun."[10] One wonders if the editor would find dressing children up in blackface equally "fun." Misapprehending the difference between not wanting children to witness racist costuming during an extracurricular event and changing the school's curriculum, the editor stated, "Raheja and other Claremont parents angry about the pageant can be forgiven for wanting their children to understand the real story of North America's colonization and conquest."[11] Timothy Lange, a Seminole tribal member living in Los Angeles, replied to the editorial:

> "Forgiven" for wanting their children and others to know the truth? Wow. Are you arguing that there is no age-appropriate way of teaching young children historical truth, and that therefore half-truths masquerading as fun are proper substitutes? Your view that complaining parents are "oversensitive" insults them, us Indians, and all Americans who want our children to understand history. We're lucky to live in a nation where we can observe our past without being shackled to it. Presenting the original Thanksgiving in its ironic context can be accomplished without harming five-year-olds, without making anybody feel guilty, and without stealing anybody's fun.[12]

Adding to the irony, the *Los Angeles Times* printed an article that contradicted the editorial's position on the opposing page. In it, historian Karl Jacoby contends that the U.S. Thanksgiving holiday as it is currently celebrated is a post–Civil War fiction. He also briefly noted the fate of Metacom, the son of Massosoit, a Wampanoag leader who was present at the so-called "first

Thanksgiving" of 1621. Once the English colonies began to thrive, they no longer honored agreements with their Native American neighbors, who had initially protected them and ensured their survival. Metacom's son and wife were sold into slavery in the British West Indies, and "Metacom met his ends at the hands of a Colonial scouting party in August of 1676. His killers quartered and decapitated his body and sent Metacom's head to Plymouth, where for two decades it would be prominently displayed on a pike outside the colony's entrance." Jacoby writes, "That same year, as the violence drew to a close, the colony of Connecticut declared a 'day of Publique Thanksgiving' to celebrate 'the subdueing of our enemies.'"[13] Jacoby advocates thinking about the U.S. holiday "not as a perpetual reenactment of the "first Thanksgiving" of 1621 but instead as a dynamic event whose meaning has shifted over time."[14]

Although the principals at both schools eventually decided to forego the stereotypical costumes in favor of the children dressing in their respective school t-shirts to visually emblematize encountering the "Other," some parents from both schools, as well as teachers, violated this decision and dressed children (and in some cases, themselves) in costume. My daughter attended the event as a result of the principals' decision to discontinue the costumes; however, when her father dropped her off at her classroom, a parent of an older child who had come to the school dressed in a fringed construction-paper vest and wearing red "war paint" accosted a group of kindergarteners and their parents. This parent, according to a group of parents assembled outside their children's kindergarten classroom, proceeded to perform a "war dance" complete with "war whoops" around the parents and children, including my child. She then told those gathered outside the classroom to "go to hell." With no trace of irony, this parent threatened five- and six-year-olds—at least one of whom is of Native American ancestry—and their parents with what amounts to an act of symbolic aggression with a thinly

29. Kelley Davis (*left*) and Andrew Loeffler protest school ban on Thanksgiving for kindergartners. Photograph by Allen J. Schaben, courtesy of the *Los Angeles Times*, November 25, 2008.

veiled threat of violence. The public pedagogy of the parent was intended to demonstrate to the children assembled that Native Americans are racially inferior (they do not communicate using words, but through war whoops and the occasional curse) and, in a perversion of Bakhtin's notion of carnival, that redfacing and other forms of racial masquerade and their attendant "anonymity" are acceptable forms of acting out violence against subordinate, and/or resistant, nonassimilationist groups.

This parent engaged in a long-standing, contradictory practice of defining U.S. national identity (and "tradition") both in opposition to and closely identified with Native American culture. On the one hand, standard pedagogy on American origins, from elementary school to college, begins alternately with Columbus's landfall in 1492 or the Pilgrims' debarkation at Plymouth Rock, conveniently eliding thousands of years of Indigenous history and presence in the Americas. On the other hand, Americans have created a national identity through appropriating fantastical revisions of Native American history and culture. As Rayna Green argues, "One of the oldest and most pervasive forms of American cultural expression, indeed one of the oldest forms of affinity with American culture at the national level, is a 'performance' I call 'playing Indian.'"[15] "Playing Indian," in Green's estimation, is a crucial way "in which we demarcate the boundaries of an American identity distinct from that which affiliates with Europe."[16] The parent in redface exemplified this love-hate relationship by dressing up in Indian costume and performing a dance sequence patterned on Hollywood films in order to display her support for this long-standing minstrel tradition, while at the same time disavowing concerns expressed by parents that this tradition promotes cultural and historical ignorance and racial stereotypes.

As a result of the publicity surrounding the school event, I received hundreds of messages of support from parents, Native American community members, students, and other individuals, some of whom are engaged in similar social justice and educational struggles in their respective communities. An Indigenous youth filmmaking collective, Outta Your Backpack Media, was also inspired to create a video entitled "Thanks Taking" in response to the events of November 2008.[17] On the local level, the school district created a cultural advisory board, of which I was chosen a member, to ensure that other parents who raise similar concerns in the future will be protected from this kind of retribution. In addition, a local retirement community for former missionaries, which had for over sixty years staged a Thanksgiving pageant complete with elderly residents in stereotypical redface and rides on the "Massasoit Super Chief Train" and the "Mayflower-on-Wheels," changed its program as a result in November 2009. The new program featured a Seneca man who spoke about life on the reservation and a Japanese American internment camp survivor who narrated his experiences during World War II.[18]

Yet unfortunately parents who objected to the costumes were also the targets of retaliation. I received hundreds of hateful and threatening telephone calls, faxes, and letters, some of which labeled me with misogynist and racist terms, advocated violence against my daughter, demonstrated an ignorance of U.S. history, and supported genocide of Native Americans. For example, an anonymous individual using the appellation "The Conquistador," evoked the purported practice of delivering smallpox-infested blankets to Native Americans as a form of germ warfare when he wrote to the *Los Angeles Times* online opinion section suggesting that Native Americans be given "blankets as a token of our goodwill to them." Increased police patrols were required at my home, and precautionary measures were taken at my place of employment as a result. It is ironic that the defenders of the Thanksgiving myth, which purports to celebrate peaceful coexistence, would employ hateful speech and threats of violence and intimidation in an attempt to stamp out any open discourse about this holiday. Many of the anonymous online posts responding to news coverage reflected genocidal sentiments and indicated that public opinion of Native Americans promotes a kind of discursive violence in the twenty-first century as fervently as the physical violence that was advocated in the nineteenth century, when in 1850 California passed the ironically named Act for the Government and Protection of the Indians. This Act permitted the seizure and enslavement of Indigenous adults and children in the state.[19] In addition, in 1853 the *Yreka (CA) Herald*, published an essay entreating the U.S. government to send funds and troops to "enable the citizens of the north to carry on a war of extermination until the last redskin of these tribes has been killed. Extermination is no longer a question of time—the time has arrived, the work has commenced and let the first man who says treaty or peace be regarded as a traitor."

In light of these historical, legislative, and discursive imperatives, the contemporary pageants of Thanksgiving indicate that the dominant culture has created and is deeply invested in comforting fantasies of racial harmony and historical amnesia, as well as institutionalized unequal power dynamics predicated on racial masquerade as a form of sanctioned appropriation and cultural ownership. If the dominant U.S. culture continues to violently perpetuate and relentlessly support the egregious stereotypes generated during Thanksgiving—by sports mascots or in other forms of visual culture such as film—then there remains very little room for Native American self-representations to be visible. What happened at my daughter's school is not an isolated or anomalous incident. In 2006 an Omaha parent who requested that her son's San Francisco area school not perform Thanksgiving reenactments was also the target of threats and intimidation, and in 2008 a young Chumash man in Santa Barbara County received death threats and hate mail for protesting his high school's stereotypical Indian mascot.[20] This limited range of visibility and threat of violence explains how early Native American cinematographers such as Edwin Carewe or James Young Deer operated primarily within the bounds of hegemonic discourses out of fear of violent reprisal, while also subtly critiquing Indian images.

Although it was incredibly painful to be the target of such anger, misunderstanding, and ignorance—all of which was exacerbated by the media—and to feel so unsafe and vulnerable in the small town where I live, both of my daughters were largely shielded from the ugliness of the school event and its aftermath through the support of our friends and colleagues. Yet the event also encouraged my school-age daughter to view dominant images of people of color such as herself more critically. A few months afterward, she requested to be removed from her class when the teacher screened Disney's *Peter Pan* (1953) because of its stereotypical images of Native Americans, and she subsequently questioned the framing of historical narratives about the U.S. on several other occasions in the classroom. Although she did not feel protected by her teachers during the ordeal, it has caused her to become more outspoken in the face of injustice of many kinds.

I hope that this book encourages a reconsideration of images of Native Americans and other minority groups, from elementary school to the university classroom, that are grounded in dominant-culture fantasies toward images that reflect more complex and empowering self-representations, such as the exciting new work being created by filmmakers and video artists and being disseminated through electronic media. Perhaps through the kind of challenging, lively, and engaging work these visual culture artists are creating, my daughters' children will enter classrooms where distortions and disrespectful stereotypes are the exception and not the rule.

"Not Ready to Make Nice": History Lessons on the Virtual Reservation

Films such as *Imprint*, *It Starts with a Whisper*, and *Atanarjuat (The Fast Runner)* as well as other works by contemporary Native American filmmakers are important, sometimes-risky works that confound conventional cinema genres and present images of Native Americans on tribally specific Indigenous terms, in contradistinction to stereotypical images such as those offered up at Thanksgiving. Experimental filmmaking techniques, such as those demonstrated in these films, are ideal vehicles for staging "traditional" knowledges regarding oral narrative, spirituality, time, and culture. Simultaneously, they offer up critiques of older practices of redfacing that had been initiated by Indigenous film actors and directors. While these independent films participate in the project of visual sovereignty and provide a useful space for thinking about the virtual reservation, perhaps the very nature of their experimental style limits their dissemination beyond a university and film festival audience.

Although I am aware of the Internet's limitations as a "digital racial-abolitionist strategy,"[21] an online community on the virtual reservation has coalesced as a generative space for creating Indigenous media whose accessibility stretches far beyond what has been possible with cinema. Kyra Landzelius has questioned the effects of electronic information-communication technologies on Indigenous communities: "Can the info-superhighway be a fast track to greater empowerment for the historically disenfranchised? Or do they risk becoming 'roadkill': casualties of hyper-media and the drive to electronically map everything?"[22] Digital technologies can, in Faye Ginsburg's estimation, increase the gap between the powerful and the powerless. She argues, "*The digital age* stratifies media hierarchies for those who are out of power and are struggling to become producers of media representations of their lives. It is an issue that is particularly salient for Indigenous people who, until recently, have been the object of other peoples' image-making practices in ways damaging to their lives."[23] While Landzelius's and Ginsburg's concerns are understandable given the unequal distribution of power and access to technology within settler nations, Indigenous peoples' relationship to modernity, new technologies, and new media is ongoing, and there is plenty of evidence to suggest already that Native American communities are utilizing online communication technologies to advance and reconfigure cultural and linguistic traditions, despite the shortcomings of employing the Internet as a means of cultural and social revitalization. There have been similar concerns about the print medium as a forum for Indigenous literature, as well as the impact of technologies such as radio, cinema, and television in Indigenous communities. Hanay Geiogamah anticipates how Internet technologies will affect Native American communities while at the same time noting that Indigenous communities are already using information-communication technologies and new media to their advantage. "Whether this fundamental change in communication modes and systems will prove a positive, beneficial advancement for Indian people and their traditional cultures and belief systems is a question that won't be answered completely any time in the near future," he notes, "but already this revolution is redefining the identity and role of American Indian communicators and artists, and a productive track record from it has been established and is growing."[24]

Of course, there are important issues with digital media that have not yet been resolved adequately, particularly around intellectual and cultural copyright issues and universal access to knowledges and images that have a limited audience in Indigenous communities. For example, some Aboriginal Australian communities practice restricted knowledge in regard to digital images. Some images, particularly those of deceased persons, cannot be universally viewed, so community members are understandably anxious about issues of electronic accessibility and cultural theft.[25] Yet in cases where knowledge is not restricted by gender, age, or those who have been initiated, the virtual reservation provides a way for filmmakers and other artists to reach audiences to which they may not otherwise have access.

The American Indian Film Institute (AIFI), a nonprofit media organization in San Francisco, offers Native American youth the opportunity to learn digital filmmaking and editing techniques as well as networking skills through its Tribal Touring Program (TTP) every summer. Students present their work at film festivals as well as over the Internet as a project of community building and as a means of disseminating their work beyond conventional circuits.[26] Thomas M. Yeahpau, for example, a Kiowa filmmaker and author of the young adult collection of short stories *X-Indian Chronicles: The Book of Mausape*, has posted *Retort* (2007) on YouTube, a nine-minute black-and-white, experimental, and unscripted film created by his collective, Hosstyle Films, that thematizes domestic violence and female empowerment.[27]

Sites like YouTube and rezKast (a native video and music sharing site) allow Native media-makers to post seemingly endless representations of Indigenous subjects that draw from older stereotypes, reworking and undermining them through music videos, film shorts, language lessons, dance performances, and video clips to present individuals and communities as dynamic, living cultures. No longer simply a recorded live performance, music videos can be considered a mixed-media tradition often innovative in their use of experimental sound and narrative techniques. "Music video," according to Carol Vernallis, "belongs somewhere among music, film, television studies, cultural studies, ethnic studies, and communication studies, as well as philosophy, theater, and dance."[28] Native American music videos also create an aesthetics and discursive tradition that engages the spectator in issues beyond the context of the production. Blackfire, for example, a Flagstaff-based Navajo band composed of two brothers and a sister (Clayson, Klee, and Jeneda Benally) that incorporates traditional Native American and punk rock musical styles, uses their music videos to educate audiences about issues as far-ranging as environmental destruction, police brutality, sexism, and racism.[29] *Rolling Stone* states that the band connects "their distortion-warrior originals to the traditional songs of their people."[30] Joey Ramone collaborated with the band, and "his final recordings were his guest vocals on *[Silence] Is a Weapon,"* released in 2007.[31] A music video from this album, *Overwhelming,* narrates the story of a young woman (played by band member Jeneda Benally) who is abducted and subjected to a series of state-sponsored medical experiments that evoke the coerced sterilization of Native American women and metaphorize the destruction of the environment broadly and the desecration of the sacred San Francisco Peaks in the southwestern United States in particular.[32] The lyrics highlight this connection between issues of women's health and the environment: "So restless / she's shaking / can't you feel her temperature rising? / We're so complacent / and apathetic / while she's given us everything." Band member Klee Benally is also the founder of Indigenous Action Media, an organization that produces documentaries about social justice and environmental protection.[33]

Another example of what Ginsburg calls "cultural activist"[34] work that has employed digital media is musician and Lakota language instructor Redwing Thomas (who goes by the name Red). His three-minute video, *Still Alive* (2008), uses images of Native American children, young adults, and elders to foster cultural pride in the face of "over 500 years of attempted genocide." Employing hip hop music to convey a message of political empowerment and cultural survival, Thomas sings, "the worst possible scenario / USA just couldn't get us to go / hell no! / We are still alive / I say we are still alive." The video was produced by NervousWreck Productions, a Native American video and music production company based in Ukiah, California, and filmed on the Pine Ridge Reservation in South Dakota.

NervousWreck has also posted a nine-minute video of the making of *Still Alive* to YouTube that underscores the kind of productions based in visual sovereignty by contemporary media artists.[35] In a recording studio, Thomas notes that "a lot of people are embarrassed of the reservation," but that he is invested in living and recording in his home territory rather than in New York or Los Angeles. He claims, "you don't even need a fucking professional studio" to produce high-quality music and video that can be digitally uploaded and viewed by an audience of millions. The reservation here is both literal and territorial—a sovereign Lakota space in South Dakota—but also virtual as the work that NervousWreck Productions and the musician Red create connect to the larger on-line and off-line communities of young Indigenous people worldwide who use the idioms of hip hop, as well as their own traditional music and languages, to reconfigure images and represent histories of Indigenous people. Although it can lack the temporal simultaneity of a concert or face-to-face meeting, the text comments offered on sites like YouTube allow individuals to comment on, critique, and connect with media producers and the images they generate. The anonymity afforded by this practice both protects an individual's identity and permits her or him to enter into the conversation with less inhibition. Conversely, however, anonymity also opens up a space for the kinds of hateful, negative comments posted on digital media sites that feature work by Native American film and video artists.

The media created and disseminated through the Internet by Native American amateur and professional artists does not offer a technologically mediated alternative from their constraints of culture. Lisa Nakamura argues that the Internet is not "a place to escape from reality, especially racial realities."[36] Rather, it engages in what Tiziana Terranova has termed the "'outernet'—the network of social, cultural, and economic relationships which criss-crosses and exceeds the Internet—surrounds and connects the latter to larger flows of labour, culture, and power."[37] She continues, "It is fundamental to move beyond the notion that cyberspace is about escaping reality in order to understand how the reality of the Internet is deeply connected to the development of late postindustrialist societies as a whole."[38] If videos posted on the Internet present a fragmented notion of Indigenous identity and culture, they do so within a larger representational regime that supplements, critiques, and engages these images.

Missy Whiteman's music video *Indigenous Holocaust* (2008), for example, featuring the work of hip hop artist Wahwahtay Benais and the Dixie Chicks ("Not Ready to Make Nice"), exemplifies how Indigenous media creates virtual reservations.[39] These spaces open up imaginative sites where Indigenous people can contest, reconfigure, and revisit media representations. Whiteman, an Arapaho and Kickapoo media advocate, artist, and filmmaker, directed and produced the video with her company, Independent Indigenous Film and Media (IIFM).

The video opens with a blurry, ghostly figure that gradually focuses to reveal Benais, an Anishinabe musician. The shot reverses the dominant trope of the vanishing Indian. Benais emerges out of the shadows to narrate the story of Indigenous genocide and survival at federal boarding schools in the United States and residential schools in Canada, a traumatic history that shapes contemporary Native American existence. Benais utilizes the idioms of hip hop to Indigenous ends—his bling is an oversized handmade beaded and fringed medallion that features a black bear paw and his name against a white background, and he is accompanied by young men and women jogging in First Nations United t-shirts.[40]

The lyrics of the song narrate the history of forcibly removing Native American children from their homes from the eighteenth through the twentieth centuries and the kinds of physical, sexual, cultural, and spiritual violence they endured (what Benais and Whiteman refer to as an "Indigenous holocaust"). Contemporary, vibrant images of Benais are juxtaposed with archival photographs of children at schools such as Carlisle demonstrating how events

30. Image from *Indigenous Holocaust* (2008).

that took place a hundred or more years ago still affect Native communities in the present.

As virtual reservation, this video invites the spectator to participate in the process of healing from this genocide, using the Dixie Chicks' lyrics as a prompt: "Forgive, sounds good / Forget, I'm not sure I could / They say time heals everything / but I'm still waiting." The video transforms the lyrics from an experience of grief and alienation to a community's process of grievance and use of media as resistance. This collective form of activism cites the Dixie Chicks' refusal to apologize or retreat for their impromptu onstage criticism of George W. Bush and the U.S. invasions of

Afghanistan and Iraq during a performance in England in 2003. In the wake of these comments, the band members were critiqued in the U.S. media, received hate mail and death threats, and were the victims of an economic boycott of their work. This uncritical jingoism, violent reprisal, and nationalist fervor underscore the increased intolerance for dialogue and debate in national discourse, as the Thanksgiving event also exemplifies.

Native American filmmakers continue to create work that radically expands the kinds of images that were available to early twentieth- century spectators and media makers. The way these images are disseminated through film festival circuits, in Indigenous territory, in university classrooms, and on the Internet will continue to shape exciting new possibilities for critically engaging and creating representations of Indigenous people. Moving in tandem with the production of new media technologies, Native American film, video-makers, and cultural artists are doing more than simply resisting and surviving, they are interrogating the powers of the state, providing nuanced and complex forms of self-representation, imagining a futurity that militates against the figure of the vanishing Indian, and engaging in visual sovereignty on virtual reservations of their own creation.

Notes

1. Since there is no single appropriate or accurate term to refer to the Indigenous peoples of what is now known as the Americas, unless one refers specifically to a particular nation or tribe, I follow the conventional usage of "Native American" and "American Indian" in the context of the northern United States to refer to members of autochthonous communities; "First Nations" and "Aboriginal" in a Canadian context; "Indigenous" in a broad transnational and hemispheric context; and "Indian" to refer to the mass-mediated Hollywoodean image of Native peoples. I do so fully aware of the problematic origins of the terms and their homogenizing tendencies. For more on Indigenous identity terminology preferences, see Berkhofer, *White Man's Indian*; Nagel, *American Indian Ethnic Renewal*; and Yellow Bird, "What We Want to Be Called," 1–21. Likewise, I employ the terms "white," "West(ern)," and "Euro-American" as interchangeable placeholder terms, with the understanding that these categories represent a broad spectrum of cultural histories and national-ethnic origins.

2. Sherman Alexie, "I Hated Tonto (Still Do)," *Los Angeles Times*, June 28, 1988.

3. Vizenor defines survivance in *Fugitive Poses* as "more than survival, more than endurance or mere response; the stories of survivance are an active presence. . . . The native stories of survivance are successive and natural estates; survivance is an active repudiation of dominance, tragedy, and victimry" (15).

4. Smith, "Land of a Thousand Dances." This essay has been reprinted in Smith's *Everything You Know About Indians Is Wrong*, a collection of new and previously published essays.

5. Ethnic spectatorship, according to Chow, takes into account both a critical examination of the stubborn, intractable, and egregious stereotypical spectacles of racialized popular images and a politics of identification that radically re-reads ethnic spectatorship as an affirming exercise. See Chow, *Woman and Chinese Modernity*, 24.

6. Chow, *Woman and Chinese Modernity*, 24.

242 Notes to pages xii-1

7. The history of this process of invisibilization and its attendant violence has been written about at length. See, for example, Drinnon, *Facing West*; Meyer and Royer, *Selling the Indian*; and Mihesuah, *American Indians*.

8. In *Playing Indian*, Philip Deloria discusses the long history of Euro-American strategic appropriations of Indianness. He argues that images of Indians have been employed to justify Euro-American presence in the so-called "New World" and subsequent independence from the British monarch, even while Native Americans were represented as vanishing or tragically absent. At the same time as Native Americans were absented from discourses surrounding nationhood and sovereignty, African American presence was deployed by Euro-American writers to underwrite white supremacy and legitimize Euro-American relationships to property and land. See Jefferson's *Notes on the State of Virginia* (1787), especially the queries "Aborigines" and "Laws," and Morrison's *Playing in the Dark*, a text that argues strongly and persuasively for critical reflection on the discourses of slavery and African American oppression at the expense of a discussion of Native Americans.

9. What G. Harrison Orians called the "cult of the vanishing American" began as soon as European settlers first washed up on the shores of the Americas. Alongside the fact of population decimation due to disease, violence, and displacement, the fiction of Indigenous people as existing in a state of continual decline and often-total disappearance arose. From Columbus to James Fenimore Cooper to nineteenth-century photographs to western films, Native Americans have been envisioned as disappearing. See Orians, *Cult of the Vanishing American*. See also Dippie, *Vanishing American*; Lyman, *Vanishing Race and Other Illusions*; and Romero, "Vanishing Americans."

10. Smith, "Ghost in the Machine," 9. This essay has been reprinted in Smith, *Everything You Know About Indians Is Wrong*.

1. TOWARD A GENEALOGY OF INDIGENOUS FILM THEORY

1. John del Valle, "Umatillas Lose a Chance for Glory," *New York Herald Tribune*, November 17, 1940. Cited in Friar and Friar, *The Only Good Indian*.

2. While Thunder Cloud was identified as Cherokee and Muscogee in print sources and self-identified as Cherokee, neither tribe lists him on its membership rolls, and his exact tribal affiliation has proven to be elusive.

See Aleiss, *Making the White Man's Indian*, 185–86. I do not mean to dispute his Native American identity but rather to point to the ways that his petition for recognition by a Hollywood Indian tribe reflects the vexed relationship to archivally verifiable legal status that has troubled Native American communities since Europeans introduced and enforced new categories of juridically based identity in the Americas. For a concise discussion of the complexities of Native American identity and the politics of enrollment, see Garroutte, *Real Indians*.

3. The War Paint Club (WPC) constituted the first organization dedicated to Native American performers in Southern California. It was founded in 1926 by a group of actors that included Cherokee actor Chief Tahachee (Jeff Davis Tahchee Cypert). A decade later Tahachee and Blackfeet actor Bill Hazlett co-founded the Indian Actors Association (IAA), an organization dedicated to assisting Indigenous actors with employment and attempting to ensure that production companies hired Native American actors for Indian roles. Mohawk actor Jay Silverheels would continue the work of the IAA in the 1960s through his Indian Actors Workshop, an organization that trained Native American actors and advocated for a stronger Indigenous presence on film and in television. Another nonprofit advocacy organization, American Indians in Film and Television (AIF&T), was founded in 1995 by Lakota actor Sonny Skyhawk and is still active, as are First Americans in the Arts (FAITA), the American Indian Film Institute (AIFI), and InterTribal Entertainment (ITE), an initiative of the Southern California Indian Center Inc. to train actors and technicians. The American Indian Registry for the Performing Arts, founded in 1983 by Zoe Escobar and Will Sampson, created a casting agency for Native American performers until its demise in 1992. Currently, there is a SAG caucus dedicated to Native American issues. For more on the history of Native American actors in Hollywood, see Price, "The Stereotyping of North American Indians"; and Rosenthal, "Representing Indians."

4. For a detailed description of one nation's attempts at federal recognition, see Clifford's "Identity in Mashpee" in *The Predicament of Culture*, 277–346.

5. The Americas, of course, have always been an "international" space. Native American communities in North America in particular were recognized as sovereign nations by invader-settlers working from European models of jurisprudence, and this sovereign status is reflected in the many treaties signed by the colonies and later Canadian and U.S. states from the sixteenth through the nineteenth centuries. But even prior to this, Native

America could be considered a transnational site because Indigenous peoples theorized multiple concepts of sovereignty in order to distinguish themselves from the other human, spirit, animal, and inanimate communities surrounding them through linguistic practice, performance, songs, stories, dreams, and visual and legal texts such as wampum belts and pictographs. Native American performers who entered Hollywood did so recognizing that it was a kind of new territory on many levels, and they negotiated their relationships with the United States as well as other Indigenous nations of Southern California (particularly the Acjachemen, Cahuilla, Chemehuevi, Chumash, Kumeyaay, Luiseño, Mojave, Serrano, and Tongva Nations) from this vantage point. Although Native Americans have continually inhabited what is now known as Los Angeles County for thousands of years, relocation policies from the 1950s to the 1970s brought many more Native people to Southern California, making it home to the largest urban Native American population in North America. By using the term "transnational" here, I wish to point to the fact that Indigenous actors from across the Americas participated in the Hollywood film production economy in ways that often troubled the United States's desire for a nonthreatening, domestic vision of Indianness contained within its national borders. Also, the Americas are inherently a transnational Indigenous space because each of the actors hailed from Native American nations who recognize themselves as sovereign and are often recognized as such by the settler nation in which they reside. Thus, the existence of sovereign nations within the boundaries of the larger settler-nation calls into question the legitimacy of the United States and Canada, a subject invoked with much anxiety in Hollywood films by the constant rehearsal of the cowboys and Indians trope.

6. For more on the federal acknowledgement process and history of tribes not recognized by the state, see Miller, *Forgotten Tribes*.

7. Taken from the website of the National Congress of American Indians, http://www.ncai.org (accessed January 2, 2010).

8. Collins, *Understanding Tolowa Histories*, 168.

9. Archivists at the Indian Records Division of the National Archives and Records Administration in Washington DC and Riverside, California, as well as the Office of Federal Acknowledgement in Washington DC, have found no record of it. Beverly R. Singer, however, states that the "petition was rejected by the BIA," which most likely would have been the case had the Office of Indian Affairs received it. See Singer, *Wiping the War Paint Off the Lens*, 20.

10. Native Americans have had a long history with various performative venues and genres beginning before European contact and extending through world's fairs, circuses, and Wild West shows. Native American actors had a sophisticated understanding of the politics, pleasures, and perils of the stage prior to the advent of film. Raymond Corbey asserts that Indigenous peoples exhibited in anthropological spectacles at world's fairs often "actively resisted the roles that were forced on them, for instance by running away." See Corbey, "Ethnographic Showcases," 348. These performative spaces served as proving grounds for a generation of actors who began their careers in silent films.

11. White, *unInvited*, xv.

12. White, *unInvited*, xv.

13. White, *unInvited*, xvii.

14. I borrow this phrase from Jacquelyn Kilpatrick's incisive study of Native Americans in film, *Celluloid Indians*.

15. A number of important volumes on images of Native Americans in film have been produced in the past three decades that portray the figure of the Indian as the site of harmful stereotype and victimization. The titles of these texts often reflect this notion. See Aleiss, *Making the White Man's Indian*; Bataille and Silet, *Pretend Indians*; Buscombe, *"Injuns"!*; Churchill, *Fantasies of the Master Race*; Friar and Friar, *The Only Good Indian*; Kilpatrick, *Celluloid Indians*; and Singer, *Wiping the War Paint Off the Lens*.

16. Shohat and Stam, *Unthinking Eurocentrism*, 118–19.

17. Native Americans have a long pre- and post-European contact history of celebrity figures who enjoyed widespread status in what is now known as the Americas. In the postcontact period, Indigenous people have entertained international audiences, sometimes willingly, but more often under duress. In *Marvelous Possessions*, Stephen Greenblatt details the history of the trade in Native American entertainers, many of whom performed against their volition, beginning with Christopher Columbus's kidnapping of Carib Indians. Pocahontas, who was kidnapped by English colonists in 1613, traveled to England in 1616 where she entertained and was entertained by prominent members of society and may have been presented to King James's court. For a lively history of Pocahontas from a Native American perspective, see Allen, *Pocahontas*. Samson Occom was a Mohegan who converted to Christianity and attended Moor's Charity School (later Dartmouth College). He later was ordained as a Presbyterian

minister and traveled to England in 1766 to fundraise for the school. There he delivered more than three hundred well-attended sermons. He was so popular that both King George III and the Earl of Dartmouth contributed to his cause. His "Short Narrative of My Life" (1768) is considered one of the first autobiographies written by a Native American in English. See Brooks, *The Collected Writings of Samson Occom, Mohegan*. Also a Christian minister and missionary, George Copway was an Ojibwe writer from Canada who lectured to large crowds in Europe, Canada, and the United States. His autobiography, speeches, and correspondence are collected in Ruoff and Smith, *Life, Letters & Speeches*. Copway's fellow Canadian, E. Pauline Johnson, a highly popular and successful Mohawk entertainer and poet, gained international recognition in England, the United States, and Canada. She was the first aboriginal poet from Canada to be published. See Gray, *Flint and Feather*.

18. Harrold Weinberger Papers, Margaret Herrick Library, Academy of Motion Picture Arts and Sciences, Beverly Hills CA.

19. Harrold Weinberger Papers, Margaret Herrick Library, Academy of Motion Picture Arts and Sciences, Beverly Hills CA.

20. Deloria, *Indians in Unexpected Places*, 68.

21. DuBois, *Souls of Black Folk*, 1.

22. DuBois, *Souls of Black Folk*, 1.

23. Sheridan vigorously denied making this statement, according to biographer Roy Morris Jr. See Morris, *Sheridan*. John Wayne's character Ethan Edwards in *The Searchers* (1956) utters the more popular version of the phrase, "The only good Indian is a dead Indian."

24. Friar and Friar, *The Only Good Indian*, 2, 203.

25. Singer, *Wiping the War Paint Off the Lens*, 33.

26. Aleiss, *Making the White Man's Indian*, xvii.

27. Only a handful of full-length texts have addressed the rich and growing history of North American Indigenous filmmaking practices. These include Leuthold's *Indigenous Aesthetics*; Singer's *Wiping the War Paint Off the Lens*; and Lewis's *Alanis Obomsawin*, the first full-length consideration of a Native American documentary filmmaker. Rob Schmidt's "Newspaper Rock" blog on his Blue Corn Comics page (http://www.bluecorncomics. com) is an indispensible source of information about recent releases of Native American media and news, as well as the source of critical analysis of current events in Indian Country.

28. Between the silent era and the 1960s, Native Americans worked on

the set of films as actors and technicians, but except for Sol Worth and John Adair's experiment in ethnographic filmmaking on the Navajo Reservation, documented in *Through Navajo Eyes*, no known Native American filmmakers gained prominence in the years between the rise of sound technology in film and the civil rights era. Native American filmmakers of the late 1960s and early 1970s include Alanis Obomsawin, George Burdeau, Larry Cesspooch, Sandra Osawa, Harriet Skye, and Richard Whitman. Singer chronicles the rise of Native American filmmakers, most of whom work in nonfiction documentary, since the 1960s in *Wiping the War Paint Off the Lens*.

29. See Solanas and Gettino, "Towards a Third Cinema." Solanas and Gettino define "third cinema" as a revolutionary "guerrilla" (278) movement against Hollywood, colonialism, and capitalism that evolved out of bourgeois, neocolonial national film production.

30. Freya Schiwy terms this shift from Third Cinema to Indigenous cinema in a Latin American context "Indianizing" in *Indianizing Film*. See also Wilson and Stewart, *Global Indigenous Media*, for analysis of transnational Indigenous media production.

31. Leuthold cites Masayesva and elaborates his concept of Indigenous aesthetics in *Indigenous Aesthetics*, Kilpatrick discusses a number of contemporary Native American filmmakers and their particular uses of Indigenous aesthetics in the last chapter of *Celluloid Indians*, and Christian spoke of Indigenous aesthetics in February 2008 at UCR during a screening of her film, *a spiritual land claim* (2006). She is currently working on a project that theorizes Indigenous aesthetics.

32. Barclay, "Celebrating Fourth Cinema," 11. Manuel Michel in 1965 introduced the concept of "Fourth Cinema" as the status of Mexico's super-8 (*superochero*) motion picture production: "A marginal cinema, a cinema to fill up space" in "Toward a Fourth Cinema: Prologue," 73. Wresting the term from a broader cinema of the oppressed to the more specific transnational Indigenous context, Barclay reimagines Fourth Cinema as a utopic movement that weds Indigenous epistemologies with new visual media technologies.

33. Barclay, "Celebrating Fourth Cinema," 11.

34. Lorde, "The Master's Tools," 110–13. Lorde was referring specifically to women of color in what Andrea Smith has called the "academic industrial complex," yet this admonition can be equally applied to other contexts. See Smith, "Social-Justice Activism."

35. Barclay, "Celebrating Fourth Cinema," 11.

36. Chadwick Allen has theorized about such "*trans*-Indigenous" possibilities and what an analysis across narrative practices might look like. He does not advocate dismissing dominant critical paradigms for thinking about Indigenous texts, demonstrating instead how "Indigenous writers appropriate and innovate both Indigenous and dominant (in some cases, colonial) artistic and rhetorical traditions to produce texts in all genres." See "Engaging the Politics and Pleasures," 151; and *Blood Narrative*.

37. See Ballinger, *Living Sideways*; Hyde, *Trickster Makes This World*; and Vizenor, "Trickster Discourse."

38. Dozier, *The Pueblo Indians*, 184.

39. Moses cites several examples of Native actors' refusal to conform to Hollywood expectations in *Wild West Shows*.

40. For more on the history of minstrelsy and blackface performances, see Lott, *Love and Theft* and Roediger, *The Wages of Whiteness*.

41. Scott, *Domination and the Arts*, 3. "Public transcript," as Scott defines it, is "a shorthand way of describing the open interaction between subordinates and those who dominate" (2). Film, in this sense, would constitute a public transcript. In *Covering*, Kenji Yoshino similarly draws attention to not only the ways that queer, gendered, and racialized subjects interact with the public transcripts of the state, but also the more intimate ones found within families, at the workplace, and in the military with its compulsory, assimilationist "don't ask, don't tell" policies.

42. Yamamoto, *Masking Selves, Making Subjects*, 5.

43. Carewe (born Jay Fox) began his acting career with the Lubin Company and worked for Rolfe-Metro, Dearborn Stock Company, MGM, and First National Studios. He directed, produced, and starred in over sixty films until his career ended in 1934, one of the casualties of the introduction of sound technology in cinema. Carewe is credited with discovering Dolores Del Rio, Francis X. Bushman, and Gary Cooper. Angela Aleiss notes that he and his two brothers, also motion picture writers and producers, are on the 1907 Chickasaw Rolls (*Making the White Man's Indian*, 180). Carewe was such an integral part of the fabric of Hollywood during the early decades of film that he is included in Carolyn Lowrey's 1920 list of influential actors and directors, *The First One Hundred Noted Men and Women of the Screen*. Young Deer (born J. Younger Johnston) directed and starred in over a dozen motion pictures, including the first extant film by a Native American director, *White Fawn's Devotion* (1910). Young Deer was not an enrolled member of the Ho-Chunk (Winnebago) Tribe, but,

as Philip Deloria suggests, he may have been enrolled under a different name, may have accidentally been left off the rolls, or may not have met enrollment requirements, for a variety of reasons. See Deloria, *Indians in Unexpected Places*, 258–59.

44. Deloria, *Indians in Unexpected Places*, 94. Emphasis in original. For more on the fascinating lives and work of Young Deer and Red Wing, see Hearne, "'The Cross-Heart People,'"; Simmon, *The Invention of the Western Film*; and Smith, *Shooting Cowboys and Indians*.

45. There is extensive scholarship on the history of the boarding school system in the United States and the residential school system in Canada. For example, see Fear-Segal, *White Man's Club*; and Miller, *Shingwauk's Vision*. DeMille initially cast Princess Mona Darkfeather (born Josephine Workman) to play the lead female role Nat-U-Rich in *The Squaw Man*, but Darkfeather turned him down. Darkfeather, a non-Indian, starred in over one hundred silent melodramas and westerns with Bison Motion Pictures, Selig Polyscope, Nestor Studios, Kalem Studios, and Universal Studios.

46. Jean Sanders, "Lillian St. Cyr (Princess Red Wing) and James Young Deer: First Native American Silent Movie 'Power Couple'" on the Nebraska State Education Association website, http://www.nsea.org/news (accessed May 20, 2008).

47. Ann Fienup-Riordan has written about Mala's life and career in *Freeze Frames*.

48. Strongheart played primarily uncredited minor roles in films; however, his work off-screen is critical to understanding how Native American actors operated within a visual sovereignty paradigm. After performing in Buffalo Bill Cody's Wild West Show and Major Lillie's Pawnee Bill Shows, Strongheart developed an interest in film while attending Carlisle in Pennsylvania. He was hired by the Lubin Film Company to manage Native student actors and to serve as ethnographic advisor to the director. "This was my first introduction to the movies," Strongheart wrote in a lengthy study of Hollywood representations of Native Americans, "and directly after the Lubin Co. left the Carlisle grounds, the news got around, even in those infant days, and the Vitagraph Co. from Brooklyn came to Carlisle, and History [*sic*] repeated itself and NIPO [*sic*] fell an innocent victim, and liked it!" See Strongheart, "History in Hollywood," 10–16, 41–46. Strongheart later used his position as an actor to propel his activism. He hosted Native American students from Sherman Institute and

led planning meetings at his home that would lead to the creation of the Indian Center of Los Angeles in the 1930s. See Rosenthal, "Representing Indians," 5; and the publication of the Indian Center of Los Angeles for more on Strongheart's career.

49. Lesser-known supporting cast Native actors had equally fascinating lives. Hundreds of uncredited extras starred in films from the earliest moving images through the 1970s. Many of their stories have yet to be told since they did not leave much of an archival trail, but they played an important part in the larger drama of Native Americans in cinema. Jim Thorpe, the renowned Sac and Fox athlete, had a twenty-year film career after competing in the 1912 Olympics. He starred in over sixty films, including *King Kong* (1933) and *They Died with Their Boots On* (1941). Chauncey Yellow Robe, a Lakota from the Rosebud Reservation and graduate of Carlisle Indian School, starred in only one film, *The Silent Enemy* (1930). Yet as a reformer, activist, and vocal member of the Society of American Indians, he criticized representations of Native Americans in Wild West shows and films. See Yellow Robe, "The Menace of the Wild West Show," a speech printed in *The Quarterly Journal of the Society of American Indians* and his critical analysis of film quoted in Moses, *Wild West Shows and the Images of American Indians, 1883–1933*, 239. Chief Thunderface (Miguel Soto Holguin), an Apache actor, began his career in the circus and later starred in several of Buster Keaton and Tom Mix's silent films. He posed in photographs with well-known actors and directors of the period, demonstrating that on the set he was more than an anonymous extra.

50. DuPea (1849–1970) is credited as being the oldest person buried at Forest Lawn Memorial Park in Glendale, California. For a brief biography, see Robertson, "Tatzumbie Was Born in the Tragic Year," 25.

51. See Sherman Institute Student File Case, National Archives and Records Administration, Riverside.

52. According to Michael Tsosie, director of the Colorado River Indian Tribes (CRIT) Museum, young Southern California Indian women participating in Sherman's outing program frequently were placed as domestic workers in the homes of Hollywood actors, directors, and executives. Michael Tsosie, conversation with author, Riverside CA, August 25, 2008.

53. Malécot, a University of Pennsylvania linguist, credits her as an informant in "Luiseño, A Structural Analysis I: Phonology."

54. James Sr. and Gertrude Chorre note on their children's application

to Sherman that they chose an Indian boarding school over the local Los Angeles public school. This choice complicates conventional wisdom on boarding school histories, demonstrating that while some Native children were forcibly removed from their parents to attend boarding school, others saw it as a site of cultural survival and renewal. See the Chorre school file at the National Archives Record Administration, Riverside branch.

55. Lewis, *Alanis Obomsawin*. This text represents the first full-length study of a single Native American or First Nations filmmaker. For a broader discussion of what might be called "aesthetic," "cultural," or "discursive" sovereignty—conceptions of sovereignty beyond strictly legal discourses—see Lyons, "Rhetorical Sovereignty"; Rickard's call for thinking about sovereignty's relationship to the arts in "Sovereignty: A Line in the Sand"; Singer, *Wiping the War Paint Off the Lens*; Cliff Trafzer's and Anthony Madrigal's definitions of cultural sovereignty in Trafzer, *The People of San Manuel*; Madrigal, *Sovereignty, Land and Water*; Vizenor, *Wordarrows*; and Robert Allen Warrior's "intellectual sovereignty" in *Tribal Secrets* and his discussion of sovereignty in "Organizing Native American and Indigenous Studies."

56. Lewis, *Alanis Obomsawin*, 175.

57. Moses, *Wild West Shows*, 8.

58. Deloria, *Indians in Unexpected Places*, 69. Some Native American actors lived on film sets, ranches, and barrios such as Inceville, Corriganville, and Gower Gulch while others made enough money to purchase their own homes in more affluent neighborhoods.

59. Rosaldo, *Culture and Truth*, 69–70.

60. See Fixico, *Termination and Relocation*. Kent Mackenzie's recently released narrative film, *The Exiles* (1961) also documents relocation-era Indians as they negotiate the community in and around Bunker Hill in Los Angeles.

61. Thunderbird's archival materials were donated to the Southwest Museum in Los Angeles by his widow and are housed in Manuscript Collection 641. See Rosenthal, "Representing Indians," for more on Thunderbird.

62. For examples of visual representations of Native Americans from the sixteenth through the early-twentieth century, see the work of Jan van der Straet, Theodor de Bry, John White, Charles Bird King, Paul Kane, Jan Verelst, Karl Bodmer, George Catlin, Charles M. Russell, Frank Schoonover, Maynard Dixon, Frederic Remington, Seth Eastman, Edward Curtis, Frank

Matsura, and Gertrude Käsebier. For historical and critical studies of these images, see Bank, "Representing History"; Berkhofer, *White Man's Indian*; Bokovoy, *The San Diego World's Fairs*; Bush, *The Photograph and the American Indian*; Gaudio, *Engraving the Savage*; Hiesinger, *Indian Lives*; Lippard, *Partial Recall*; McClintock, *Imperial Leather*; Moses, *Wild West Shows*; and Shea Murphy, "*The People Have Never Stopped Dancing*."

63. Filmmakers were intrigued with using new visual technologies to record raced images generally. Asian Americans, African Americans, and Latinos were the subjects of many early films, as were "exotic" people located outside the borders of the United States.

64. Jacqueline Shea Murphy notes that the U.S. government was partially responsible for the way Wild West shows fixed Native Americans as anachronistic through the enacting of laws that "polic[ed] authenticity" (57).

65. Angela Aleiss terms these films "surprising silents" because they portray images of Native Americans that are more nuanced than representations in most of the films produced after the introduction of sound technology. She surveyed the over 200 fiction and nonfiction films featuring Native American characters catalogued by the Motion Picture, Broadcasting, and Record Sound Division at the Library of Congress and found, "This treasure trove allows us to rethink that early era and to speculate realistically on what later brought about more negative images" in "Native Americans: The Surprising Silents," 34.

66. Smith, *Shooting Cowboys and Indians*, 72.

67. Smith, *Shooting Cowboys and Indians*, 72.

68. Baudrillard, *Simulations*, 2. Gerald Vizenor engages with the trade in images of Native Americans using Baudrillard's theory of simulation in *Manifest Manners*. He critiques the imposition and use of the term "Indian," substituting for it "postindian," an ambiguous neologism that encompasses both those who have capitulated to the Indigenous reality crafted by the colonizer as well as those "postindian warriors of survivance" who attempt the balancing act of simultaneously deconstructing the fabricated hyperreality of mass-mediated Native American experience and serving Native American communities in the embodied, material world as they confront political, cultural, and spiritual crises.

69. Seigworth, "Banality for Cultural Studies," 229.

70. Morris, "Banality in Cultural Studies."

71. Seigworth, "Banality for Cultural Studies," 231.

72. Womack, *Red on Red*, 11.

73. Dench, *Making the Movies*, 94.

74. Slotkin, *Regeneration Through Violence*, 5.

75. Standing Bear, *My People the Sioux*, 284.

76. Some of these films include *The Invaders* (1912), *The Indian Massacre/Heart of an Indian*, and *Battle of the Red Men* (1912).

77. Standing Bear, *My People the Sioux*, 288.

78. Standing Bear, *My People the Sioux*, 137–38.

79. Standing Bear, *My People the Sioux*, 128.

80. Some of these theaters were Native-owned. Alexander Tallchief, prima ballerina Maria Tallchief's father, for example, owned a cinema in Fairfax, Oklahoma.

81. Smith, "Shooting Cowboys and Indians," 71.

82. Shively, "Cowboys and Indians," 353.

83. Basso, *Portraits of "the Whiteman,"* 37. For more sustained discussions of "Indian humor," see Clastres, "What Makes Indians Laugh"; Lincoln, *Indi'n Humor*; the National Museum of the AmericanIndian online exhibition, "Indian Humor," http://www.nmai.si.edu/exhibitions (accessed June 2, 2008); and Taylor, *Me Funny*.

84. Basso, *Portraits of "the Whiteman,"* 37–38.

85. Rodríguez, *Forced Passages*, 3.

86. *Moving Picture World*, March 18, 1911, 581.

87. *Moving Picture World*, March 18, 1911, 581.

88. Hansen, *Babel and Babylon*. She discusses silent cinema as "an alternative public sphere" (101) that allowed spectators from disparate social, linguistic, ethnic, and religious backgrounds to coalesce around a homogenizing sense of the nation.

89. Deleuze, *Proust and Signs*, 57.

90. Seigworth, "Banality for Cultural Studies," 236.

2. IDEOLOGIES OF (IN)VISIBILITY

1. Turner first delivered "The Significance of the Frontier in American History" at the World's Columbian Exhibition in Chicago in 1893 and published it as *The Frontier in American History* in 1921. Scholars such as Patricia Nelson Limerick have critiqued Turner's thesis for privileging a racist, ethnocentric view of American expansion, colonialism, and dispossession of Native Americans. See Limerick, *The Legacy of Conquest*.

2. Cohen, *Silent Film*, 81. Although Turner's frontier thesis has been criticized by scholars, Cohen notes that it has had an enduring shelf-life in the American imagination. "One reason," she contends, "may be the pleasure of having it both ways: it allows moral righteousness to coexist with individualistic assertiveness and ambition, and it supports an idealism that is rhetorical and naïve" (81).

3. Shohat and Stam, *Unthinking Eurocentrism*, 115.

4. Sedgwick describes the "homosocial" as "social bonds between persons of the same sex" that may or may not involve sexual relations in *Between Men*, 1.

5. Allmendinger, "The Queer Frontier," 223.

6. Allmendinger, "The Queer Frontier," 224.

7. Marubbio, *Killing the Indian Maiden*.

8. McClintock, *Imperial Leather*, 26. In addition to articulating this image as a double site of sexual and colonial conquest through the conflation of women's bodies with conquered lands, McClintock suggests that the drawing also suggests a scene of "male anxiety and paranoia" as the female cannibal figures in the background pose the prospect of emasculation through dismemberment (26).

9. Regardless of their reception within their own tribal communities and concomitant leadership roles, La Malinche, Pocahontas, and Sacajewea form the points of an unholy traitor-whore trinity in the American imagination. For productive, feminist revisions of these figures as enemies of Indigenous peoples, see Alarcón, "Chicana's Feminist Literature"; Gunn Allen, *Pocahontas*; Kidwell, "Indian Women as Cultural Mediators"; Lopez, "María Cristina Mena"; and Saldívar-Hull, *Feminism on the Border*.

10. McClintock, *Imperial Leather*, 26.

11. The female cannibal figure is central in colonial European literature of the sixteenth century, regardless of whether or not this figure was predicated on a historical "fact" of anthropophagy or the colonial imagination. The female cannibal, as expressed in literature and visual culture, serves to indict both Indigenous communities that do not submit easily to European authority and Indigenous women whose bodies served as sites of sexual conquest and pleasure, as well as fear and repulsion of gender attitudes and practices that radically differed from European mores. For example, Jean de Léry's sixteen-century account, *History of the Voyage to the Land of Brazil*, depicts Indigenous women engaging in what are described as cannibal practices: "Now after all the pieces of the body, including the guts,

have been thoroughly cleaned, they are immediately put on the *boucans*. While it all cooks according to their style, the old women (who, as I have said, have an amazing appetite for human flesh) are all assembled beside it to receive the fat that drips off along the posts of the big, high wooden grills. . . . Licking their fingers, they say . . . 'It is good'" (126). de Léry is less horrified by the act of cannibalism, an act he most likely engaged in during his time among the Tupinamba, than by the fact that such "useless" women would openly and actively benefit from the privilege of a protein-rich meal and the labors of men.

12. For more on the visual, literary, and sexual traffic in colonized Indigenous women's bodies, see also Bouvier, *Women and the Conquest of California*; Faery, *Cartographies of Desire*; Green, "The Pocahontas Perplex"; Kolodny, *The Lay of the Land*; Smith, *Conquest*; and Valaskakis, "Sacajawea and Her Sisters." For studies of the masculinization of the frontier and its impact on literature and culture, see Slotkin's trilogy: *The Fatal Environment*, *Gunfighter Nation*, and *Regeneration Through Violence*. For speculation about how Native North Americans interpreted contact with European colonizers, see Trigger, "Early Native North American Responses," and Vizenor, *The Heirs of Columbus*.

13. In early American literature, Native American women were reviled as drudges who held positions little higher than slaves in traditional cultures, despite anthropological and tribal historical evidence to the contrary. And in film texts, particularly those produced after 1930, Indigenous women were employed primarily as sexual pawns between men, were used as comic relief, or remained invisible and uncredited.

14. Bouvier, *Women and the Conquest of California*, 12.

15. See, for example, Hansen, *Babel and Babylon*, who uses the metaphor of the biblical Tower of Babel to suggest that the idea of the spectator emerged at the turn of the twentieth century as a strategy created by the film industry to incorporate select "outsider" social groups, such as white women and recent immigrants from Europe, into the body politic as consumers of particular forms of knowledge and culture.

16. Other Native American female actors from the early film period include Madeline Theriault Katt (Anishinabe); Lillian St. Cyr, aka Princess Red Wing (Ho-Chunk); Humming Bird (Chickasaw); Margaret Camp (Abenaki); Beulah Tahamont Parker (Abenaki and Seneca); Gertrude Chorre (Luiseño); Tatzumbie DuPea (Paiute); Atalie Unkalunt (Cherokee); and Aphed (alternately spelled Apid in some sources) Elk (Penobscot and Maliseet), Molly Spotted Elk's sister.

17. I elaborate on the term "virtual reservation" in chapter four of this book.

18. Taylor, *The Archive and the Repertoire*, 19. Emphasis in original. Gallop's *Anecdotal Theory* has also been helpful in sorting out the absences and excesses I find surrounding the lives and work of these performers. In her work, Gallop relates her "attempt to theorize from a different place," a place that permits seemingly quirky pairings such as dreams and poststructuralist texts, legal documents and personal narrative (11). Because Native American knowledge practices rely on and are built upon a scaffolding that consists of a broad understanding of what constitutes reality—written texts, dreams, oral narrative, folk genealogy, photographs, and dance, for example—all of these texts (the archive and the para-archival) inform contemporary Indigenous culture and, in turn, structure our access to other historical contexts.

19. I am referring here to Aleiss, "Native Americans"; Bachman and Slater, *American Silent Film*; Bernardin, *The Birth of Whiteness*; Butters, *Black Manhood on the Silent Screen*; Hansen, *Babel and Babylon*; Hearne, "'The Cross-Heart People'"; Musser, *Before the Nickelodeon*; Rabinowitz, "Past Imperfect"; Rosen, *Change Mummified*; Ross, *Working-Class Hollywood*; and Smith, *Shooting Cowboys and Indians*.

20. See Berumen, *Brown Celluloid*; Feng, *Identities in Motion*; Francis, "Embodied Fiction, Melancholy Migrations"; Gaines, "Fire and Desire"; Guerrero, *Framing Blackness*; Marez, "Subaltern Soundtracks"; Miyao, *Sessue Hayakawa*; Noriega, *Chicanos and Film*; and Sturtevant, "'But Thing's is Changin' Nowadays.'"

21. Taylor, "Black Silence," 7.

22. Marubbio, *Killing the Indian Maiden*, 6. See also Green, who defines the "Pocahontas Perplex" as "a model for the national understanding of Indian women . . . with her darker, negative viewed sister, the Squaw—or anti-Pocahontas," 17. "Squaw" is a controversial and outdated term that many Native Americans find obscene and demeaning. While the exact etymology of the term is contested, originating perhaps from an Algonquian word, it has been associated with a sexualized, inferior image of Native American women.

23. Marubbio, *Killing the Indian Maiden*, 7.

24. Very little has been published about Minnie Ha Ha. The biographical information I reference in this chapter comes from an interview published in the *Mack Sennett Weekly*, 1 (February 12, 1917) n.p., and from telephone

conversations with her granddaughter, Shari Holland, a filmmaker who lives on the Northern Cheyenne Reservation near the cabin her grandmother built once she returned to the reservation.

25. *Mack Sennett Weekly*, 1 (February 12, 1917), n.p.

26. *Mack Sennett Weekly*, 1 (February 12, 1917), n.p.

27. *Mack Sennett Weekly*, 1 (February 12, 1917), n.p.

28. According to Bunny McBride in *Molly Spotted Elk*, Spotted Elk was originally selected for lead roles in W. S. VanDyke's *Laughing Boy* and Cecil B. DeMille's *The Squaw Man*, but neither of those roles materialized. McBride, *Molly Spotted Elk*, 239.

29. Spotted Elk was encouraged to attend the University of Pennsylvania by Frank Speck, who considered her a potential ethnographic informant and assistant. She first attended Swarthmore Preparatory School and began auditing classes at the University of Pennsylvania in 1924 while living with Speck's family, who claimed her as a dependent. Both Spotted Elk and Gladys Tantaquidgeon, a Mohegan classmate, worked as Speck's assistants. Unlike Tantaquidgeon, Spotted Elk did not matriculate, but left the university to work for the 101 Ranch, a Wild West show, in 1925. She did so because while Speck often asked her to perform Indianness in an academic setting, she was unable to survive on what little she earned on her stipend. "She was hungry and needed to [perform to survive]," according to an interview with Speck's son conducted by McBride, "Those [Penobscot] people were *poor* . . . struggling for an existence, trying to do something, anything, to get by." See McBride, *Molly Spotted Elk*, 58–64.

30. Spotted Elk kept a diary, which she began at the age of thirteen. Her diary is partially published in McBride, *Molly Spotted Elk*. She also wrote a series of oral narratives and a dictionary. This material was recently published in *Katahdin: Wigwam's Tales of the Abnaki Tribe and a Dictionary of Penobscot and Passamaquoddy Words with French and English Translations*.

31. McBride, *Molly Spotted Elk*, 164.

32. Martin, "'Remembering the Jungle,'" 311.

33. McBride, *Molly Spotted Elk*, 164.

34. McBride, *Molly Spotted Elk*, 167.

35. Letter from Robert Valentine to the Selig Polyscope Company, May 13, 1911. William Selig Collection, Folder 474, Correspondence (United States government), Margaret Herrick Library, Academy of Motion Picture Arts and Sciences.

36. See Abel, *Americanizing the Movies*. Abel cites Herbert Blau's observa-

tion that the "usable past" separates what was "commonly remembered and adhered to, or thought of as better forgotten" from what was not (62).

37. Reference to the Ghost Dance is significant here not only because so many films with Native American plots are located on the Great Plains, where the Ghost Dance religion and its key proponent, the Paiute prophet Wovoka, was embraced in the late-nineteenth century, but because both performances of the Ghost Dance and the Wounded Knee Massacre that resulted from the United States Cavalry's fears and misreadings of the new religion were documented photographically and circulated as incredibly powerful visual markers of alterity and violence. In *Ghost Dances and Identity* Gregory Ellis Smoak counters conventional readings of the Ghost Dance as a pathetic last gasp of a vanishing race by reading it as a creative and influential means of expressing a multiple register of social identities that radically revised historical conceptions of race and ethnicity at the turn of the twentieth century. See also Mike Davis's chapter on the Ghost Dance in *Dead Cities and Other Tales* and L. G. Moses's essay "'The Father Tells Me So!'"

38. Leuthold, "Rhetorical Dimensions," 65. See also Morris and Wander, "Native American Rhetoric."

39. Shea Murphy, *The People Have Never Stopped Dancing*, 34.

40. See Moses, *Wild West Shows*, for more on the prohibitions on travel enforced on Native people living on reservations. Moses also argues that the Wild West shows, one of film's precursors, became a site of anxiety for government officials invested in programs of assimilation because it encouraged and permitted a space where Native Americans could continue practices that were discouraged or outlawed by the U.S. government.

41. By "sympathetic" and "sensitive" here I do not mean to imply that the films did not uphold racist ideologies and were not exploitative, because they most certainly did and were. There is a large body of work on the racist portrayals of Native Americans in film. See Aleiss, "Native Americans"; Bataille and Silet, *The Pretend Indians*; Brownlow, *The War, the West, and the Wilderness*; Buscombe, "*Injuns!*"; Friar and Friar, *The Only Good Indian*; Hilger, *From Savage to Nobleman*; Jay, "'White Man's Book No Good,'"; Kilpatrick, *Celluloid Indians*; and Rollins and O'Connor, *Hollywood's Indian*.

42. Smith, *Shooting Cowboys and Indians*, 5.

43. Smith, *Shooting Cowboys and Indians*, 57.

44. *Northern Exposure* also starred Darren E. Burrows, Apesanahkwat, Graham Greene, and Floyd Westerman in key roles.

45. For a history of Mohawks in New York City, see Rasenberger, *High Steel*. Other recent televisual representations of Native Americans include TNT's six-episode television series *Into the West* (2005) a dramatization of frontier expansion and Indian-white relations that intertwined Lakota and Euro-American histories, manifest destiny, the Ghost Dance, and Native American boarding school experiences from the historical period 1825–90. *Into the West* features a large cast of Native American actors including Irene Bedard, Tonantzin Carmelo, Russell Means, Raoul Trujillo, Kalani Queypo, Michael Spears, Graham Greene, and Sheila Tousey. Yet like many of its predecessors, it fixes Native American people in the past with no viable future. Likewise, HBO's made-for-television movie, *Bury My Heart at Wounded Knee* (2007), covers roughly the same historical period as *Into the West* and also features an impressive Native American cast that includes Adam Beach, August Schellenberg, Wes Studi, Eric Schweig, and Gordon Tootoosis. It likewise traffics in a tragic view of Native American history. In 2007 Raoul Trujillo played Raw, a Lion-like character, in the Syfy channel's miniseries *Tin Man*, based on L. Frank Baum's *The Wonderful Wizard of Oz*. In an interview, Trujillo identifies Dorothy's motley group as a "tribal society" and likens the role to one he played in *Apocalypto*. Yet Raw is not an explicitly Native American character (although his name connotes the "savagery" associated with Indian people in mass media and the anthropological distinction between those who eat raw food and those who eat cooked food). See Ian Spelling, "Neal McDonough, Alan Cumming and Company Are Off to See the Wizard in Sci Fi's New Miniseries, *Tin Man*," *Sci Fi Weekly*, www.scifi.com (accessed January 13, 2008). Trujillo also played Long Shadow, a Native American vampire, in HBO's *True Blood* for four episodes in 2008. Most recently, PBS released a five-part series, *We Shall Remain* (2009), directed by Chris Eyre and featuring a large cast of Native American actors.

46. Roscoe Pond, "Native Americans Still at the Bottom in Hollywood." An Associated Content article published by Newspaper Rock, http://news paperrock.bluecorncomics.com (accessed April 2, 2010).

47. See Roth, *Something New in the Air*, for a history of televisual representations of Native Americans in Canada. Isuma TV (http://www.isuma .tv) is the latest Internet media outlet for Indigenous video production in Canada. The site offers a variety of programming, from language instruction to full-length feature films. Faye Ginsburg notes that it is a "free internet portal for global Indigenous media, available to local audiences and world-

wide viewers." See her essay on Isuma TV, "Beyond Broadcast: Launching NITV on Isuma TV," at In Media Res: A Media Commons Project, http://mediacommons.futureofthebook.org (accessed May 4, 2009).

48. I became aware of many of the films discussed in this chapter through Karen C. Lund's comprehensive guide to over 130 silent films that focus on Native American plots and characters. See "American Indians in Silent Film," http://www.loc.gov/rr. Her guide helped me locate these films in the Library of Congress's Motion Picture, Broadcasting, and Recorded Sound Division collections, the British Film Institute, and archives in Los Angeles.

49. For more on the representational and institutional race practices and contexts of world's fairs and International Expositions, see Bank, "Representing History"; Bokovoy, *San Diego World's Fairs*; Fowler and Fowler, "The Uses of Natural Man in Natural History"; L. G. Moses, *Wild West Shows*; and Rydell, *All the World's a Fair*. For an excellent study of precinematic actualities and ethnographic films and their intersection with anthropological discourses, see Griffiths, *Wondrous Difference*.

50. Contrary to dominant narratives about Native American demographics, Indigenous populations in the 1920s were in recovery and have steadily increased since then. Shoemaker's *American Indian Population Recovery in the Twentieth Century* examines the increase in Native American numbers in the United States from a low point of 237,000 in 1900. See also Snipp, *American Indians* for an analysis of the 1980 census information on Native Americans.

51. For more on the Dawes Act, see Black, "Remembrances of Removal"; Taylor, *The New Deal and American Indian Tribalism*; and Washburn, *Assault on Indian Tribalism*. Following on the heels of other policies to enforce assimilation, such as the creation of the Carlisle Indian Industrial School, the Dawes Act further devastated tribal communities through the policy of dividing up tribally held lands into individual parcels. This essentially effected a massive land transfer to rapacious white settlers as individual Native Americans were deemed to require much less land than the collective. It also instituted a paradigm shift from the communal to the nuclear family. The Merriam Report of 1928 declared allotment to be a complete failure and chastised the U.S. government for the epidemic of poverty, despair, violence, and discontent that followed in the wake of the Dawes Act.

52. Hearne, "'The Cross-Heart People,'" 182–83.

53. Simpson, "On Ethnographic Refusal," 74.

54. For an insightful analysis of *White Fawn's Devotion*, see Hearne, "'The Cross-Heart People.'"

55. Shohat and Stam point out that one of the western's conventional ways of representing Indians was "by making Native Americans appear intruders on their own land" (133).

56. *Red Love* was produced by the short-lived independent Lowell Film Production Company, created by actor John Lowell, who plays the part of Thunder Cloud. The only other extant film by the company is *Floodgates* (1924), a film that stars many of the same actors as *Red Love*. Lowell's daughter, Evangeline Russell, played the part of Starlight in *Red Love*, and his wife, Lillian Case Russell, wrote the screenplay.

57. See Schlereth, *Victorian America*. Schlereth examines a number of everyday household products in Victorian America to demonstrate how these items helped shape bourgeois notions of the self and individualism. The Victorian moralistic worldview was predicated on the individual's triumph over nature through the assistance of new forms of technology, Schlereth contends. "The availability of cheap cameras and inexpensive film," he notes, allowed individuals to perpetuate a form of visual colonization on the world through these new methods of recording, storing, and owning representations of the "other" (199).

58. Jay, "'White Man's Book No Good,'" 3.

59. See Deloria's chapter on the Boston Tea Party in *Playing Indian* and Jones, "The First but Not the Last of the 'Vanishing Indians.'"

60. Lott, *Love and Theft*, 6, 234. See also Roediger's chapter on antebellum minstrelsy in *The Wages of Whiteness*.

61. Rogin, *Blackface, White Noise*, 5.

62. Deloria poses a similar argument in *Playing Indian* in chapters devoted to earlier performances of whites in Indian roles, such as the Boston Tea Party, and literary appropriations such as Lewis Henry Morgan's Grand Order of the Iroquois.

63. See the depiction of Indigenous peoples in *Eirik's Saga*, a twelfth-century narrative that purports to record the Norse invasion of the eastern seaboard of what is now known as Canada and the United States five centuries before Christopher Columbus, in Magnusson and Pálsson, *The Vinland Sagas*.

64. Barthes, *Mythologies*, 125. Italics in original.

65. Barthes, *Mythologies*, 121. Italics in original.

66. Dunn, "I Am the Real Hollywood Indian," 238.

67. A few of these non-Indians who played Native American roles include Henry Brandon, Charles Bronson, Jeff Chandler, Tony Curtis, Richard Dix, Sessue Hayakawa, Nobel Johnson, Burt Lancaster, Elsa Martinelli, J. Carrol Naish, and Debra Paget.

68. Chude-Sokei, *The Last "Darky"*, 3.

69. Chude-Sokei, *The Last "Darky"*, 3.

70. Marubbio, *Killing the Indian Maiden*, 12.

71. If this character is her father or serves as a paternal figure, it would make sense that Minnie wore a simple dress. According to Luther Standing Bear in his 1928 autobiography, *My People the Sioux*, the role of chief among Plains tribes required generosity and self-sacrifice: "His family did not come first. He received no salary" and was therefore often poor in material goods because of his role as wealth distributor (59).

72. Vestal, "The Hollywoodean Indian," cited in Bataille and Silet, *The Pretend Indians*, 63–67.

73. Both the Sun Dance and the dog sacrifice sometimes associated with it are often misunderstood by non-Indians as violent, "savage" practices. See Stover, "Postcolonial Sun Dancing at Wakpamni Lake," and Jorgensen, *The Sun Dance Religion*.

74. Although *Fatty & Minnie He-Haw* was filmed in California, Mack Sennett was born in Quebec, Canada and grew up in New England, so he likely was familiar with popular stories about the Haudenosaunee (Iroquois) White Dog Sacrifice during Midwinter ceremonies. See Wallace, *Death and Rebirth of the Seneca*; and Johansen and Mann, *Encyclopedia of the Haudenosaunee*.

75. Wallace and Hoebel, *The Comanches*, 69.

76. Wallace and Hoebel, *The Comanches*, 69.

77. McCaffrey and Jacobs, *Guide to the Silent Years of American Cinema*, 241.

78. *Mickey* was the Mabel Normand Feature Film Company's first and only release. According to Simon Louvish in *Keystone: The Life and Clowns of Mack Sennett*, *Mickey* was a box office success when it was released and is considered to be Mabel Normand's best film (156). Louvish notes, "In a country undergoing the gloom both of war and influenza, some months before the armistice that would end the Great War, the film's simple romance, recognizable heroine and villains, the triumph of the downtrodden and the virtues of rural against city life struck a familiar chord" (160). See Mahar's

Women Filmmakers in Early Hollywood for more on the vexed production
history of *Mickey* and the Mabel Normand Feature Film Company.

79. Louvish, *Keystone*, 160.

80. Elmer, "A Response to Jonathan Arac," 15.

81. See Smith's *Conquest* for a detailed discussion of the history of
sexual violence against Indigenous women in the Americas. She argues that
European colonizers "have historically used sexual violence as a primarily
tool of genocide" (3) by imagining Native women as "polluted with sexual
sin" or as sexually rapacious (10).

82. Marubbio, *Killing the Indian Maiden*, 29.

83. As Native peoples not associated with either the Plains or the Southwest, California Indians were, with rare exception, outside of the representational realm of Hollywood images. Therefore, it is not surprising that
Minnie's costume does not conform to stereotypical notions of "Indianness."
Moreover, because of the extreme population decline of California Indians
during the mission era and the Gold Rush, Minnie's seeming disconnection
from a tribal community may have reflected less her outsider status and more
the threat of violence that such an association might have caused her.

84. Native people of California were called "Digger Indians" because of
the term's semblance to an epithet for African Americans, as well as their
supposed inferiority. Native Californians were considered inferior because
they ate edible roots rather than engaging in agricultural practices that
were deemed by the dominant culture to be more civilized. The Act for the
Government and Protection of Indians permitted the seizure and enslavement of California Indians and was not repealed until sixteen years later,
when in 1866 California had to comply with the Fourteenth Amendment
to the U.S. Constitution. For more on Native California history during the
mission system and Gold Rush period, see Almaguer, *Racial Fault Lines*;
Heizer, *The Destruction of California Indians*; Jackson and Castillo, *Indians,
Franciscans and Spanish Colonization*; Lightfoot, *Indians, Missionaries,
and Merchants*; and Trafzer and Hyer, *"Exterminate Them!"*

85. Gold was discovered in the historical Feather River in the 1840s
by General John Bidwell, a potential source for the figure of Mickey's
deceased father. Louisa Amelia Knapp Smith Clapp, a white writer who
lived near Feather River, records the history of Bidwell, whose life trajectory
resembled that of Mickey's biological father, in letters that were published
in *The Pioneer* and the *Marysville Herald* in 1851 and 1852. According to
Lori Lee Wilson, Clapp may have met writers Helen Hunt Jackson and

Louisa Mae Alcott. Bret Harte read her letters to her sister, which inspired him to write *The Luck of Roaring Camp and Other California Gold Rush Stories*, another possible source for *Mickey*'s screenwriters. See Wilson, "A Lady's Life in the Gold Rush." Bidwell was the founder of Chico, California, and a friend of John Sutter. He owned Rancho Chico Arroyo, a ranch that encompassed a Mechoopda Maidu village that was "protected" from further white encroachment in exchange for labor that, according to Mechoopda descendants, "resembled that of a plantation society to some." See www.mechoopda-nsn.gov (accessed January 13, 2008). While Bidwell's Rancho Arroyo Chico serves as an example of Native dispossession and white paternalism, it was also a very complicated site given its historical context. According to the ranch's ledger books, cited on the Mechoopda website, Native workers from Mechoopda and surrounding communities were "paid the same rate as non-Indian workers performing the same or similar work." Moreover, the ranch served as a respite from the violence of the region as murder of Native Californians was sanctioned in the mid-nineteenth century. In 1863, for example, Bidwell commissioned soldiers from San Francisco to be stationed for twelve months around the ranch "to protect the native population . . . from threats of extermination by local militias." Bidwell's relationship to the Mechoopda may have been more than economic, however, as it has been speculated that he engaged in a long-term relationship with an Indigenous woman named Nuppani that was "recognized as marriage" by the community. Nuppani is alternately spelled "Nupani" and "Nopani" in other sources. See Gillis and Magliari, *John Bidwell and California*. According to Gillis and Magliari, Bidwell and Nuppani had a daughter, Amanda Wilson, who was granted land upon Bidwell's death. In *Mickey*, Minnie's role reflects this condition: she is protected or indentured first under Mickey's father's household and then later under Joe's. While the Bidwell story may not have been a direct influence on *Mickey*'s writers, the anguished and violent history of northern California does provide a useful context for reading Minnie's complicated relationship to Joe and Mickey. Concomitant with the film's romantic comedy plot is a Native American subplot that provides an alternative reading of the "vanishing Indian" trope.

86. Aleiss, *Making the White Man's Indian*, 23.

87. The Anishinabe have also been referred to as the Chippewa and Ojibway. See Vizenor, *The People Named the Chippewa*.

88. Burden, *Look to the Wilderness*.

89. For more biographical information on Yellow Robe, see Fielder, *Sioux Indian Leaders*; Yellow Robe's obituary (*New York Times* April 8, 1930); Weinberg, *The Real Rosebud*; and the introduction to *Tonweya and the Eagles and Other Lakota Tales*, written by his daughter, Rosebud Yellow Robe.

90. According to McBride in *Molly Spotted Elk*, "Yellow Robe wrote and delivered the film's opening narrative" (103).

91. Smith, in *Writing Tricksters*, defines the "trickster aesthetic" as public pedagogy disseminated "through comic example and . . . by transgressing [culture's] boundaries" (8).

92. Murray, *Forked Tongues*, 14.

93. Murray, *Forked Tongues*, 6.

94. Ruby, *Picturing Culture*, 9.

95. Meek, "And the Injun Goes 'How!'" 103.

96. Sobchack, "The Scene of the Screen," 146.

97. Sobchack, "The Scene of the Screen," 146 (emphasis in original); Simpson, "On Ethnographic Refusal," 71.

98. McBride, *Molly Spotted Elk*, 108.

99. McBride, *Molly Spotted Elk*, 108.

100. Theriault, *Moose to Moccasins*, 58. Beaver trapping had already been prohibited in 1923.

101. For more on the Indian Acts, see Miller, *Sweet Promises*.

102. McBride, *Molly Spotted Elk*, 112. McBride notes that Burden and Chandler most likely only interviewed men as Madeline Katt Theriault, an Anishinabe actor in the film whose opinion had not been solicited, objected to some of the film's ethnographic details (312).

103. McBride, *Molly Spotted Elk*, 96.

104. Long Lance was born Sylvester Long on December 1, 1890, in Winston-Salem, North Carolina. According to his biographer, Donald B. Smith, Long Lance's parents were most likely of African American, European American, and Lumbee ancestry, although he claimed to be Blackfoot in his autobiography, *Long Lance*. Smith intimates that Long Lance committed suicide in 1932 in Los Angeles in order to escape imminent public exposure as a fraud. See Smith, *Long Lance*; Smith, *Chief Buffalo Child Long Lance*; and Micco, "Tribal Re-Creations." Molly Spotted Elk was born Mary Alice Nelson on the Penobscot Reservation in Maine in 1903. According to McBride, Spotted Elk spent time in mental institutions after she returned from living and performing in Europe. See McBride, *Molly Spotted Elk*, 282–83.

105. McBride, *Molly Spotted Elk*, 124.
106. McBride, *Molly Spotted Elk*, 40.
107. McBride, *Molly Spotted Elk*, 83.
108. McBride, *Molly Spotted Elk*, 121.
109. Burden chose not to include a miscegenation plot in the film because of his negative views of intermarriage. In *Dragon Lizards of Komodo*, Burden is dismayed by the lack of miscegenation laws in the Dutch colony: "Where is this getting the world, this intermarriage between race and race, this breaking down of the barriers of race consciousness? In the long run, as intermarriage becomes more and more frequent, does it not lead inevitably to one grand hodge podge, one loathsome mixture of all races into a pigsty breed? An unattractive thought, perhaps, but sure of fulfillment, as long as racial intermarriage continues" (166).
110. McBride, *Molly Spotted Elk*, 125.
111. I thank Jacqueline Shea Murphy for drawing my attention to Miguel and Olson's work, which was staged as a work-in-progress entitled *April in Paris* at UCR's Red Rhythms: Contemporary Methodologies in American Indian Dance Conference in 2004, a conference Shea Murphy and I co-organized. The version of the dance piece I cite from here was performed at NOZHEM: First Peoples Performance Space at Trent University in March 2005 where it premiered.
112. McBride, *Molly Spotted Elk*, 268.
113. Janet Smith, "Struggles Along Road to Paris: Molly Spotted Elk's Groundbreaking Journey Inspires Multidisciplinary Performance," www.straight.com (accessed January 30, 2008).
114. Shea Murphy, "*The People Have Never Stopped Dancing*," 225.
115. Shea Murphy, "*The People Have Never Stopped Dancing*," 272.
116. Mildred Bailey (née Mildred Rinker), nicknamed "Mrs. Swing," was a groundbreaking female jazz vocalist popular in the 1930s and 1940s. Julia Keefe, a Nez Perce jazz singer, performed a retrospective of Bailey's work, "Thoroughly Modern: Mildred Bailey Songs," at the National Museum of the American Indian in April 2009. See Kara Briggs, "Julia Keefe Spins Songs of Native Jazz Pioneer," http://colorsnw.com/colors (accessed June 11, 2009), and "Mildred Balley."

3. TEARS AND TRASH

1. Aleiss, "Native Son," *New Orleans Times-Picayune*, May 26, 1996, D1.
2. Green, "A Tribe Called Wannabee."

3. Jolson, Wayne, and Brando performed various racialized characters in their films, as did many actors. Jolson infamously wore blackface in *The Jazz Singer* (1927), John Wayne played Genghis Khan in *The Conqueror* (1956), and Marlon Brando starred as the eponymous hero in *Viva Zapata!* (1952). But none of these actors claimed the ethnic identity of the character they played in the film as their own biological identity.

4. Chapter 4 addresses this reconfiguration of the ghost figure in contemporary Native American films.

5. Deloria, *Playing Indian*; Green, "A Tribe Called Wannabee"; and Huhndorf, *Going Native*. Deloria, Green, and Huhndorf eloquently describe this long history of strategically inhabiting "Indian" identities in North America. See also the following texts that discuss the phenomenon of "playing Indian" as central to the formation and maintenance of Euro-American identity: Baird, "Going Indian"; and Mechling, "'Playing Indian.'" Euro-Americans have defined the Native American "Other" in terms of authenticity and imitation but have also couched their own identity vis-à-vis Europe (the authentic) and technology (the imitation) in the same terms. See, for example, Orvell, *The Real Thing*.

6. Green, "A Tribe Called Wannabee," 30.

7. Huhndorf, *Going Native*, 6.

8. See Warrior and Smith, *Like a Hurricane*; and *Alcatraz Is Not an Island* (James M. Fortier, 2001), a documentary film, for more on the history of the takeover of Alcatraz and its aftermath.

9. For more on AIM and the 1973 Wounded Knee occupation, see Gonzalez and Cook-Lynn, *The Politics of Hallowed Ground*; and Johnson and Fixico, *The American Indian Occupation of Alcatraz Island*. See also *Incident at Oglala* (Michael Apted, 1992), and *Wounded Knee*, the fifth episode of the PBS series, *We Shall Remain* (Chris Eyre, 2009), featuring rare archival footage of the events.

10. Rosaldo, *Culture and Truth*, 69–70.

11. I discuss both of these films at length in chapter four.

12. For more on cultural patrimony, see Arnold Krupat's discussion of cultural property in *The Turn to the Native*, 19–24 and Michael F. Brown's case study of Indigenous intellectual property rights in *Who Owns Native Culture?*.

13. Wilson, "Blood Quantum," 109.

14. Weaver, "Indigenous Identity," 240.

15. Archuleta, "Refiguring Indian Blood," 1.

16. Archuleta, "Refiguring Indian Blood," 1.

17. Weaver, Indigenous Identity," 249.

18. See Weaver, "More Light than Heat." For more on the complexities of Native American identity, see Garroutte, *Real Indians*; Harmon, *Indians in the Making*; Lyons, *X-Marks*; Strong and Van Winkle, "'Indian Blood'"; Tallbear, "DNA, Blood, and Racializing the Tribe"; Weaver, "Indigenous Identity"; and Weaver, *That the People May Live*.

19. Cheng, *The Melancholy of Race*, 24.

20. Cody also published *Indian Talk* and *Iron Eyes Cody*, among other short works.

21. Cody, *Iron Eyes*, 9.

22. Cody, *Iron Eyes*, 10.

23. Owens, *Mixedblood Messages*, 129.

24. Cody, *Iron Eyes*, 245.

25. Brumble, *American Indian Autobiography*, 73.

26. Cody, *Iron Eyes*, 90.

27. Cody, *Iron Eyes*, 250. Italics in original.

28. Cody, *Iron Eyes*, 71. Emphasis in original.

29. Bertha's mother acted in many silent films and died in California in 1945. She also served as an ethnographic informant during her young adulthood. At sixteen, she told an "Abenaki Witch Story" to M. Raymond Harrington, who published it in the *Journal of American Folklore* in 1901. Bertha's mother's name appears in print sources alternately as Beulah and Beatrice Tahamont. Joy Porter identifies her as Beulah Tahamont in *To Be an Indian*. According to Porter, Beulah was an enrolled Abenaki born in 1904 (54). Daniel F. Littlefield and James W. Parins identify Parker's wife as Beatrice Tahamont in *A Biobibliography of Native American Writers, 1772–1924* (263). Arthur C. Parker was the author of *The Code of Handsome Lake, the Seneca Prophet, Seneca Myths and Folk Tales*, and *Skunny Wundy*, among other publications, and he served as curator of the Rochester Museum of Science. His uncle, Ely S. Parker, was a Seneca statesman and sachem who served under President Ulysses S. Grant and became the first Native American to head the Federal Commission on Indian Affairs, which later became the BIA. Bertha Parker's publications include "Yurok Tales," "California Indian Cradles," and *Indian Legends*, which was published posthumously with Iron Eyes Cody. Harrington discusses her work in an article about an almost all-Native archaeological dig sponsored by the Southwest Museum in 1940 in "Man and Beast in Gypsum Cave." She

also served as a film consultant on a set of motion pictures with Indian plots and cohosted a television program in the 1950s on Native American culture with her husband.

30. Standing Bear, *My People the Sioux*, 284.

31. Dench, *Making the Movies*, 61–62.

32. Bergland, *The National Uncanny*, 19.

33. Keep America Beautiful Inc., "Famous Tear and Environmental Icon Return to tv after a 20-Year Absence!" September 21, 1998. The ad originally played from 1971 to 1985, but channels like Nickelodeon still play it, and the anti-litter organization recently filmed a new television announcement that features the same Indian image.

34. There are a number of books on representations of Indians by Europeans. See, for example, Berkhofer, *White Man's Indian*; Bird, *Dressing in Feathers*; Fiedler, *The Return of the Vanishing American*; Francis, *The Imaginary Indian*; Green, "The Indian in Popular Culture"; Greenblatt, *Marvelous Possessions*; Honour, *New Golden Land*; Jennings, *Invasion of America*; and Pearce, *Savagism and Civilization*.

35. There are, of course, exceptions to this rule, as I point out elsewhere in this book. *The Silent Enemy*, a 1930 silent film directed by H. P. Carver and cosponsored by the New York Museum of Natural History, is a rare example of an early film that features an all-Indian cast with "speaking" parts.

36. One of the first and most well-known "vanishing Indians" is Jefferson's eloquent, but interminably tragic Logan described in appendix 4 of *Notes on the State of Virginia*.

37. Kilpatrick, *Celluloid Indians*, 2.

38. It should be noted here that while scholars debate the veracity of the speech and question the issue of its translation into English, the Suquamish Tribe has argued that the words are authentic and praise the speech as "one of the greatest statements ever made concerning the relationship between a people and the earth." This information comes from the Suquamish Tribe's home page, www.suquamish.nsn.us (accessed September 24, 1998).

39. Keep America Beautiful Inc.

40. Bergland, *The National Uncanny*, 1.

41. Bergland, *The National Uncanny*, 4.

42. McGarry, *Ghosts of Futures Past*, 97.

43. Bergland, *The National Uncanny*, 16.

44. Benjamin, "The Work of Art in the Age of Mechanical Reproduction."

45. Cody, *Iron Eyes*, 22.

46. Aleiss, "Native Son," *New Orleans Times-Picayune*, May 26, 1996, D1.

47. Aleiss, "Native Son," *New Orleans Times-Picayune*, May 26, 1996, D1. Ron Russell followed up on Aleiss's allegations and conducted further research he published in "Make-Believe Indian," *New Times Los Angeles*, April 8–14, 1999, 14. According to Russell, Cody and his brothers, also film actors, changed their surname to Cody, ironically adopting the surname of the Wild West shows' most famous performer and publicist, William F. Cody (Buffalo Bill). Both Aleiss and Russell assert that Iron Eyes Cody's father struggled to succeed in the land of his dreams but became involved with the mafia in Louisiana and abandoned the family by escaping to Texas. After his mother remarried, Cody and his siblings also moved to Texas.

48. Russell, "Make-Believe Nation," *New Times Los Angeles*, April 8–14, 1999, 16.

49. Sieg, *Ethnic Drag*, 6.

50. Ginsburg, *Passing and the Fictions of Identity*, 2.

51. Bennett, *Passing Figure*, 36.

52. Bennett, *Passing Figure*, 36.

53. See Robinson, "Forms of Appearance of Value," 250. Harper engages Robin's question more fully in "Passing for What?" 382.

54. Sieg, *Ethnic Drag*, 17.

55. Robinson, "Forms of Appearance of Value," 250.

56. Larsen, *Passing*, 56.

57. Yamamoto, *Masking Selves*, 31.

58. Yamamoto, *Masking Selves*, 31.

59. Quoted in Russell, 16.

60. Quoted in Russell, 16.

61. Andrade, Reply to H-Net List for American Indian Studies. Internet. April 21, 2000.

62. Quoted in Russell, 16. Red Elk's film career has spanned over forty years, and she has starred in productions ranging from the television series *The Virginian* in 1968 to Chris Eyre's *Skins* in 2002.

63. Quoted in Russell, 16.

64. Quoted in Russell, 16.

65. From Robert Tree Cody's website, www.treecody.com (accessed May 31, 2007).

66. Ahhaitty, Reply to H-Net List for American Indian Studies. Internet. April 21, 2000.

67. Ahhaitty, Reply to H-Net List for American Indian Studies. Internet. April 21, 2000.

68. Cody also had a small eponymous role in *The Spirit of '76* (1990).

69. Berlant, *The Female Complaint*, 110.

70. See Bill Donovan, "Iron Eyes Cody Dead at 94," *Navajo Times* 38 (January 17, 1999): A5; and Douglas Casgraux, "Iron Eyes Cody Memorial Held in LA: Los Angeles Indian Community Remembers a Great Man," *News from Indian Country* 13 (May 15, 1999): 9:1A.

71. Donovan, "Iron Eyes Cody Dead at 94," *Navajo Times* 38 (January 17, 1999), A5.

72. Cody and Thompson, *Iron Eyes Cody*, 84.

73. Vizenor, *Manifest Manners*, 62.

74. In Canada individuals of Aboriginal ancestry are not recognized legally because members of their nations are referred to as nonstatus Indians. In the United States, individuals who do not meet eligibility requirements are known as nonenrolled Indians. A. T. Anderson terms those tribes not federally recognized and those individuals not enrolled in any tribe "the Uncounted." See his study of the American Indian Policy Review Commission for more on "the Uncounted, *"Nations Within a Nation.* See also Miller's work on the politics of federal recognition in *Invisible Indigenes*.

75. Eco, *Travels in Hyperreality*, 8. See also Vizenor on the "postindian" in *Manifest Manners*.

76. Owens, *Mixedblood Messages*, 128.

77. An exciting recent movement in critical Native American Studies advocates an examination of Indigenous knowledge production and praxis in order to demonstrate how autochthonous communities embed the philosophical, literary, and cultural precepts of transformation and change into traditional and contemporary intellectual and quotidian practices. See, for example, Acoose, et al., *Reasoning Together*; Allen, *Pocahontas*; Brooks, *The Common Pot*; Justice, *Our Fire Survives the Storm*; Kelsey, *Tribal Theory in Native American Literature*; Turner, *This Is Not a Peace Pipe*; Vizenor, *The People Named the Chippewa*; Warrior, *Tribal Secrets*; and Wong, *Sending My Heart Back Across the Years*.

78. Leuthold, *Indigenous Aesthetics*, 1.

79. Silko, *Ceremony*, 126.

80. Sturken, in *Tangled Memories*, contends that while the United States is imagined as an amnesiac nation dedicated to the process of forgetting rather than remembering, cultural memory is embedded where "cultural

arenas such as art, popular culture, activism, and consumer culture intersect" (3).

81. African Americans have also developed creative responses to "playing Indian." The Mardi Gras Indians of New Orleans are perhaps the best example of this. See, for example, Joseph Roach, "Mardi Gras Indians and Others." George Lipsitz argues that the Mardi Gras Indians, who possess no "direct Indian ancestry," challenge "the core dualism of American racism that defines people as either black or white" in "Mardi Gras Indians." While African American participants may intend to honor "heroic warriors resisting domination" (103) in a mass cultural form acceptable to Euro-American spectators in ways a staged slave uprising would not be, the effect of a group of Native Americans performing blackface in a parade ostensibly to honor what the dominant culture perceives of as African American dances, costumes, or physical traits remains unquestioned.

82. OutKast's performance was one of the more recent examples of what some have called racist appropriations of Native American cultures. Dressed in neon green Mardi Gras Indian regalia and dancing before smoking tipis to their hit "Hey Ya!," African American musicians Andre and Big Boi were interpreted by many Native American activists and organizations—including the Oneida Nation, Suzan Shown Harjo, and Andrew Brother Elk—to be denigrating Native American powwow traditions rather than poking fun at Hollywood stereotypes. See Cristina Verán, "Rap, Rage, and REDvolution," *The Village Voice*, April 20, 2004. Internet access. May 29, 2007.

83. Deloria, *Playing Indian*, 5.

84. See Stahl, "Shania Twain," 29; and Helligar, "Against All Odds." According to an interview with Helligar, Twain changed her first name to Shania, contending that it is an Anishinabe word for "I'm on my way" and states, "My dad's side of the family was the side we grew up with. So it was the Indians that were really our family" (109), although she has been criticized for not being more forthcoming with her racial identity as a white woman.

85. Garroutte, *Real Indians*, 38.

86. Vizenor has termed these mixed-descent individuals "crossbloods" and contends that the narratives that "crossblood" writers create are "invitation[s] to new theories of tribal interpretation" and celebrate communal "survivance" of the vagaries of colonization. See *Manifest Manners*, 14.

87. Roach, "Mardi Gras Indians and Others," 481.

88. See Sollors, *Beyond Ethnicity*, 133.

89. For more on Sylvester Long, see Smith, *Long Lance*.

90. For more on Carter, see Huhndorf's chapter, "The Making of an Indian: 'Forrest' Carter's Literary Inventions," in *Going Native*; Jack Anderson, "Lots of Smoke Rises Around This Indian," *Washington (DC) Post* (February 16, 1984, DC11); Browder, "What Does It Tell Us that We Are so Easily Deceived?"; and Henry Louis Gates, "'Authenticity,' or the Lesson of Little Tree," *New York Times Book Review* 1 (November 24, 1991): 26–30. Other complex "Indian" figures include: William McNary (aka Okah Tubbee), a slave born in Mississippi ca. 1810 who escaped his condition by assuming a Choctaw identity and traveling north where he met his wife, Laah Ceil Manatoi Elaah, a Mohawk-Lenni Lenape missionary, who wrote his 1852 autobiography, *The Life of Okah Tubbee*; Sacheen Little Feather (born Maria Louise Cruz), the Apache- and Yaqui-identified actress who accepted Marlon Brando's 1973 Academy Award for his role in *The Godfather* in a beaded buckskin dress that looked like it may have been borrowed from a western film; Jamake Highwater (born Jay Marks), who published several influential works on Native American philosophy and spirituality, was revealed to be Greek American in the 1980s, and later wrote an autobiography, *Shadow Show*; and Grey Owl (born Archie Belaney), who claimed Apache ancestry but was born in England, developed a childhood fascination with American Indians, and moved to Canada as a young man where he assumed his Indigenous persona. After meeting his Mohawk wife, Gertrude Anahareo Bernard, Grey Owl became a conservationist and published several books. See Bernard, *Devil in Deerskins* and Smith's *From the Land of the Shadows*. More recently, scholar Ward Churchill has been the subject of debate due to his contested claim that he is Cherokee. See Byrd, "'Living My Native Life Deadly'" and Jodi Rave, "Former Professor Churchill Perceived as Impostor by Many," http://www.missoulian.com (accessed June 25, 2009).

4. PROPHESIZING ON THE VIRTUAL RESERVATION

1. Behdad, *A Forgetful Nation*, x and xiii.
2. Gordon, *Ghostly Matters*, 63.
3. Lim, "Spectral Times," 287.
4. This desire to overturn the image of the ghostly Indian on the part of Native Americans is not unique to filmmakers. Nineteenth century Pequot Methodist minister, activist, and writer William Apess employed the image

of the spectral Indian ironically in his autobiography, *A Son of the Forest* (1829). As a child indentured to a white family as a result of poverty and child abuse, Apess narrates a tale of his fears of dark-skinned Indians whom he was told "haunted" the forests surrounding the clearing where he lived. Apess employs this memory to critique the dominant culture not only for instilling a psychological fear of self in Apess, but for not understanding that Euro-Americans are, in Apess's mind, the lurking monsters of which Native Americans should be afraid, given historical evidence. Several years later, Apess wrote a political document, *Indian Nullification* (1835), that reads an Indigenous graveyard not as the final resting place of a culture, but as a repository of connection between past and present. In *Eulogy on King Philip* (1836), Apess completes the process of turning the ghostly Indian on its head by arguing that "King Philip" (the Wampanoag sachem Metacomet) becomes "immortal" (144) through a prophetic narrative that reinvigorates Native American culture in New England, whereas the Puritans become the long-faced, vanished specters of a long-forgotten past. For the collected work of Apess, see O'Connell, *On Our Own Ground*.

5. Lim, "Spectral Times," 288.

6. Roth, "Crossing of Borders and the Building of Bridges."

7. McMaster, "Living on Reservation X," 19.

8. Soja, *Thirdspace*, 5.

9. Soja, *Thirdspace*, 65.

10. Soja, *Thirdspace*, 70.

11. See Embry, *America's Concentration Camps*. For more on the creation and history of reservations, see Deloria and Wilkins, *Tribes, Treaties, and Constitutional Tribulations*; Fixico, *The Invasion of Indian Country in the Twentieth Century*; Frantz, *Indian Reservations in the United States*; and Parchemin, *The Life and History of North America's Indian Reservations*.

12. Agamben, *Homo Sacer*, 159.

13. Gordon, *Ghostly Matters*, 8.

14. Gordon, *Ghostly Matters*, 18.

15. Scheckel, *Insistence of the Indian*, 3.

16. Ryan, *Narrative as Virtual Reality*, 13.

17. Weaver, in *That the People Might Live*, coined the term "communitarian" to refer to the commitment of Native American writers to their respective communities. I propose here that there is a shared "communitarian" impulse on the virtual reservation to interact with, share, and forge

connections both within one's own tribal boundaries as well as through transnational Indigenous movements.

18. González, *Subject to Display*, 36.

19. Pratt defines autoethnographic texts as "instances in which colonized subjects undertake to represent themselves in ways that engage with the colonizer's own terms" in *Imperial Eyes*, 7. In her film, Bowman attempts to document the life of her grandmother, who is clearly an unwilling participant. The film forces the spectator to occupy the position of the prying, persistent, and insensitive ethnographer capturing images of a resistant subject. While this is a productive space through which to rethink the politics of documentary film, the project is controversial and discomfiting because the urban, educated, seemingly progressive filmmaker becomes pathologized in the process.

20. Ginsburg, "Indigenous Media," 95.

21. Singer, *Wiping the War Paint Off the Lens*, 34.

22. Masayesva's films include *Hopi Traditions* (1980), *Hopiit* (1982), and *Ritual Clowns* (1988). He has also published *Hopi Photographers, Hopi Images* (Tucson: University of Arizona Press, 1983) and *Husk of Time: The Photographs of Victor Masayesva* (Tucson: University of Arizona Press, 2006).

23. Singer, *Wiping the War Paint Off the Lens*, 62.

24. For more on Masayesva's work, see Sands and Lewis, "Seeing with a Native Eye."

25. Other Native American filmmakers who have produced experimental work include Jeff Barnaby (Mi'kmaq), Melanie Printup Hope (Tuscarora), Zachary Longboy (Sayasi Dene), Randy Redroad (Cherokee), and Deron Twohatchet (Kiowa/Comanche).

26. Turner, *This Is Not a Peace Pipe*, 110. Emphasis in original.

27. See Fabian, *Time and the Other*.

28. Turner, *This Is Not a Peace Pipe*, 110.

29. Turner, *This Is Not a Peace Pipe*, 110. For more information on Crazy Horse, see Sandoz, *Crazy Horse*.

30. Eyre coproduced *Imprint* with Carolyn Linn and Michael Linn while Michael Linn served as the director, screenplay writer (along with Keith Davenport, another member of Linn Productions), editor (with Marc Linn), and musical score writer. Other Linn family members—Carolyn Linn (executive producer), Marc Linn (assistant director and editor), and Eric Linn (postproduction special effects)—assisted as production and postproduction

crew on the film. Other media produced by Linn Productions include a full-length feature film with a Christian theme, *Into His Arms* (1999); public service videos; television advertisements; and websites. At the West Coast premier of the film in the Zanuck Theater at Fox Studios in Los Angeles, Michael Linn suggested that the film's budget was $50,000—significantly less than most independently produced films.

31. Carolyn Linn, email message to author, July 10, 2009. Because the film crew was so small, Carolyn also "got the movie funded, handled legal issues, hired actors, arranged locations, did scheduling, budget, etc., and then getting distributors."

32. This type of collaboration has historical antecedents in films such as *In the Land of the War Canoes* (1914), *Nanook of the North* (1922), *Dances with Wolves* (1990), and *Black Robe* (1991). *Imprint*'s difference, however, is that Linn Productions is much more transparent about crediting Native American consultants and cocollaborators, and the film's success hinges on the reputation of the Native American producer, Chris Eyre, who is much more well known than the Linn family.

33. Pine Ridge features prominently in Dee Brown's germinal book *Bury My Heart at Wounded Knee* (1970), Johnny Cash's song "Big Foot" (1972), Redbone's single "We Were All Wounded at Wounded Knee" (1973), Buffy Sainte-Marie's song "Bury My Heart at Wounded Knee" (1996), Michael Apted's fiction film *Thunderheart* (1992), Apted's documentary *Incident at Oglala* (1992), the made-for-television biopic *Lakota Woman: Siege at Wounded Knee* (1994), Steven Spielberg's miniseries *Into the West* (2005), and HBO's *Bury My Heart at Wounded Knee* (2007). See also Reinhardt, *Ruling Pine Ridge*; and Jensen, Paul, and Carter, *Eyewitness at Wounded Knee*.

34. Carole Quattro Levine contends that "*Imprint*'s biggest imprint is its portrayal of women; neither victims nor backdrops, they are the force and the soul of the entire story." See "*Imprint* Redefines Native Women in Film," www.nativevue.org (accessed May 31, 2007).

35. Cited in William Goss, "SXSW '07 Interview: *Imprint* Director Michael Linn," http://efilmcritic.com (accessed May 31, 2007); and Joe Leydon, "Imprint," *Variety*, April 9, 2007.

36. Sam Stonefeather is played by Charlie White Buffalo, a Lakota actor and language consultant. Sam's disease is left ambiguous in the film to make his catatonic state with intermittent outbursts seem all the more terrifying. The film's website, however, indicates that he has suffered a stroke. See www.imprintmovie.com (accessed May 31, 2007).

37. Lim, "Spectral Times," 288.

38. *It Starts with a Whisper*, directed by Shelley Niro and Anna Gronau, Women Make Movies (Canada, 1992). The Haudenosaunee Confederacy (also known as the Iroquois or Six Nations) is comprised of the Seneca, Cayuga, Onondaga, Oneida, Mohawk, and Tuscarora Nations. See Bruce Elliott Johansen and Barbara A. Mann, *Encyclopedia of the Haudenosaunee*. The Six Nations Reserve was created in 1784 to shelter the Haudenosaunee survivors of attacks on their villages by George Washington, James Clinton, John Sullivan, and Daniel Brodhead during the so-called American Revolutionary War. The original land grant, known as the Haldimand Grant, was created for the Haudenosaunee followers of Mohawk leader Joseph Brant and is an L-shaped tract of land that stretches from Mohawk Point on Lake Erie north to the Grand River's head past Dundalk and six miles west and east on either side of the river. Since 1847, however, the current reserve occupies only twenty thousand hectacres of land southeast of Brantford. See the Six Nations Reserve's homepage at www.sixnations.ca for more information.

39. Larry Abbott, *A Time of Visions: Interviews with Larry Abbott*, www.britesites.com (accessed May 25, 2007). This online book is a supplement to Abbott's *I Stand in the Center of the Good*.

40. For more on Haudenosaunee conceptions of gender, see Doxtator, *Godi'nigoha,'* a collection of essays that grew out of a symposium and exhibit by the same name; Noel, "Power Mothering"; Spittal, *Iroquois Women*; and Wagner, *Sisters in Spirit*.

41. Serres and Latour, *Conversations on Science, Culture, and Time*, 60.

42. There are several different versions of the Haudenosaunee creation story. See, for example, Converse, *Myths and Legends of the New York State Iroquois*; Cusick, "Creation of the Universe"; Norton, "Iroquois Creation Myth"; and Parker, *Seneca Myths and Folk Tales*. For a critical and comparative account of these creation narratives, see White, *Haudenosaunee Worldviews through Iroquoian Cosmologies*.

43. Doxtator, *Godi'Nigoha,'* 29.

44. Doxtator, *Godi'Nigoha,'* 30.

45. Sobchak, "The Scene of the Screen," 146. Emphasis in original.

46. The Tutelo are a nation related to the Saponi and Ocaneechi whose original homelands are in present-day Virginia and North Carolina. As a result of displacement by other nations and European invaders, they sought

refuge among the Haudenosaunee in the 1740s. They established a village with the Cayuga, which was destroyed in 1779 during what is known as the Sullivan/Clinton campaign, a violent sweep through Haudenosaunee territory ordered by George Washington. After their homes and crops were burned, they scattered with the Cayuga to Ohio and Canada, settling in Canada on the Six Nations Reserve. Although they are considered by some historians to be an "extinct" tribe, descendants live in Virginia, North Carolina, and Canada and continue to revitalize their language and culture. See Vest, "An Odyssey among the Iroquois."

47. Nichols, *Introduction to Documentary*, 39.

48. Varga, "Seeing and Being Seen in Media Culture," 53.

49. Molly Brant was an eighteenth-century Mohawk leader and older sister of Joseph Brant who married Sir William Johnson and helped broker peace between the British and the Iroquois Confederacy. See Carson, "From Clan Mother to Loyalist Chief"; Earle, *The Three Faces of Molly Brant*; and Kenny, *Tekonwatoni/Molly Brant*. E. Pauline Johnson was an internationally recognized poet, fiction writer, and stage performer born on the Six Nations Reserve in the nineteenth century. See Gray, *Flint and Feather* and Strong-Boag and Gerson, *Paddling Her Own Canoe*. Emily General was a twentieth-century teacher and mentor born on the Six Nations Reserve who was fired for refusing to sign the pledge to the Queen in the 1960s. She organized theater productions on the reservation and was considered a traditional spokesperson. For more on Emily General, see Thomas, "Six Articulations on Being Iroquois." Thanks to Shelley Niro for clarifying these figures.

50. Deleuze, *Cinema 2*, 41, 272.

51. Elijah Harper came to national prominence when he refused to sign the Meech Lake Accords in 1990 because the Canadian government had not solicited aboriginal participation in drafting the agreement. His distinguished career began in 1978 when he served as Band Chief of the Red Sucker Lake Reserve in northern Manitoba. He has also served as a Member of Parliament, was appointed Minister of Northern Affairs, encouraged Canadians to work together toward spiritual and cultural healing through national meetings termed "Sacred Assemblies," and was appointed Commissioner of the Indian Claims Commission. For more on Harper, see Turpel and Monture, "Ode to Elijah."

52. Stam, "Beyond Third Cinema," 34.

53. Stam, "Beyond Third Cinema," 37.

54. Shields, *Places on the Margin*, 118.

55. Lear, *Radical Hope*.

56. This project was cocreated by Indigenous artists and scholars Shelley Niro, Lori Blondeau, Ryan Rice; curator and scholar Nancy Marie Mithlo; and anthropologist Elisabetta Frasca.

57. Nancy Marie Mithlo, http://www.nancymariemithlo.com (accessed July 2, 2007).

58. Nancy Marie Mithlo, http://www.nancymariemithlo.com (accessed July 2, 2007).

59. According to one of Shenandoah's visions, the end of the world would be marked by maple trees "dying from the top down." Wall, *To Become a Human Being*, 72.

60. For more on Native American science, see Aikenhead, "Towards a First Nations Cross-Cultural Science and Technology Curriculum"; and Lambert, "From 'Savages' to Scientists." For more on European and Euro-American notions of time and space, see Casey, *The Fate of Place*; Fabian, *Time and the Other*; and Kern, *The Culture of Time and Space*.

61. Talk presented at the University of California–Riverside, February 26, 2007, "Traditional American Indian Medicine: How Culture Can Heal."

62. Reineke, "Overturning the (New World) Order," 66.

63. Reineke, "Overturning the (New World) Order," 70–71.

64. Both Anne McClintock's *Imperial Leather* and Annette Kolodny's *The Lay of the Land* detail the ways in which the "New World" was figured as female and sexually available for colonial conquest, often drawing on nuanced readings of visual culture to demonstrate how European colonial writers deployed the triangulation of race, gender, and geography in order to mark Indigenous peoples as inferior.

65. Silko, *Almanac of the Dead*, 14. I find this very truncated description of prophecy to be problematic because it relies on markers of European "progress"—urban spaces and transportation networks—in order to render the Maya, Aztec, and Inca commensurable with their colonizers. Not only does this replicate the historical elision of other tribal groups in the area, it assumes the inferiority of Indigenous nations whose social, political, and intellectual traditions do not so easily match up with those considered technologically advanced by European standards, but who nonetheless have profoundly complex epistemological systems.

66. See Irwin, *Coming Down from Above*; Mould, *Choctaw Prophecy*; Nabokov, *Native American Testimony*; and Wood, *Transcending Conquest*.

67. Silko, *Storyteller*, 130.
68. Silko, *Storyteller*, 132.
69. Silko, *Storyteller*, 133. Emphasis in original.
70. Silko, *Storyteller*, 135–36. Emphasis in original.
71. Silko, *Storyteller*, 137. Emphasis in original.
72. See Tzvetan Todorov's description of Hernán Cortés as reported by Moctezuma in *The Conquest of America*.
73. See Cave, *Prophets of the Great Spirit*; Peterson, *Native American Prophecies*; and Trafzer, *American Indian Prophets*.
74. Mould, *Choctaw Prophecy*, xxxi.
75. Mould, *Choctaw Prophecy*, 2.
76. Doxtater, "Indigenous Knowledge in the Decolonial Era," 620.
77. Wiget, "Reading Against the Grain," 226.
78. Smith, *Decolonizing Methodologies*.

5. VISUAL SOVEREIGNTY, INDIGENOUS REVISIONS
OF ETHNOGRAPHY, AND *ATANARJUAT*

1. *Nanook of the North* is alternately considered the first documentary and the first ethnographic film, and Flaherty is often credited as the "father of documentary." See Ruby's *Picturing Culture* for a critical analysis of the film's production. For more on the complexities of defining ethnographic and its relationship to Indigenous media productions, see Crawford and Turton, *Film As Ethnography*; Ginsburg, "Screen Memories"; Griffiths, *Wondrous Difference*; Heider, *Ethnographic Film*; and MacDougall, *The Corporeal Image*.

2. Rony, *The Third Eye*, 111. Rony cites an interview with Nayoumealuk, a contemporary Inuit community member, in Claude Massot and Sebastien Regnier's film *Nanook Revisited* (1988): "Each time a scene was shot, as soon as the camera was starting to shoot, [Allakariallak] would burst out laughing. He couldn't help it. Flaherty would tell him—'Be serious.' He couldn't do it. He laughed each time" (123). There is some controversy over the use of the terms "Eskimo" and "Inuit." While "Eskimo" is still employed as a self-designation in some communities in Alaska and particularly among the Yupik, Canadian Indigenous people have preferred the descriptor "Inuit" as a result of conversations begun at the Inuit Circumpolar Conference in 1977. See Gabriella Golinger, "Inuit to Form World Organization," *Nunatsiaq News*, June 22, 1977. "Inuit," in Inuktitut, one of the languages

of Nunavut, Canada's newest territory, means "The Living Ones Who Are Here," according to Inuktitut speaker Rachel Qitsualik, while there is some debate whether "Eskimo" means the less flattering "eater of raw meat" or the more positive Montagnais "snowshoe net-weaver." See Qitsualik, "Esquimaux," *Nunatsiaq News*, June 27, 2003.

3. Rothman, "The Filmmaker as Hunter," 32–33.

4. For more on the ways anthropologists manipulate time in order to make non-Western peoples appear primitive, see Fabian, *Time and the Other*. For more on how the Inuit have been represented in visual and literary culture, see Fienup-Riordan, *Freeze Frame* and Oswalt, *Eskimos and Explorers*.

5. Deloria Jr., *Custer Died for Your Sins*; Rickard, "Sovereignty"; Singer, *Wiping the War Paint Off the Lens*; and Warrior, *Tribal Secrets*.

6. Warrior, "Native Nationalism and Criticism." Warrior prefers the term "intellectual health" to the more commonly used "community healing." See also Warry, *Unfinished Dreams*.

7. The list of contemporary North American Indigenous filmmakers is much too lengthy to list here but includes artists who work in many different genres, from experimental video to full-length feature films, and who treat a remarkable array of subjects, from awareness of gay, lesbian, bisexual, and transgender issues to land rights activism. These include Shelley Niro, Clint Alberta, Chris Eyre, Zachary Longboy, Malinda Maynor, Jeff Barnaby, Alanis Obomsawin, Shirley Cheechoo, Victor Masayesva Jr., Sandra Osawa, Sterlin Harjo, Thirza Cuthand, Randy Redroad, and the collective production companies Arnait Video Productions and Igloolik Isuma. There were at least two Native American directors active during the silent period whose work might also be considered as participating in the project of visual sovereignty—Edwin Carewe and James Young Deer.

8. Ginsburg, "Screen Memories," 39.

9. Ruby, *Picturing Culture*, 88–89. Ruby, however, disagrees with Ginsburg and Rony that Inuit working with Flaherty served as camera operators. He argues that there is no evidence to support this claim, although he provides documentation that Inuit consulted with Flaherty about scenes and future film ideas and that their input was valued (283).

10. For more on Pitseolak's work, see Pitseolak and Eber, *People from Our Side*. I am indebted to Stephanie Fitzgerald for drawing my attention to Pitseolak's work.

11. For more on the history of Inuit Tapirisat and early Inuit interventions into satellite broadcasting service, see Ginsburg's "Screen Memories."

See also Ginsburg and Roth, "First Peoples' Television," 130–31; Roth, *Something New in the Air*; and Sorenson, "The Inuit Broadcasting Corporation and Nunavut."

12. Quoted in Ruby, *Picturing Culture*, 92–93.

13. The photographer Edward S. Curtis later changed the name of his film to the more palatable (at least to twentieth-century white audiences) *In the Land of the War Canoes: A Drama of Kwakiutl Life in the Northwest*. The restored version of a surviving 1972 print was edited by Bill Holm and features new original music and dialogue by Kwakiutl (Kwakwaka'wakw) community members, many of whom consider the film important not only for its visual record of their relatives who were actors in the film, but because of its interpretation of a Kwakiutl story. More recently, Aaron Glass, Brad Evans, and Andrea Sanbord produced a restored version of *In the Land of the Headhunters* featuring the original musical score and intertitles from incomplete original footage held by the Field Museum and UCLA's Film and Television Archive, www.curtisfilm.rutgers.edu (accessed November 8, 2008). The producers make a strong case that Curtis's original film was narrative cinema, not documentary. See also Anne Makepeace's *Coming to Light: Edward S. Curtis and the North American Indians* (coproduction of Anne Makepeace and WNET, 2000), a documentary that discusses Kwakiutl involvement in the production of *In the Land of the Headhunters*, and Wakeman, "Becoming Documentary," which argues against reading *In the Land of the Headhunters* as an authentic artifact of unadulterated Native American culture. I do not read these films as fragments of authenticity but rather as texts that are—to some extent—collaborative, similar to the "as told to" autobiographies of Indigenous people who worked with white amanuenses. In both cases the texts are animated sites of internal investigation into Native American culture and knowledges, however problematic their production and transmission might be.

14. For more on the visual traffic in violence around the Wounded Knee Massacre, see Jensen, Paul, and Carter, *Eyewitness at Wounded Knee*. Much more devastating in its large-scale effects on thousands of Indigenous families, the federal Indian boarding school (or residential school, as it is called in Canada) period of the late-nineteenth and twentieth centuries, during which thousands of children were forced to attend school, assimilate mainstream societal precepts, and be subjected to enforced Christianity, was also a time of intense visual documentation with its "before and after" photographs used to record and legitimate the children's movement from

"savage" to "civilized" subject. For more on the history of boarding schools or residential schools, see Adams, *Education for Extinction*; Child, *Boarding School Seasons*; Grant, *No End of Grief*; Lomawaima, *They Called It Prairie Light*; Miller, *Shingwauk's Vision*; and Trafzer, Keller, and Sisquoc, *Boarding School Blues*.

15. Wilkins and Lomawaima, *Uneven Ground*, 5.

16. For more on sovereignty and its associated discourses, see Deloria and Lytle, *The Nations Within*; Wilkins, *American Indian Sovereignty and the Supreme Court*; and Wunder, *Native American Sovereignty*.

17. Lyons, "Rhetorical Sovereignty."

18. I find Grande's discussion in *Red Pedagogy* constructive for the way it calls for such a continued rethinking of sovereignty as grounded only in Western jurisprudence. She suggests that we "detach and *dethink* the notion of sovereignty from its Western understandings of power and relationships and base it on Indigenous notions of power" (52, emphasis in original). Grande draws from the work of Alfred, whose *Peace, Power, Righteousness* militates against this dependence on conventional understandings of sovereignty. Other Native American scholars have also called for a broader understanding of sovereignty beyond the relationship of tribes to the U.S. judicial system. Following Singer's lead, Clifford Trafzer and Anthony Madrigal term this understanding "cultural sovereignty" and ground it in Indigenous—specifically Serrano—songs, stories, relationships to plants and animals, and geography. See Trafzer, *The People of San Manuel* and Madrigal, *Sovereignty, Land and Water*. In addition, see Barker, *Sovereignty Matters* and Weighill, "The Two-Step Tales of Hahashka."

19. G. Peter Jemison, "Two Row Wampum: Symbol of Sovereignty; Metaphor of Life," http://www.pbs.org/warrior (accessed July 12, 2005).

20. See Spivak's critical definition of "strategic essentialism" in "Subaltern Studies."

21. Igloolik is a northern village in Nunavut, located to the west of Baffin Island on Melville Peninsula. Igloolik is the cultural hub of Nunavut ("our land" in Inuktitut). For more information, see www.gov.nu.ca/nunavut. Dahl, Hicks, and Jull have also collected a series of powerful and engaging essays on the creation and future of Nunavut in *Nunavut: Inuit Regain Control of Their Lands and Their Lives*.

22. Ginsburg, "*Atanarjuat* Off-Screen: From 'Media Reservations' to the World Stage," *American Anthropologist* 105(4): 827–30.

23. Zacharias Kunuk, "The Art of Inuit Storytelling," http://www.isuma .ca/about_us/isuma (accessed February 12, 2003).

24. See Isuma TV's mission statement at http://www.isuma.tv/hi (accessed June 1, 2009). Faye Ginsburg also writes about Isuma TV in her essay, "Beyond Broadcast: Launching NITV on Isuma TV," *In Media Res*, http://mediacommons.futureofthebook.org (accessed May 4, 2009).

25. See http://www.isuma.tv/hi/en/about-us.

26. Igloolik Isuma Inc. and Arnait Video Productions have released over twenty documentary, experimental, and dramatic feature films. Inuit refer to mainstream, European-Canadian culture as "southern," a geographic, rather than racial, ethnic, or economic designation.

27. Faye Ginsburg's "Screen Memories," for example, puts Inuit filmmaking practices into productive dialogue with those of Indigenous filmmakers in Australia.

28. See Solanas and Gettino, "Towards a Third Cinema." See also Ginsburg, "Indigenous Media."

29. Leigh, "Curiouser and Curiouser," 88.

30. While the Inuit occupy a geographically isolated space and have been perceived as archaic hunter-gatherers, Inuit communities do not conceive of technology and new media as external threats to their culture. According to Joe Mauryama of the Inuit-owned Internet service provider Nunavut www Communications, about half the homes in Nunavut's capital, Iqaluit, have Internet access. See Mark Bourrie, "Technology: Internet Heats Up Debate on Arctic Traditions," *Terra Viva Online*, http://www.ipsnews.net (accessed April 10, 2005). Inuit communities employ the Internet for a variety of uses: language preservation (there are many websites that publish in the Inuktitut syllabary and phonetic Inuktitut); updates on local, national, and international news; medical information; online entrepreneurship; and connecting with far-flung villages. Moreover, Christensen writes that the Internet has a "cultural and identity affirming use" among the Inuit. See *Inuit in Cyberspace*, 12. See also Bessire's review of Atanarjuat that discusses the film's multiple audiences, "Talking Back to Primitivism."

31. I use the term "aberrant" here to signal both the sometimes unintentional way that visual anthropology has represented the non-Western world as "Other" through portrayals of unfamiliar (to the West) sartorial, culinary, familial, etc. cultural mores and Umberto Eco's understanding of the "aberrant decoder" as a potentially liberating site that separates the author-filmmaker's intentions from those of the reader-spectator. See Eco, *The Role of the Reader*. Wilton Martinez has explored the possibilities for spectators of reading the putative "aberrant" in ethnographic film as an

invitation to explore the limits of filmic verisimilitude and realism. See Martinez, "Who Constructs Anthropological Knowledge?"

32. Floyd Red Crow Westerman, "Here Come the Anthros" from *Custer Died for Your Sins/The Land Is Your Mother* (Trikont, 1991). Originally released in 1970.

33. Recorded *BBC* Talks, London, June 14, July 25, September 5, 1949. In Ruby, "A Reexamination," 448.

34. Biolosi and Zimmerman, *Indians and Anthropologists*, 3.

35. See Clifford and Marcus, *Writing Culture* for a collection of essays that rethinks the process of fieldwork and the ethnographer's relationship to the ethnographic subject.

36. Hansen, *Babel and Babylon*, 7.

37. Salvage anthropology stressed that Indigenous people were destined to disappear off the face of the earth in a matter of years; therefore, great pains should be taken to preserve any Indigenous material or linguistic artifact. This anxiety-driven form of anthropology was less concerned with representing Indigenous culture as the Indigenous peoples interpreted themselves, but more with the value of future scientific research on tribal/non-Western cultures. James Clifford has criticized salvage anthropology, which was first practiced by Franz Boas and his contemporaries, but whose effects are still felt: "The rationale for focusing one's attention on vanishing lore, for rescuing in writing the knowledge of old people, may be strong (though it depends on local circumstances and cannot any longer be generalized). I do not wish to deny the specific cases of disappearing customs and languages, or to challenge the value of recording such phenomena. I do, however, question the assumption that with rapid change something essential ('culture'), a coherent differential identity, vanishes." See Clifford and Marcus, *Writing Culture*, 112–13. Clifford also charges salvage ethnography with insisting on a binary opposition where Indigenous cultures are presented as dependent, defenseless, and in need of protection by an outsider.

38. White, "Arguing with Ethnography."

39. Key exceptions include Kilpatrick, *Celluloid Indians*; Lewis, *Alanis Obomsawin*; Schiwy, *Indianizing Film*; and Singer, *Wiping the Warpaint*.

40. See Victor Masayesva Jr.'s film *Imagining Indians* (1992) and his interviews with Native American actors detailing their treatment by Hollywood filmmakers, as well as the example of Tonto on *The Lone Ranger* television series, and a whole host of relatively recent films such as *The*

Mission (1986), *Dances with Wolves* (1990), *The New World* (2005), and *Avatar* (2009).

41. "Isuma Feature to Be Launched December 14–16 in Igloolik," *Nunatsiaq News*, December 1, 2000.

42. Ward Churchill argues in *Fantasies of the Master Race* that films with Native American themes must be set in the present in order to do any positive political work. If a film "would alter public perceptions of Native Americans in some meaningful way," he argues, it must be focused on "the real struggles of living native people to liberate themselves from the oppression that has beset them in the contemporary era" (246). I contend, however, that *Atanarjuat* provides a powerful political message about rethinking ethnography and contemporary notions of visual sovereignty precisely through its setting in the past.

43. Senungetuk, *Give or Take a Century*, 25.

44. Fienup-Riordan, *Freeze Frame*, xi–xiii.

45. Claude Levi-Strauss quoted in Angilirq, *Atanarjuat/The Fast Runner*, 9.

46. Even in their publicity decisions, Igloolik Isuma must contend with the vestiges of colonialism and Western conventions. Kunuk has been identified as the director of the film in most media accounts. But because Igloolik Isuma works collaboratively and attempts to engage with Inuit epistemes of the collective and nonhierarchical production style, it would be more appropriate not to focus on a single director.

47. See Robinson, *Isuma*, as well as Huhndorf's discussion of *Atanarjuat's* reception in her review of the film, "*Atanarjuat, The Fast Runner.*"

48. Rony, *The Third Eye*, 12.

49. Ted Mala, a Native Alaskan physician and the son of Inuit film actor Ray Mala, states that not all Inuit communities use the term "shaman" to designate a healer or medicine person (conversation with author, Washington DC, June 22, 2006). However, since Igloolik Isuma Productions employs it in their press materials, I use it here. The Inuktitut word for shaman is *angakoq* (pl. *angakkuit*) and is not loaded with the kinds of negative Christian biases associated with the term "shaman" as evil or as a figure of Satan.

50. Robinson, *Isuma*, 37 and 39.

51. In her dissertation, *Inuit Postcolonial Gender Relations in Greenland*, Karla Jessen Williamson, an Inuit scholar from Greenland, asserts that traditional conceptions of gender equality and complementarity among the Inuit inform contemporary structures of gender equality and, among other things, attitudes towards sexual orientation in Arctic communities.

52. In *Sex Objects*, Doyle locates a queer reading of Herman Melville's *Moby-Dick* in the novel's "boring parts," such as the "Cetology" chapter. I do not find these passages of *Atanarjuat* boring but have screened the film with students who have found the non-Hollywood-action sequences tedious.

53. Leuthold, *Indigenous Aesthetics*, 124–25.

54. Fleming, "Igloolik Video."

55. Fleming, "Igloolik Video," 27.

56. Griffiths, *Wondrous Difference*, xxix.

57. *Igloolik Isuma Production Diary*, http://atanarjuat.com/produc tion_diary (accessed January 14, 2003). Emphasis in original.

58. Faris, "Anthropological Transparency," 171–82.

6. EPILOGUE

1. According to the former school district superintendent, a previous principal at the participating school ended the costuming aspect of the school's observation of the holiday because of the stereotypes it perpetuates. Apparently, he did not want his elementary school–age child to participate in this kind of racist event. The "tradition" was reinstated under his successor.

2. Jonathan Walton, "Giving Thanks to Genocide," blog on *Religion Dispatches*, November 27, 2008. http://www.religiondispatches.org/blog/ humanrights (accessed November 27, 2008).

3. Deloria, *Playing Indian*, 187.

4. For more on the Wampanoag and the historical roots of the Thanksgiving holiday, see Calloway, *After King Philip's War*; Calloway and Salisbury, *Reinterpreting New England Indians and the Colonial Experience*; Jennings, *The Invasion of America*; Salisbury, *Manitou and Providence*; and Siskind, "The Invention of Thanksgiving." See also "After the Mayflower," one of five films in the *We Shall Remain* (2009) PBS series directed by Chris Eyre. For a contemporary Wampanoag perspective on Thanksgiving and Indian costumes, see Fran Fifis, "Native Americans Still Fighting Ignorance at Plimouth," posted on November 28, 2008 at CNN.com, http://e.a.cnn .net/2008/TRAVEL/11/28 (accessed November 28, 2008). According to the article, Linda Coombs and Paula Peters, Mashpee Wampanoag docents at the reconstructed Plimouth Plantation and descendants of the Native Americans whose homelands the Puritans invaded and colonized, regularly face the dominant culture's ignorance about their community. Peters states

that visitors often remark, "I thought we killed all of you," and that they must constantly ask children not to come to the site dressed in Indian costume.

5. There are hundreds of print and online sources about the teaching of Thanksgiving myths to children and alternatives to this practice. Some of these include Bigelow and Peterson, *Rethinking Columbus*; Brouillet, et al, "Teaching About Thanksgiving," (http://cwis.org/fwdp/Americas/tchthnks.txt); Dorris, *American Indian Stereotypes in the World of Children*; Education World, "Are You Teaching the Real Story of the 'First Thanksgiving?'" (http://www.education-world.com); Keeler, "A Native American View—Thanksgiving, Hope, and the Hidden Heart of Evil," Pacific News Service (http://www.pacificnews.org); Williams, "The Politics of Ignorance in Our Schools," *Indian Country Today* June 2, 2009, http://www.indiancountrytoday.com/opinion (accessed June 5, 2009); Oyate, "Deconstructing the Myths of 'The First Thanksgiving'" (www.oyate.org); and Swamp and Printup Jr., *Giving Thanks*. Debbie Reese, a Nambe Pueblo scholar, writes an engaging and important blog on this issue, "American Indians in Children's Literature: Critical Perspectives of Indigenous Peoples in Children's Books, the School Curriculum, Popular Culture, and Society-at-Large" (http://americanindiansinchildrensliterature.blogspot.com).

6. Barbara Gray, "Racism & Stereotyping: The Effects On Our Children, Our Future," http://www.tuscaroras.com (accessed November 14, 2008).

7. Fryberg, "Of Warrior Chiefs and Indian Princesses." For more on Native American intergenerational trauma and the ways in which stereotypes exacerbate this condition, see Duran and Duran, *Native American Postcolonial Psychology*.

8. Fryberg, "Of Warrior Chiefs and Indian Princesses," 216.

9. John Chester Kobylt and Kenneth Robertson Chiampou are the hosts of the *John & Ken Show*, which is broadcast on kfi am-640 in Southern California.

10. "Give Kindergartners a Break: Can't We Spare Children that Young a Thanksgiving Controversy about Political Correctness?" *Los Angeles Times*, November 26, 2008, http://www.latimes.com/news/opinion (accessed November 29, 2008).

11. "Give Kindergartners a Break: Can't We Spare Children that Young a Thanksgiving Controversy about Political Correctness?" *Los Angeles Times*, November 26, 2008, http://www.latimes.com/news/opinion (accessed November 29, 2008).

12. Timothy Lange, Letter to the Editor, *Los Angeles Times*, December 2, 2008, http://www.latimes.com/news/printedition (accessed December 4, 2008).

13. Karl Jacoby, "Which Thanksgiving?" *Los Angeles Times*, November 26, 2008, http://www.latimes.com/news/opinion (accessed December 4, 2008).

14. Karl Jacoby, "Which Thanksgiving?" *Los Angeles Times*, November 26, 2008, http://www.latimes.com/news/opinion (accessed December 4, 2008).

15. Green, "A Tribe Called Wannabee," 30.

16. Green, "A Tribe Called Wannabee," 30.

17. See http://oybm.org for more information about Outta Your Backpack Media. Their video, "Thanks Taking," can be viewed on their website and on YouTube (http://www.youtube.com/watch?v=UQwgyi2UV4o).

18. John Pixley, "These Pilgrims Remind Us of Our Progress." *Claremont (CA) Courier*, December 2, 2009.

19. The Act was not repealed until sixteen years later when in 1866 California had to comply with the Fourteenth Amendment to the U.S. Constitution. It is estimated that hundreds of Native people were enslaved by European settlers and militia, many of whom murdered parents in order to enslave children. For more on nineteenth-century newspaper accounts and the history of the Act, see Heizer, *The Destruction of California Indians*; and Trafzer and Hyer, *"Exterminate Them."*

20. See the following news sources for information about these two events: http://indiancountrynews.info/fullstory.cfm-ID=524.htm and http://www.independent.com/news/2009/mar/12.

21. Nelson, "Introduction: Future Texts."

22. Landzelius, "Introduction: Native on the Net."

23. Ginsburg, "Rethinking the Digital Age." Italics in original.

24. Geiogamah, "American Indian Tribes in the Media Age."

25. See Christen's discussion of a digital economy of knowledge production in her essay "Gone Digital."

26. The AIFI website states that the TTP's purpose is to "develop a *community* of Native media-makers," www.aifisf.com/ttp (accessed November 11, 2008). Emphasis in original.

27. http://www.youtube.com/watch?v=umCzl9_85Vg.

28. Vernallis, *Experiencing Music Video*, ix.

29. See www.blackfire.net for more information about the band. Blackfire

was in Southern California in late November 2008 on a concert tour and was very supportive of the parents who opposed the stereotypical Thanksgiving images at my daughter's school.

30. http://www.rollingstone.com/rockdaily/index.php/2007/09/11.

31. http://www.rollingstone.com/rockdaily/index.php/2007/09/11.

32. For more on the coerced sterilization of Native American women and its eugenics implications, see Carpio, "The Lost Generation"; Lawrence, "The Indian Health Service and the Sterilization of Native American Women"; and Ralstin-Lewis, "The Continuing Struggle Against Genocide." For more on the environmental devastation of the San Francisco Peaks, a mountain range sacred to many Native American nations, see www.savethepeaks.org.

33. See http://www.Indigenousaction.org for more information.

34. Ginsburg, "Rethinking the Digital Age," 302.

35. http://www.youtube.com/watch?v=UXbT8L2WCa4&feature.

36. Nakamura, "Cyberrace," 1676.

37. Terranova, *Network Culture*, 75.

38. Terranova, *Network Culture*, 75.

39. The video can be viewed on YouTube: http://www.youtube.com/watch?v=vmaSF2aIxZM.

40. First Nations United is an organization composed primarily of members of the Dakota and Red Lake Anishinabe nations dedicated to ending violence, undermining stereotypes, and protecting the environment. See http://blogs.myspace.com/waubojeeg and www.firstnationsunited.com.

Bibliography

ARCHIVES

Braun Research Library, Autry
National Center of the
American West
Library of Congress, Motion
Picture Broadcasting and
Recorded Sound Division
Margaret Herrick Library of the
Academy of Motion Picture
Arts and Sciences
William Selig Collection

Harrold Weinberger Papers
Museum of the American West,
Autry National Center of the
American West
National Archives and Records
Administration, Riverside
and Washington DC
National Library, British Film
Institute

PUBLISHED WORKS

Abel, Richard. *Americanizing the Movies and "Movie-Mad" Audiences,
1910–1914.* Berkeley: University of California Press, 2006.

Abbott, Larry. *I Stand in the Center of the Good.* Lincoln: University of
Nebraska Press, 1994.

Acoose, Janet, et al. *Reasoning Together: The Native Critics Collective.*
Norman: University of Oklahoma Press, 2008.

Adams, David Wallace. *Education for Extinction: American Indians and
the Boarding School Experience, 1875–1928.* Lawrence: University of
Kansas Press, 1995.

Agamben, Giorgio. *Homo Sacer: Sovereign Power and Bare Life.* Translated
by Daniel Heller-Roazen. Stanford: Stanford University Press, 1998.

Aikenhead, Glen S. "Towards a First Nations Cross-Cultural Science and
Technology Curriculum." *Science Education* 81:2 (1997): 217–38.

Alarcón, Norma. "Chicana's Feminist Literature: A Re-vision through
Malintzin/or Malintzin: Putting Flesh Back on the Object." In *This
Bridge Called My Back: Writings by Radical Women of Color*, by Gloria
Anzaldúa and Norma Alarcón. New York: Kitchen Table, 1981.

Aleiss, Angela. *Making the White Man's Indian: Native Americans and Hollywood Movies*. Westport CT: Praeger, 2005.

———. "Native Americans: The Surprising Silents." *Cineaste* 21:3 (Summer 1995).

Alfred, Gerald Taiaike. *Peace, Power, Righteousness: An Indigenous Manifesto*. Don Mills, Ontario: Oxford University Press, 1999.

Allen, Chadwick. *Blood Narrative: Indigenous Identity in American Indian and Maori Literary and Activist Texts*. Durham NC: Duke University Press, 2002.

———. "Engaging the Pleasures and Politics of Indigenous Aesthetics." *Western American Literature* 41:2 (Summer 2006): 146–75.

Allmendinger, Blake. "The Queer Frontier." In *The Queer Sixties*, edited by Patricia Juliana Smith, 223–36. New York: Routledge, 1999.

Almaguer, Tómas. *Racial Fault Lines: The Historical Origins of White Supremacy in California*. Berkeley: University of California Press, 1994.

Anderson, A. T. *Nations within a Nation: The American Indian and the Government of the United States*. Chappaqua NY: privately printed, 1976.

Angilirq, Paul Apak, Zacharias Kunuk, Hervé Paniaq, and Pauloosie Qulitalik, eds. *Atanarjuat (The Fast Runner)*. Toronto: Coach House and Isuma, 2002.

Archuleta, Elizabeth. "Refiguring Indian Blood through Poetry, Photography, and Performance Art." *Studies in American Indian Literatures* 17:4 (Winter 2005): 1–26.

Bachman, Gregg Paul, and Thomas J. Slater, eds. *American Silent Film: Discovery of Marginalized Voices*. Carbondale: Southern Illinois University Press, 2002.

Baird, Robert. "Going Indian: Discovery, Adoption, and Renaming toward a 'True American' from *Deerslayer* to *Dances with Wolves*." In *Dressing in Feathers: The Construction of the Indian in American Popular Culture*, edited by S. Elizabeth Bird, 195–209. Boulder: Westview, 1996.

Ballinger, Franchot. *Living Sideways: Tricksters in American Indian Oral Traditions*. Norman: University of Oklahoma Press, 2004.

Bank, Rosemary K. "Representing History: Performing the Columbian Exposition." *Theatre Journal* 54 (2002): 589–606.

Barclay, Barry. "Celebrating Fourth Cinema." *Illusions* 35 (Winter 2003): 7–11.

Barker, Joanne. *Sovereignty Matters: Locations of Contestation and Possibility in Indigenous Struggles for Self-Determination*. Lincoln: University of Nebraska Press, 2005.

Barthes, Roland. *Mythologies*. Translated by Annette Lavers. New York: Noonday, 1972.

Basso, Keith. *Portraits of "the Whiteman": Linguistic Play and Cultural Symbols among the Western Apache*. New York: Cambridge University Press, 1979.

Bataille, Gretchen M., and Charles L. P. Silet. *The Pretend Indians: Images of Native Americans in the Movies*. Ames: Iowa State University Press, 1980.

Baudrillard, Jean. *Simulations*. Translated by Paul Foss, Paul Patton, and Philip Beitchman. New York: Semiotext(e), 1983.

Behdad, Ali. *A Forgetful Nation: On Immigration and Cultural Identity in the United States*. Durham NC: Duke University Press, 2005.

Bennett, Juda. *The Passing Figure: Racial Confusion in Modern American Literature*. New York: Peter Lang, 1998.

Benjamin, Walter. "The Work of Art in the Age of Mechanical Reproduction." In *Illuminations: Essays and Reflections*, edited and with an introduction by Hannah Arendt, and translated by Harry Zohn. New York: Schocken, 1969.

Bergland, Renée. *The National Uncanny: Indian Ghosts and American Subjects*. Hanover NH: University Press of New England, 2000.

Berkhofer, Robert F. *The White Man's Indian: Images of the American Indian from Columbus to the Present*. New York: Random House, 1979.

Berlant, Lauren. *The Female Complaint: The Unfinished Business of Sentimentality in American Culture*. Durham NC: Duke University Press, 2008.

Bernard, Gertrude Anahareo. *Devil in Deerskins: My Life with Grey Owl*. Toronto: Paperjacks, 1972.

Bernardin, Daniel, ed. *The Birth of Whiteness: Race and the Emergence of U.S. Cinema*. New Brunswick NJ: Rutgers University Press, 1996.

Berumen, Frank Javier Garcia. *Brown Celluloid: Latino/a Film Icons and Images in the Hollywood Film Industry*. New York: Vantage, 2003.

Bessire, Lucas. "Talking Back to Primitivism: Divided Audiences, Collective Desires." In *American Anthropologist* 105:4 (2003): 832–37.

Bigelow, Bill, and Bob Peterson, eds. *Rethinking Columbus: The Next 500 Years*. Milwaukee: Rethinking Schools, 1998.

Biolosi, Thomas, and Larry Zimmerman. *Indians and Anthropologists: Vine Deloria Jr. and the Critique of Anthropology*. Tucson: University of Arizona Press, 1997.

Bird, S. Elizabeth, ed. *Dressing in Feathers: The Construction of the Indian in American Popular Culture*. Boulder: Westview, 1996.

Black, Jason Edward. "Remembrances of Removal: Native Resistance to Allotment and the Unmasking of Paternal Benevolence." In *Southern Communications Journal* 72:2 (April 2007): 185–203.

Bokovoy, Matthew F. *The San Diego World's Fairs and Southwestern Memory, 1880–1940*. Albuquerque: University of New Mexico Press, 2005.

Bouvier, Virginia Marie. *Women and the Conquest of California, 1542–1840: Codes of Silence*. Tucson: University of Arizona Press, 2001.

Brooks, Lisa. *The Common Pot: The Recovery of Native Space in the Northeast*. Minneapolis: University of Minnesota Press, 2008.

Browder, Laura. "'What Does It Tell Us that We Are so Easily Deceived?': Imposter Indians." In *American Indian Studies: An Interdisciplinary Approach to Contemporary Issues*, edited by Dane Morrison, 313–34. New York: Peter Lang, 1997.

Brown, Dee. *Bury My Heart at Wounded Knee: An Indian History of the American West*. New York: Holt, Rinehart and Winston, 1970.

Brown, Michael F. *Who Owns Native Culture?* Cambridge: Harvard University Press, 2003.

Brownlow, Kevin. *The War, the West, and the Wilderness*. New York: Knopf, 1978.

Brumble, H. David, III. *American Indian Autobiography*. Berkeley: University of California Press, 1988.

Burden, William Douglas. *Dragon Lizards of Komodo: The Expedition to the Lost World of the Dutch Indies*. New York: Putnam, 1927.

———. *Look to the Wilderness*. Boston: Little Brown, 1960.

Buscombe, Edward. *"Injuns!": Native Americans in the Movies*. London: Reaktion, 2006.

Bush, Alfred L. *The Photograph and the American Indian*. Princeton: Princeton University Press, 1994.

Butters, Gerald R. Jr. *Black Manhood on the Silent Screen*. Lawrence: University of Kansas Press, 2002.

Byrd, Jodi. "'Living My Native Life Deadly': Red Lake, Ward Churchill, and the Discourses of Competing Genocide." *American Indian Quarterly* 31:2 (2007): 310–32.

Calloway, Colin G. *After King Philip's War: Presence and Persistence in Indian New England*. Hanover NH: Dartmouth College Press, 1997.

——,and Neil Salisbury. *Reinterpreting New England Indians and the Colonial Experience*. Charlottesville: University of Virginia Press, 2003.

Carpio, Myla Vicenti. "The Lost Generation: American Indian Women and Sterilization Abuse," *Social Justice* 31:4 (2004): 40–53.

Carson, James Taylor. "From Clan Mother to Loyalist Chief." In *Sifters: Native American Women's Lives*, edited by Theda Perdue, 48–59. New York: Oxford, 2001.

Casey, Edward S. *The Fate of Place: A Philosophical History*. Berkeley: University of California Press, 1997.

Cave, Alfred A. *Prophets of the Great Spirit: Native American Revitalization Movements in Eastern North America*. Lincoln: University of Nebraska Press, 2006.

Cheng, Anne Anlin. *The Melancholy of Race: Psychoanalysis, Assimilation, and Hidden Grief*. New York: Oxford University Press, 2001.

Child, Brenda. *Boarding School Seasons: American Indian Families, 1900–1940*. Lincoln: University of Nebraska Press, 2000.

Chow, Rey. *Woman and Chinese Modernity: The Politics of Reading between East and West*. Minneapolis: University of Minnesota Press, 1991.

Christen, Kimberly. "Gone Digital: Aboriginal Remix and the Cultural Commons." *International Journal of Cultural Property* 12 (2005): 315–45.

Christiansen, Neil Blair. *Inuit in Cyberspace: Embedding Offline Identities Online*. Copenhagen: Museum Tusculanum Press, 2003.

Chude-Sokei, Louis. *The Last "Darky" Bert Williams, Black-on-Black Minstrelsy, and the African Diaspora*. Durham NC: Duke University Press, 2006.

Churchill, Ward. *Fantasies of the Master Race: Literature, Cinema, and the Colonization of American Indians*. Monroe ME: Common Courage, 1992.

Clastres, Pierre. "What Makes Indians Laugh." *Society Against the State*. Translated by Robert Hurley in collaboration with Abe Stein. New York: Zone, 1987.

Clifford, James. "On Ethnographic Allegory." In *Writing Culture: The Poetics and Politics of Ethnography*, edited by James Clifford and George E. Marcus. Berkeley: University of California Press, 1986.

——. *The Predicament of Culture: Twentieth-Century Ethnography, Literature, and Art*. Cambridge: Harvard University Press, 1988.

Cody, Iron Eyes. *Indian Talk: Hand Signals of the American Indian*. Happy Camp CA: Naturegraph, 1970.

———. *My Life as a Hollywood Indian*. New York: Everest, 1982.

———, and Bertha Parker Cody. *Indian Legends*. New York: Noteworthy, 1980.

Cody, Iron Eyes, and Marietta Thompson. *Iron Eyes Cody, The Proud American*. Madison NC: Empire, 1988.

Cohen, Paula Marantz. *Silent Film and the Triumph of the American Myth*. New York: Oxford University Press, 2001.

Collins, James. *Understanding Tolowa Histories: Western Hegemonies and Native American Responses*. New York: Routledge, 1997.

Converse, Harriet Maxwell. *Myths and Legends of the New York State Iroquois*. Edited and annotated by Arthur C. Parker. Albany: University of the State of New York, 1908.

Corbey, Raymond. "Ethnographic Showcases, 1870–1930." *Cultural Anthropology* 8:3 (1993): 338–69.

Crawford, Peter Ian, and David Turton. *Film As Ethnography*. Manchester UK: Manchester University Press, 1992.

Cusick, David. *David Cusick's Sketches of Ancient History of the Six Nations*. Edited by William Beauchamp. Fayetteville NY: Beauchamp, 1892.

Dahl, Jens, Jack Hicks, and Peter Jull, eds. *Nunavut: Inuit Regain Control of Their Lands and Their Lives*. Copenhagen: International Work Group for Indigenous Affairs, 2000.

Davis, Mike. *Dead Cities and Other Tales*. New York: The New Press, 2002.

de Léry, Jean. *History of a Voyage to the Land of Brazil*. Translated by Janet Whatley. Berkeley: University of California Press, 1990.

Deleuze, Gilles. *Cinema 2: The Time-Image*. Translated by Hugh Tomlinson and Robert Galeta. Minneapolis: University of Minnesota Press, 1989.

———. *Proust and Signs*. Translated by Richard Howard. Minneapolis: University of Minnesota Press, 2000.

Deloria, Philip. *Indians in Unexpected Places*. Lawrence: University of Kansas Press, 2004.

———. *Playing Indian*. New Haven: Yale University Press, 1999.

Deloria, Vine Jr. *Custer Died for Your Sins: An Indian Manifesto*. New York: Avon Books, 1969.

———, and Clifford M. Lytle. *The Nations Within: The Past, Present, and Future of American Indian Sovereignty*. Austin: University of Texas Press, 1984.

Deloria, Vine Jr., and David E. Wilkins. *Tribes, Treaties, and Constitutional Tribulations*. Austin: University of Texas Press, 2000.

Dench, Ernest A. *Making the Movies*. New York: Macmillan, 1915.

Dippie, Brian W. *The Vanishing American: White Attitudes and U.S. Policy*. Middletown CT: Wesleyan University Press, 1982.

Dorris, Michael A. *American Indian Stereotypes in the World of Children: A Reader and Bibliography*. Lanham MD: Scarecrow, 1999.

Doxtator, Deborah. "Godi'nigoha': The Women's Mind and Seeing through to the Land." In *Godi'nigoha': The Women's Mind*. Brantford, Ontario: Woodland Cultural Center, 1997.

Doxtater, Michael. "Indigenous Knowledge in the Decolonial Era." *American Indian Quarterly* 28:3–4 (2004): 618–33.

Doyle, Jennifer. *Sex Objects: Art and the Dialectics of Desire*. Minneapolis: University of Minnesota Press, 2006.

Dozier, Edward P. *The Pueblo Indians of North America*. New York: Holt, Rinehart and Winston, 1970.

Drinnon, Richard. *Facing West: The Metaphysics of Indian-Hating and Empire-Building*. Minneapolis: University of Minnesota Press, 1980.

DuBois, W. E. B. *The Souls of Black Folk*. Chicago: McClurg, 1903.

Dunn, Carolyn. "I Am the Real Hollywood Indian (or The Trick Is Going Home) *for Paula Gunn Allen*." In *Through the Eye of the Deer: An Anthology of Native American Women Writers*, edited by Carolyn Dunn and Carol Comfort. San Francisco: Aunte Lute, 1999.

Duran, Eduardo, and Bonnie Duran. *Native American Postcolonial Psychology*. Albany: State University of New York Press, 1995.

Earle, Thomas. *The Three Faces of Molly Brant: A Biography*. Dallas: Quarry, 1997.

Eco, Umberto. *The Role of the Reader: Explorations in the Semiotics of Texts*. Bloomington: Indiana University Press, 1979.

———. *Travels in Hyperreality*. San Diego: Harcourt Brace Jovanovich, 1986.

Elmer, Jonathan. "A Response to Jonathan Arac." *American Literary History* 20:1–2 (2008).

Embry, Carlos B. *America's Concentration Camps: The Facts about Our Indian Reservations Today*. New York: McKay, 1956.

Fabian, Johannes. *Time and the Other: How Anthropology Makes Its Object*. New York: Columbia University Press, 1983.

Faery, Rachel Blevins. *Cartographies of Desire: Captivity, Race, and Sex in the Shaping of an American Nation*. Norman: University of Oklahoma Press, 1999.

Faris, James C. "Anthropological Transparency: Film, Representation, and Politics." In *Film As Ethnography*, edited by Peter Ian Crawford and David Turton. Manchester UK: Manchester University Press, 1992: 171–82.

Fear-Segal, Jacqueline. *White Man's Club: Schools, Race, and the Struggle of Indian Acculturation*. Lincoln: University of Nebraska Press, 2007.

Feng, Peter X. *Identities in Motion: Asian American Film and Video*. Durham NC: Duke University Press.

Fiedler, Leslie A. *The Return of the Vanishing American*. New York: Stein and Day, 1968.

Fielder, Mildred. *Sioux Indian Leaders*. Seattle: Superior, 1975.

Fienup-Riordan, Anne. *Freeze Frame: Alaska Eskimos in the Movies*. Seattle: University of Washington Press, 1995.

Fixico, Donald L. *Termination and Relocation: Federal Indian Policy, 1945–1960*. Albuquerque: University of New Mexico Press, 1986.

———. *The Invasion of Indian Country in the Twentieth Century: American Capitalism and Tribal Natural Resources*. Boulder: University Press of Colorado, 1998.

Fleming, Kathleen. "Igloolik Video: An Organic Response from a Culturally Sound Community." *Inuit Art Quarterly* 11:1 (1996): 26–34.

Fowler, Don D., and Catherine S. Fowler, "The Uses of Natural Man in Natural History." In *Columbian Consequences: The Spanish Borderlands in Pan-American Perspective, vol. 3*, edited by David Hurst Thomas, 37–71. Washington DC: Smithsonian Institution Press, 1990.

Francis, David. *The Imaginary Indian: The Image of the Indian in Canadian Culture*. Vancouver: Arsenal Pulp, 1995.

Francis, Terri. "Embodied Fiction, Melancholy Migrations: Josephine Baker's Cinematic Celebrity." *Modern Fiction Studies* 51:4 (2005): 824–45.

Frantz, Klaus. *Indian Reservations in the United States: Territory, Sovereignty, and Economic Change*. Chicago: University of Chicago Press, 1999.

Friar, Ralph E., and Natasha A. Friar. *The Only Good Indian . . . The Hollywood Gospel*. New York: Drama Book Specialists, 1972.

Fryberg, Stephanie A. "Of Warrior Chiefs and Indian Princesses: The Psychological Consequences of American Indian Mascots." *Basic and Applied Social Psychology* 30 (2008): 208–18.

Gaines, Jane. "Fire and Desire: Race, Melodrama, and Oscar Micheaux." In *Black American Cinema*, edited by Manthia Diawara, 49–70. New York: Routledge, 1993.

Gallop, Jane. *Anecdotal Theory*. Durham NC: Duke University Press, 2002.

Garroutte, Eva Marie. *Real Indians: Identity and the Survival of Native America*. Berkeley: University of California Press, 2003.

Gaudio, Michael. *Engraving the Savage: The New World Techniques of Civilization*. Minneapolis: University of Minnesota Press, 2008.

Geiogamah, Hanay. "American Indian Tribes in the Media Age." In *Native America: Portrait of the Peoples*, edited by Duane Champagne, 701–10. Detroit: Visible Ink, 1994.

Gillis, Michael, and Michael Magliari. *John Bidwell and California: The Life and Writings of a Pioneer, 1841–1900*. Spokane WA: Arthur H. Clark, 2003.

Ginsburg, Elaine. *Passing and the Fictions of Identity*. Durham NC: Duke University Press, 1996.

Ginsburg, Faye. "Atanarjuat Off-Screen: From 'Media Reservations' to the World Stage." *American Anthropologist* 105:4 (2004): 827–30.

——. "Indigenous Media: Faustian Contract or Global Village?" *Cultural Anthropology* 6:1 (February 1991): 92–112.

——. "Rethinking the Digital Age." In *Global Indigenous Media: Cultures, Poetics, Politics*, edited by Pamela Wilson and Michelle Stewart, 287–305. Durham NC: Duke University Press, 2008.

——. "Screen Memories: Resignifying the Traditional in Indigenous Media." In *Media Worlds: Anthropology on New Terrain*, edited by Faye Ginsburg, Lila Abu-Lughod, and Brian Larkin, 39–57. Berkeley: University of California Press, 2002.

——, and Lorna Roth. "First Peoples' Television." In *Television Studies*, edited by Toby Miller. London: British Film Institute, 2002.

González, Jennifer A. *Subject to Display: Reframing Race in Contemporary Installation Art*. Cambridge: Massachusetts Institute of Technology Press, 2008.

Gonzalez, Mario, and Elizabeth Cook-Lynn. *The Politics of Hallowed Ground: Wounded Knee and the Struggle for Indian Sovereignty*. Champaign: University of Illinois Press, 1998.

Gordon, Avery. *Ghostly Matters: Haunting and the Sociological Imagination*. Minneapolis: University of Minnesota Press, 1996.

Grande, Sandy. *Red Pedagogy: Native American Social and Political Thought*. Lanham MD: Rowan and Littlefield, 2004.

Grant, Agnes. *No End of Grief: Indian Residential Schools in Canada*. Winnipeg: Pemmican Publications, 1992.

Gray, Charlotte. *Flint and Feather: The Life and Times of E. Pauline Johnson*. Toronto: HarperCollins, 2002.

Green, Rayna. "A Tribe Called Wannabee: Playing Indian in America and Europe." *Folklore* 99:1 (1988).

———. "The Indian in Popular Culture." In *The Handbook of North American Indians IV*, edited by Wilcomb Washburn. Washington DC: Smithsonian Institution Press, 1988.

———. "The Pocahontas Perplex: The Image of Indian Women in American Culture." In *Native Women's History in Eastern North America before 1900*, edited by Rebecca Kugel and Lucy Eldersveld Murphy. Lincoln: University of Nebraska Press, 2007.

Greenblatt, Stephen. *Marvelous Possessions: The Wonder of the New World*. Chicago: University of Chicago Press, 1991.

Griffiths, Alison. *Wondrous Difference: Cinema, Anthropology, and Turn-of-the-Century Visual Culture*. New York: Columbia University Press, 2002.

Guerrero, Ed. *Framing Blackness: The African American Image in Film*. Philadelphia: Temple University Press, 1993.

Gunn Allen, Paula. *Pocahontas: Medicine Woman, Spy, Entrepreneur, Diplomat*. San Francisco: Harper, 2003.

Hansen, Miriam. *Babel and Babylon: Spectatorship in American Silent Film*. Cambridge: Harvard University Press, 1991.

Harmon, Alexandra. *Indians in the Making: Ethnic Relations and Indian Identities around Puget Sound*. Berkeley: University of California Press, 1998.

Harper, Phillip Brian. "Passing for What? Racial Masquerade and the Demands of Upward Mobility." *Callaloo* 21:2 (Spring 1998).

Harrington, M. Raymond. "Abenaki Witch Story." *Journal of American Folklore* 14:54 (July–September 1901): 160.

———. "Man and Beast in Gypsum Cave." *The Desert Magazine* 4:6 (April 1940): 3–5, 34.

Hearne, Joanna. "'The Cross-Heart People': Race and Inheritance in the Silent Western." *Journal of Popular Film and Television* 30 (Winter 2003): 181–96.

Heider, Karl. *Ethnographic Film*. Austin: University of Texas Press, 1976.

Heizer, Robert F., ed. *The Destruction of California Indians*. Lincoln: University of Nebraska Press, 1993.

Helligar, Jeremy. "Against All Odds." *People Weekly* 51 (June 14, 1999): 108–12.

Hiesinger, Ulrich W. *Indian Lives: A Photographic Record from the Civil War to Wounded Knee*. New York: Prestel, 1994.

Highwater, Jamake. *Shadow Show: An Autobiographical Insinuation*. New York: Alfred Van Der Marek Editions, 1986.

Hilger, Michael. *From Savage to Nobleman: Images of Native Americans in Film*. Lanham MD: Scarecrow, 1995.

Honour, Hugh. *The New Golden Land: European Images of America from the Discovery to the Present Time*. New York: Pantheon, 1975.

Huhndorf, Shari M. "*Atanarjuat, The Fast Runner*: Culture, History, and Politics in Inuit Media," in *American Anthropologist* 105:4 (2003): 822–26.

———. *Going Native: Indians in the American Cultural Imagination*. Ithaca NY: Cornell University Press, 2001.

Hyde, Lewis. *Trickster Makes This World: Mischief, Myth and Art*. New York: North Point Press, 1999.

Irwin, Lee. *Coming Down from Above: Prophecy, Resistance, and Renewal in Native American Religions*. Norman: University of Oklahoma Press, 2008.

Jackson, Ronald H., and Edward Castillo. *Indians, Franciscans and Spanish Colonization: The Impact of the Mission System on the California Indians*. Albuquerque: University of New Mexico Press, 1995.

Jay, Gregory S. "'White Man's Book No Good': D. W. Griffith and the American Indian." *Cinema Journal* 39:4 (2000): 3–26.

Jefferson, Thomas. *Notes on the State of Virginia*. New York: Penguin, 1998. Originally published in English in 1787.

Jennings, Francis. *The Invasion of America: Indians, Colonialism and the Cant of Conquest*. Chapel Hill: University of North Carolina Press, 1975.

Jensen, Richard E., Eli Paul, and John E. Carter, eds. *Eyewitness at Wounded Knee*. Lincoln: University of Nebraska Press, 1991.

Johansen, Bruce Elliott, and Barbara Alice Mann. *Encyclopedia of the Haudenosaunee (Iroquois Confederacy)*. Westport CT: Greenwood, 2000.

Johnson, Troy, and Donald Fixico. *The American Indian Occupation of Alcatraz Island*. Lincoln: University of Nebraska Press, 2008.

Jones, Sally L. "The First but Not the Last of the 'Vanishing Indians': Edwin Forrest and Mythic Re-Creations of the Native Population." In *Dressing in Feathers: The Construction of the Indian in American Popular Culture*, edited by S. Elizabeth Bird, 13–27. Boulder: Westview, 1996.

Jorgensen, Joseph G. *The Sun Dance Religion: Power for the Powerless*. Chicago: University of Chicago Press, 1986.

Justice, Daniel Heath. *Our Fire Survives the Storm: A Cherokee Literary History*. Minneapolis: University of Minnesota Press, 2006.

Keefe, Julia. "Mildred Barley." *National Museum of the American Indian* (Summer 2009): 50–52.

Kelsey, Penelope Myrtle. *Tribal Theory in Native American Literature: Dakota and Haudenosaunee Writing and Indigenous Worldviews*. Lincoln: University of Nebraska Press, 2008.

Kenny, Maurice. *Tekonwatoni/Molly Brant (1735–1795: Poems of War)*. Buffalo: White Pine, 1992.

Kern, Stephen. *The Culture of Time and Space, 1880–1918*. Cambridge: Harvard University Press, 1983.

Kidwell, Clara Sue. "Indian Women as Cultural Mediators." *Ethnohistory* 39:2 (Spring 1992): 97–107.

Kilpatrick, Jacquelyn. *Celluloid Indians: Native Americans and Film*. Lincoln: University of Nebraska Press, 1999.

Kolodny, Annette. *The Lay of the Land: Metaphor as Experience and History in American Life and Letters*. Chapel Hill: University of North Carolina Press, 1984.

Kraut, Anthea. *Choreographing the Folk: The Dance Stagings of Zora Neale Hurston*. Minneapolis: University of Minnesota Press, 2008.

Krupat, Arnold. *The Turn to the Native: Studies in Criticism and Culture*. Lincoln: University of Nebraska Press, 1996.

Lambert, Lori. "From 'Savages' to Scientists: Mainstream Science Moves Toward Recognizing Traditional Knowledge." *Tribal College Journal* 15:1 (Fall 2003): 10–13.

Landzelius, Kyra. "Introduction: Native on the Net." In *Native on the Net:*

Indigenous and Diasporic Peoples in the Virtual Age, edited by Kyra Landzelius, 1–42. New York: Routledge, 2006.

Larsen, Nella. *Passing*. New York: Penguin, 2003.

Lawrence, Jane. "The Indian Health Service and the Sterilization of Native American Women," *American Indian Quarterly* 24:3 (2000): 400–419.

Lear, Jonathan. *Radical Hope: Ethics in the Face of Cultural Devastation*. Cambridge: Harvard University Press, 2006.

Leigh, Michael. "Curiouser and Curiouser." In *Back of Beyond: Discovering Australian Film and Television*, edited by Scott Murray, 70–89. Sydney: Australian Film Commission, 1988.

Leuthold, Steven. *Indigenous Aesthetics: Native Art, Media, and Identity*. Austin: University of Texas Press, 1998.

———. "Rhetorical Dimensions of Native American Documentary." *Wicaso Sa Review* 16:2 (2001).

Lewis, Randolph. *Alanis Obomsawin: The Vision of a Native Filmmaker*. Lincoln: University of Nebraska Press, 2003.

Lightfoot, Kent G. *Indians, Missionaries, and Merchants: The Legacy of Colonial Encounters on the California Frontiers*. Berkeley: University of California Press, 2006.

Lim, Bliss Cua. "Spectral Times: The Ghost Film as Historical Allegory." *positions* 9:2 (2001).

Limerick, Patricia Nelson. *The Legacy of Conquest: The Unbroken Past of the American West*. New York: Norton, 1987.

Lincoln, Kenneth. *Indi'n Humor: Bicultural Play in Native America*. New York: Oxford University Press, 1993.

Lippard, Lucy R., ed. *Partial Recall*. New York: New Press, 1992.

Lipsitz, George. "Mardi Gras Indians: Counter-Narrative in Black New Orleans." *Cultural Critique* 10 (Autumn 1988).

Littlefield, Daniel F., ed. *The Life of Okah Tubbee*. Lincoln: University of Nebraska Press, 1988.

Littlefield, Daniel F., and James W. Parins. *A Biobibliography of Native American Writers, 1772–1924: A Supplement*. Lanham MD: Scarecrow, 1981.

Lomawaima, Tsianina, K. *They Called It Prairie Light: The Story of Chilocco Indian School*. Lincoln: University of Nebraska Press, 1994.

Long Lance, Chief Buffalo Child. *Long Lance*. New York: Cosmopolitan, 1928.

Lopez, Tiffany. "María Cristina Mena: Turn-of-the-Century La Malinche, and Other Tales of Cultural (Re)Construction." In *Tricksterism in Turn-of-the-Century American Literature: A Multicultural Perspective*, edited by Elizabeth Ammons and Annette White-Parks, 21–45. Hanover: University Press of New England, 1994.

Lorde, Audre. "The Master's Tools Will Never Dismantle the Master's House." In *Sister Outsider: Essays and Speeches*, edited by Audre Lorde. Freedom CA: Crossing, 1984.

Lott, Eric. *Love and Theft: Blackface Minstrelsy and the American Working Class*. New York: Oxford University Press, 1993.

Louvish, Simon. *Keystone: The Life and Clowns of Mack Sennett*. New York: Faber and Faber, 2003.

Lowrey, Carolyn. *The First One Hundred Noted Men and Women of the Screen*. New York: Moffat, Yard, and Company, 1920.

Lyman, Christopher. *The Vanishing Race and Other Illusions: Photographs of Indians by Edward Curtis*. New York: Pantheon, 1982.

Lyons, Scott Richard. "Rhetorical Sovereignty: What Do American Indians Want from Writing?" *College Composition and Communication* 51:3 (2000): 447–68.

———. *X-Marks: Native Signatures of Assent*. Minneapolis: University of Minnesota Press, 2010.

MacDougall, David. *The Corporeal Image: Film, Ethnography, and the Senses*. Princeton: Princeton University Press, 2006.

Madrigal, Anthony. *Sovereignty, Land and Water*. Riverside: California Center for Native Nations Press, 2008.

Magnusson, Magnus, and Hermann Pálsson, trans. *The Vinland Sagas: The Norse Discovery of America*. New York: Penguin, 1965.

Mahar, Karen Ward. *Women Filmmakers in Early Hollywood*. Baltimore: Johns Hopkins University Press, 2006.

Malécot, André. "Luiseño, A Structural Analysis I: Phonology." *International Journal of American Linguistics* 29:2 (April 1963): 89–95.

Marez, Curtis. "Subaltern Soundtracks: Mexican Immigrants and the Making of Hollywood Cinema." *Aztlan: A Journal of Chicano Studies* 29:1 (Spring 2004): 57–82.

Martin, Wendy. "'Remembering the Jungle': Josephine Baker and Modernist Parody." In *Prehistories of the Future: The Primitivist Project and the Culture of Modernism*, edited by Elazar Barkan and Ronald Bush. Stanford: Stanford University Press, 1995: 310–25.

Martinez, Wilton. "Who Constructs Anthropological Knowledge?: Toward a Theory of Ethnographic Film Spectatorship." In *Film As Ethnography*, edited by Peter Ian Crawford and David Turton, 131–61. Manchester UK: Manchester University Press, 1992.

Marubbio, M. Elise. *Killing the Indian Maiden: Images of Native American Women in Film*. Lexington: University of Kentucky Press, 2006.

Masayesva, Victor, and Erin Younger. *Hopi Photographers, Hopi Images*. Tucson: University of Arizona Press, 1983.

——, and Beverly Singer. *Husk of Time: The Photographs of Victor Masayesva*. Tucson: University of Arizona Press, 2006.

McBride, Bunny. *Molly Spotted Elk: A Penobscot in Paris*. Norman: University of Oklahoma Press, 1995.

McCaffrey, Donald W., and Christopher P. Jacobs. *Guide to the Silent Years of American Cinema*. Westport CT: Greenwood, 1999.

McClintock, Anne. *Imperial Leather: Race, Gender, and Sexuality in the Colonial Conquest*. New York: Routledge, 1995.

McGarry, Molly. *Ghosts of Futures Past: Spiritualism and the Cultural Politics of 19th-Century America*. Berkeley: University of California Press, 2008.

McMaster, Gerald. "Living on Reservation X." In *Reservation X*, edited by Gerald McMaster. Seattle: University of Washington Press, 1999.

Mechling, Jay. "'Playing Indian' and the Search for Authenticity in Modern White America." In *Prospects 5*, edited by Jack Salzman, 17–34. New York: Burt Franklin, 1980.

Meek, Barbara A. "And the Injun Goes 'How!': Representations of Indian English in White Public Space." *Language in Society* 35:1 (2006).

Meyer, Carter Jones, and Diana Royer, eds. *Selling the Indian: Commercializing and Appropriating Indian Cultures*. Tucson: University of Arizona Press, 2001.

Micco, Melinda. "Tribal Re-Creations: Buffalo Child Long Lance and Black Seminole Narratives." In *Re-Placing America: Conversations and Constellations*, edited by Ruth Hsu, Cynthia Franklin, and Suzanna Kosanke, 74–81. Honolulu: University of Hawai'i Press, 2000.

Michel, Manuel. "Toward a Fourth Cinema: Prologue." *Wide Angle* 21:3 (1993): 70–81.

Mihesuah, Devon. *American Indians: Stereotypes and Realities*. Atlanta: Clarity, 1996.

Miller, Bruce Granville. *Invisible Indigenes: The Politics of Nonrecognition*. Lincoln: University of Nebraska Press, 2003.

Miller, J. R. *Shingwauk's Vision: A History of Native Residential Schools.* Toronto: University of Toronto Press, 1996.

———. *Sweet Promises: A Reader of Indian–White Relations in Canada.* Toronto: University of Toronto Press, 1991.

Miller, Mark Edwin. *Forgotten Tribes: Unrecognized Indians and the Federal Acknowledgement Process.* Lincoln: University of Nebraska Press, 2004.

Miyao, Daisuke. *Sessue Hayakawa: Silent Cinema and Transnational Stardom.* Durham NC: Duke University Press, 2007.

Morris, Meaghan. "Banality in Cultural Studies." In *Logics of Television,* edited by Patricia Mellencamp. Bloomington: Indiana University Press, 1990.

Morris, Richard, and Philip Wander. "Native American Rhetoric: Dancing in the Shadows of the Ghost Dance." *Quarterly Journal of Speech* 76:2 (1990): 164–91.

Morris, Roy Jr. *Sheridan: The Life and Wars of General Phil Sheridan.* New York: Crown, 1992.

Morrison, Toni. *Playing in the Dark: Whiteness and the Literary Imagination.* New York: Vintage, 1993.

Moses, L. G. "'The Father Tells Me So!' Wovoka: The Ghost Dance Prophet." *American Indian Quarterly* 9:3 (Summer 1985): 335–51.

———. *Wild West Shows and the Images of American Indians, 1883–1933.* Albuquerque: University of New Mexico Press, 1996.

Mould, Tom. *Choctaw Prophecy: A Legacy of the Future.* Tuscaloosa: University of Alabama Press, 2003.

Murray, David. *Forked Tongues: Speech, Writing & Representation in North American Indian Texts.* Bloomington: Indiana University Press, 1991.

Musser, Charles. *Before the Nickelodeon: Edwin S. Porter and the Edison Manufacturing Company.* Berkeley: University of California Press, 1999.

Nabokov, Peter, ed. *Native American Testimony: A Chronicle of Indian-White Relations from Prophecy to the Present.* New York: Penguin, 1992.

Nagel, Joanne. *American Indian Ethnic Renewal: Red Power and the Resurgence of Identity and Culture.* New York: Oxford University Press, 1996.

Nakamura, Lisa. "Cyberrace." PMLA 123:5 (October 2008): 1673–82.

Nelson, Alondra. "Introduction: Future Texts," *Social Text* 20:2 (2002): 1–15.

Nichols, Bill. *Introduction to Documentary*. Bloomington: Indiana University Press, 2001.

Noel, Jan. "Power Mothering: The Haudenosaunee Model." In *"Until Our Hearts Are on the Ground": Aboriginal Mothering, Oppression, Resistance, and Rebirth*, edited by D. Memee Lavell-Harvard and Jeannette Corbiere Lavell, 76–93. Toronto: Demeter, 2006.

Noriega, Chon, ed. *Chicanos and Film: Representation and Resistance*. Minneapolis: University of Minnesota Press, 1992.

Norton, John. *The Journal of Major John Norton, 1816*. Toronto: Champlain Society, 1970.

O'Connell, Barry. *On Our Own Ground: The Complete Writings of William Apess, A Pequot*. Amherst: University of Massachusetts Press, 1992.

Orians, G. Harrison. *The Cult of the Vanishing American: A Century View*. Toledo: Chittenden, 1934.

Orvell, Miles. *The Real Thing: Imitation and Authenticity in American Culture, 1880–1940*. Chapel Hill: University of North Carolina Press, 1989.

Oswalt, Wendell H. *Eskimos and Explorers*. Lincoln: University of Nebraska Press, 1999.

Owens, Louis. *Mixedblood Messages: Literature, Film, Family, Place*. Norman: University of Oklahoma Press, 1998.

Parchemin, Richard, ed. *The Life and History of North America's Indian Reservations*. North Dighton MA: J. G. Press, 1998.

Parker, Arthur C. *Seneca Myths and Folk Tales*. Buffalo NY: Publications of the Buffalo Historical Society, 1923. Volume 27. Reprint: University of Nebraska Press: 1989.

———. *Skunny Wundy: Seneca Indian Tales*. New York: Doran, 1926.

———. *The Code of Handsome Lake, the Seneca Prophet*. Albany: New York State Education Department, 1913.

Parker, Bertha. "California Indian Cradles." *Masterkey* 14 (1940): 89–96.

———. "Yurok Tales: Wohpekumen's Tales as Told by Jane Van Stralen to Bertha Parker Cody." *Masterkey* 15 (1941): 228–31.

Patchell, Beverly Sourjohn. "Traditional American Indian Medicine: How Culture Can Heal." Talk presented at the University of California–Riverside, February 26, 2007.

Pearce, Roy Harvey. *Savagism and Civilization: A Study of the Indian and the American Mind*. Berkeley: University of California Press, 1988.

Peterson, Scott. *Native American Prophecies*. Minneapolis: Paragon House, 1999.

Pitseolak, Peter, and Dorothy Eber. *People from Our Side: An Eskimo Life Story in Words and Photographs*. Bloomington: Indiana University Press, 1975.

Porter, Joy. *To Be an Indian: The Life of Iroquois-Seneca Arthur Caswell Parker*. Norman: University of Oklahoma Press: 2001.

Pratt, Mary Louise. *Imperial Eyes: Travel Writing and Transculturation*. New York: Routledge, 1992.

Price, John A. "The Stereotyping of North American Indians in Motion Pictures." *Ethnohistory* 20:2 (1973): 153–71.

Rabinowitz, Lauren. "Past Imperfect: Feminism and Social Histories of Silent Film." *Cinemas* 16:1 (2005): 21–34.

Ralstin-Lewis, D. Marie. "The Continuing Struggle Against Genocide: Indigenous Women's Reproductive Rights." *Wicazo Sa Review* 20:1 (2005): 71–95.

Rasenberger, Jim. *High Steel: The Daring Men Who Built the World's Greatest Skyline*. New York: HarperCollins, 2004.

Red Crow Westerman, Floyd. "Here Come the Anthros." In *Custer Died for Your Sins/The Land Is Your Mother*. Munich: Trikont, 1991.

Reineke, Yvonne. "Overturning the (New World) Order: Of Space, Time, Writing, and Prophecy in Leslie Marmon Silko's *Almanac of the Dead*." *Studies in American Indian Literatures* 10:3 (Fall 1998): 65–84.

Reinhardt, Akim D. *Ruling Pine Ridge: Oglala Lakota Politics from the IRA to Wounded Knee*. Lubbock: Texas Tech University Press, 2007.

Rickard, Jolene. "Sovereignty: A Line in the Sand." In *Strong Hearts: Native American Visions and Voices*, edited by Peggy Roalf, 51–59. New York: Aperture, 1995.

Roach, Joseph. "Mardi Gras Indians and Others: Genealogies of American Performance." *Theatre Journal* 44 (1992).

Robertson, Dorothy. "Tatzumbie Was Born in the Tragic Year." *Desert Magazine* 22 (November 1959): 25.

Robinson, Amy. "Forms of Appearance of Value: Homer Plessy and the Politics of Privacy." In *Performance and Cultural Politics*, edited by Elin Diamond. London: Routledge, 1996.

Robinson, Gillian, ed. *Isuma: Inuit Studies Reader*. Montreal: Isuma, 2004.

Rodríguez, Dylan. *Forced Passages: Imprisoned Radical Intellectuals and the U.S. Prison Regime*. Minneapolis: University of Minnesota Press, 2006.

Roediger, David R. *The Wages of Whiteness: Race and the Making of the American Working Class*. New York: Verso, 1991.

Rogin, Michael. *Blackface, White Noise: Jewish Immigrants in the Hollywood Melting Pot*. Berkeley: University of California Press, 1996.

Rollins, Peter C., and John E. O'Connor, eds. *Hollywood's Indian: The Portrayal of the Native American in Film*. Lexington: University of Kentucky Press, 1998.

Romero, Lora. "Vanishing Americans: Gender, Empire, and New Historicism." *American Literature* 63:3 (1991): 385–404.

Rony, Fatimah Tobing. *The Third Eye: Race, Cinema, and Ethnographic Spectacle*. Durham NC: Duke University Press, 1996.

Rosaldo, Renato. *Culture and Truth: The Remaking of Social Analysis*. Boston: Beacon, 1989.

Rosen, Philip. *Change Mummified: Cinema, Historicity, Theory*. Minneapolis: University of Minnesota Press, 2001.

Rosenthal, Nicholas G. "Representing Indians: Native American Actors on Hollywood's Frontier." *The Western Historical Society* 36:3 (2005): 329–52.

Ross, Stephen J. *Working-Class Hollywood: Silent Film and the Shaping of Class in America*. Princeton: Princeton University Press, 1999.

Roth, Lorna. *Something New in the Air: The Story of First Peoples Television Broadcasting in Canada*. Montreal: McGill-Queen's University Press, 2005.

———. "The Crossing of Borders and the Building of Bridges: Steps in the Construction of the Aboriginal Peoples Television Network in Canada." *International Journal of Communication Studies* 62:3–4 (2000).

Rothman, William. "The Filmmaker as Hunter: Robert Flaherty's *Nanook of the North*." In *Documenting the Documentary: Close Readings of Documentary Film and Video*, edited by Barry Keith and Jeannette Sloniowski, 23–39. Detroit: Wayne State University Press, 1998.

Ruby, Jay. *Picturing Culture: Explorations of Film & Anthropology*. Chicago: University of Chicago Press, 2000.

———. "A Reexamination of the Early Career of Robert J. Flaherty." *Quarterly Review of Film Studies* 5, no. 4 (Fall 1980): 448.

Ruoff, A. LaVonne Brown, and Donald B. Smith, eds. *Life, Letters &*

Speeches: George Copway (Kahgegagahbowh). Lincoln: University of Nebraska Press, 1997.

Ryan, Marie-Laure. *Narrative as Virtual Reality: Immersion and Interactivity in Literature and Electronic Media*. Baltimore: Johns Hopkins University Press, 2001.

Rydell, Robert W. *All the World's a Fair: Visions of Empire at American International Expositions, 1876–1916*. Chicago: University of Chicago Press, 1984.

Saldívar-Hull, Sonia. *Feminism on the Border: Chicana Gender Politics and Literature*. Berkeley: University of California Press, 2000.

Salisbury, Neil. *Manitou and Providence: Indians, Europeans, and the Making of New England*. New York: Oxford University Press, 1984.

Sands, Kathleen M., and Allison Sekaquaptewa Lewis. "Seeing with a Native Eye: A Hopi Film on Hopi." *American Indian Quarterly* 14:4 (Autumn 1990): 387–96.

Sandoz, Mari. *Crazy Horse: Strange Man of the Oglalas*. Lincoln: University of Nebraska Press, 1961.

Scheckel, Susan. *The Insistence of the Indian: Race and Nationalism in Nineteenth-Century American Culture*. Princeton: Princeton University Press, 1998.

Schiwy, Freya. *Indianizing Film: Decolonization, the Andes, and the Question of Technology*. Piscataway NJ: Rutgers University Press, 2009.

Schlereth, Thomas. *Victorian America: Transformations of Everyday Life, 1876–1915*. New York: Harper-Perennial, 1991.

Scott, James C. *Domination and the Arts of Resistance: Hidden Transcripts*. New Haven: Yale University Press, 1992.

Sedgwick, Eve Kosofsky. *Between Men: English Literature and Male Homosocial Desire*. New York: Columbia University Press, 1985.

Seigworth, Gregory J. "Banality for Cultural Studies." *Cultural Studies* 14:2 (2000): 227–68.

Senungetuk, Joseph E. *Give Or Take a Century: An Eskimo Chronicle*. San Francisco: Indian Historian, 1971.

Serres, Michel with Bruno Latour. *Conversations on Science, Culture, and Time*. Ann Arbor: University of Michigan Press, 1995.

Shea Murphy, Jacqueline. *"The People Have Never Stopped Dancing": Native American Modern Dance Histories*. Minneapolis: University of Minnesota Press, 2007.

Shields, Rob. *Places on the Margin: Alternative Geographies of Modernity*. New York: Routledge, 1991.

Shively, JoEllen. "Cowboys and Indians: Perceptions of Western Films Among American Indians and Anglos." In *Film and Theory: An Anthology*, edited by Robert Stam and Toby Miller, 345–60. Malden MA: Blackwell, 2000.

Shoemaker, Nancy. *American Indian Population Recovery in the Twentieth Century*. Albuquerque: University of New Mexico Press, 1999.

Shohat, Ella, and Robert Stam. *Unthinking Eurocentrism: Multiculturalism and the Media*. New York: Routledge, 1994.

Sieg, Katrin. *Ethnic Drag: Performing Race, Nation, and Sexuality in West Germany*. Ann Arbor: University of Michigan Press, 2002.

Silko, Leslie Marmon. *Almanac of the Dead*. New York: Penguin, 1991.

———. *Ceremony*. New York: Penguin, 1977.

———. *Storyteller*. New York: Arcade, 1981.

Simmon, Scott. *The Invention of the Western Film: A Cultural History of the Genre's First Half-Century*. Cambridge: Cambridge University Press, 2003.

Simpson, Audra. "On Ethnographic Refusal: Indigeneity, 'Voice,' and Colonial Citizenship." *Junctures* 9 (December 2007).

Singer, Beverly R. *Wiping the War Paint Off the Lens: Native American Film and Video*. Minneapolis: University of Minnesota Press, 2001.

Siskind, Janet. "The Invention of Thanksgiving: A Ritual of American Nationality," *Critique of Anthropology* 12 (1992): 167–91.

Slotkin, Richard. *Gunfighter Nation: The Myth of the Frontier in Twentieth-Century America*. New York: Maxwell Macmillan, 1992.

———. *Regeneration through Violence: The Mythology of the American Frontier, 1600–1800*. Middletown CT: Wesleyan University Press, 1973.

———. *The Fatal Environment: The Myth of the Frontier in the Age of Industrialization*. New York: Atheneum, 1985.

Smith, Andrea. *Conquest: Sexual Violence and American Indian Genocide*. Cambridge MA: South End, 2005.

———. "Social-Justice Activism in the Academic Industrial Complex." *Journal of Feminist Studies in Religion* 23:2 (2007): 140–45.

Smith, Andrew Brodie. *Shooting Cowboys and Indians: Silent Western Films, American Culture, and the Birth of Hollywood*. Boulder: University Press of Colorado, 2003.

Smith, Donald B. *Chief Buffalo Child Long Lance: The Glorious Impostor*. Red Deer, Alberta: Red Deer, 1999.

———. *From the Land of the Shadows: The Making of Grey Owl*. Seattle: University of Washington Press, 1999.

———. *Long Lance: The True Story of an Impostor*. Lincoln: University of Nebraska Press, 1983.

Smith, Jeanne Rosier. *Writing Tricksters: Mythic Gambols in American Ethnic Literature*. Berkeley: University of California Press, 1997.

Smith, Linda Tuhawai. *Decolonizing Methodologies: Research and Indigenous Peoples*. London: Zed, 1999.

Smith, Paul Chaat. *Everything You Know about Indians Is Wrong*. Minneapolis: University of Minnesota Press, 2009.

———. "Ghost in the Machine." In *Strong Hearts: Native American Visions and Voices*, edited by Peggy Roalf. New York: Aperture Foundation, 1995.

Smoak, Gregory Ellis. *Ghost Dances and Identity: Prophetic Religion in American Indian Ethnogenesis in the Nineteenth Century*. Berkeley: University of California Press, 2006.

Snipp, C. Matthew. *American Indians: The First of This Land*. New York: Russell Sage Foundation, 1989.

Sobchack, Vivian. "The Scene of the Screen: Envisioning Photographic, Cinematic, and Electronic 'Presence.'" In *Carnal Thoughts: Embodiment and Moving image Culture*, edited by Vivian Sobchack, 135–62. Berkeley: University of California Press, 2004.

Soja, Edward W. *Thirdspace: Journeys to Los Angeles and Other Real and-Imagined Places*. Malden MA: Blackwell, 1996.

Solanas, Fernando, and Octavio Gettino. "Towards a Third Cinema: Notes and Experiences for the Development of a Cinema of Liberation in the Third World," *Afterimage* 3 (Summer 1971): 16–30. Reprinted in *Film and Theory: An Anthology*, edited by Robert Stam and Toby Miller, 265–86. Malden MA: Blackwell, 2000.

Sollors, Werner. *Beyond Ethnicity: Consent and Descent in American Culture*. New York: Oxford University Press, 1986.

Sorenson, Laila. "The Inuit Broadcasting Corporation and Nunavut." In *Nunavut: Inuit Regain Control of Their Land and Their Lives*, edited by Jens Dahl, Jack Hicks, and Peter Jull. Copenhagen: International Working Group for Indigenous Affairs, 2000.

Spittal, William Guy, ed. *Iroquois Women: An Anthology*. Ohsweken, Ontario: Iroquois Publishing and Craft Supplies, 1990.

Spivak, Gayatri Chakravorty. "Subaltern Studies: Deconstructing Historiography." In *Subaltern Studies IV*, edited by Ranajit Guha. New Delhi: Oxford University Press, 1985.

Spotted Elk, Molly. *Katahdin: Wigwam's Tales of the Abnaki Tribe and a Dictionary of Penobscot and Passamaquoddy Words with French and English Translations*. Orono: Maine Folklife Center, 2003.

Stahl, Jerry. "Shania Twain." *Esquire* 125 (April 1996).

Stam, Robert. "Beyond Third Cinema: The Aesthetics of Hybridity." In *Rethinking Third Cinema*, edited by Anthony R. Guneratne and Wimal Dissanayake. New York: Routledge, 2003.

Standing Bear, Luther. *My People the Sioux*. Lincoln: University of Nebraska Press, 1975.

Stover, Dale. "Postcolonial Sun Dancing at Wakpamni Lake." In *Readings in Indigenous Religions*, edited by Graham Harvey, 173–93. New York: Continuum International, 2002.

Strong, Pauline Turner, and Barrik van Winkle. "'Indian Blood': Reflections on the Reckoning and Refiguring of Native North American Identity." *Cultural Anthropology* 11:4 (November 1996): 547–76.

Strong-Boag, Veronica, and Carole Gerson. *Paddling Her Own Canoe: The Times and Texts of E. Pauline Johnson (Tekahionwake)*. Toronto: University of Toronto Press, 2000.

Strongheart, Nipo. "History in Hollywood." *Wisconsin Magazine of History* 38 (Autumn 1954).

Sturken, Marita. *Tangled Memories: The Vietnam War, the AIDS Epidemic, and the Politics of Remembering*. Berkeley: University of California Press, 1997.

Sturtevant, Victoria. "'But Thing's is Changin' Nowadays An' Mammy's Gettin' Bored': Hattie McDaniel and the Culture of Dissemblance." *Velvet Light Trap* 44 (Fall 1999): 68–79.

Swamp, Jake, and Erwin Printup Jr. *Giving Thanks: A Native American Good Morning Message*. New York: Lee & Low, 1997.

TallBear, Kimberly. "DNA, Blood, and Racializing the Tribe." *Wicazo Sa Review* 18:1 (Spring 2003): 81–107.

Taylor, Clyde R. "Black Silence and the Politics of Representation." In *Oscar Micheaux and His Circle*, edited by Pearl Bowser, Jane Gaines, and Charles Musser, 3–10. Bloomington: Indiana University Press, 2001.

Taylor, Diana. *The Archive and the Repertoire: Performing Cultural Memory in the Americas*. Durham NC: Duke University Press, 2003.

Taylor, Drew Hayden, ed. *Me Funny*. Vancouver: Douglas & McIntyre, 2006.

Taylor, Graham D. *The New Deal and American Indian Tribalism: The Administration of the Indian Reorganization Act, 1934–1945*. Lincoln: University of Nebraska Press, 1980.

Terranova, Tiziana. *Network Culture: Politics for the Information Age*. London: Pluto, 2007.

Theriault, Madeline Katt. *Moose to Moccasins: The Story of Ka Kita Wa Pa No Kwe*. Toronto: Natural Heritage/Natural History, 1992.

Thomas, Jeffrey M. "Six Articulations on Being Iroquois." In *Lifeworlds—Artscapes: Contemporary Iroquois Art*, edited by Sylvia S. Kasprycki and Doris I. Stambrau, 45–54. Frankfurt-am-Main, Germany: Museum der Weltkulturen, 2003.

Todorov, Tzvetan. *The Conquest of America*. New York: Harper Perennial, 1984.

Trafzer, Clifford. *The People of San Manuel*. Patton CA: San Manuel Band of Mission Indians, 2002.

——,ed. *American Indian Prophets: Religious Leaders and Revitalization Movements*. Sacramento: Sierra Oaks, 1986.

——,and Joel Hyer, eds. *"Exterminate Them!": Written Accounts of the Murder, Rape, and Slavery of Native Americans During the California Gold Rush, 1848–1868*. East Lansing: Michigan State University Press, 1999.

Trafzer, Clifford, Jean Keller, and Lorene Sisquoc, eds. *Boarding School Blues: Revisiting American Indian Educational Experience*. Lincoln: University of Nebraska Press, 2006.

Trigger, Bruce G. "Early Native North American Responses to European Contact: Romantic versus Rationalistic Interpretations." *The Journal of American History* 77:4 (March 1991): 1195–1215.

Turner, Dale. *This Is Not a Peace Pipe: Towards a Critical Indigenous Philosophy*. Toronto: University of Toronto Press, 2006.

Turpel, Mary Ellen, and Patricia A. Monture. "Ode to Elijah: Reflections of Two First Nations Women on the Rekindling of Spirit at the Wake for the Meech Lake Accord." *Queen's Law Journal* 15 (1990): 345–59.

Valaskakis, Gail Guthrie. "Sacajawea and Her Sisters: Images and Native Women." *Indian Country: Essays on Contemporary Native Culture*. Waterloo, Ontario: Wilfred Laurier University Press, 2005: 125–50.

Varga, Darrell. "Seeing and Being Seen in Media Culture: Shelley Niro's *Honey Moccasin*." *CineAction* 61 (Spring 2003).

Vernallis, Carol. *Experiencing Music Video: Aesthetics and Cultural Context.* New York: Columbia University Press, 2004.

Vest, Jay Hansford C. "An Odyssey among the Iroquois: A History of Tutelo Relations in New York." *American Indian Quarterly* 29:1–2 (Winter–Spring 2005): 124–55.

Vestal, Stanley. "The Hollywoodean Indian." *Southwest Review* 21 (1936): 418–23.

Vizenor, Gerald. *Fugitive Poses: Native American States of Absence and Presence.* Lincoln, University of Nebraska Press, 1998.

———. *Manifest Manners: Postindian Warriors of Survivance.* Hanover NH: University Press of New England, 1994.

———. *The Heirs of Columbus.* Hanover NH: Wesleyan University Press, 1991.

———. *The People Named the Chippewa: Narrative Histories.* Minneapolis: University of Minnesota Press, 1984.

———. "Trickster Discourse: Comic Holotropes and Language Games." In *Narrative Chance: Postmodern Discourse on American Indian Literatures*, edited by Gerald Vizenor, 187–212. Norman: University of Oklahoma Press, 1993.

———. *Wordarrows: Native States of Literary Sovereignty.* Lincoln: University of Nebraska Press, 2003.

Wagner, Sally Roesch. *Sisters in Spirit: Haudenosaunee (Iroquois) Influence on Early American Feminists.* Summertown TN: Native Voices, 2001.

Wakeman, Pauline. "Becoming Documentary: Edward Curtis's *In the Land of the Headhunters* and the Politics of Archival Reconstruction," *Canadian Review of American Studies* 36:3 (2006): 293–309.

Wall, Steve. *To Become a Human Being: The Message of Tadodaho Chief Leon Shenandoah.* Charlottesville VA: Hampton Roads, 2001.

Wallace, Anthony F. C. *Death and Rebirth of the Seneca.* New York: Knopf, 1970.

Wallace, Ernest, and E. Adamson Hoebel. *The Comanches: Lords of the South Plains.* Norman: University of Oklahoma Press, 1952.

Warrior, Robert Allen. "Native Nationalism and Criticism." Paper presented at the University of California–Riverside, March 2007.

———. "Organizing Native American and Indigenous Studies." *PMLA* 123:5 (October 2008): 1683–91.

———. *Tribal Secrets: Recovering American Indian Literary Traditions.* Minneapolis: University of Minnesota Press, 1994.

———, and Paul Chaat Smith. *Like a Hurricane: The Indian Movement from Alcatraz to Wounded Knee.* New York: New Press, 1996.

Warry, Wayne. *Unfinished Dreams: Community Healing and the Reality of Aboriginal Self-Government.* Toronto: University of Toronto Press, 1998.

Washburn, Wilcomb E. *The Assault on Indian Tribalism: The General Allotment Law (Dawes Act of 1887).* Philadelphia: Lippincott, 1975.

Weaver, Hilary N. "Indigenous Identity: What Is It, and Who *Really* Has It?" *American Indian Quarterly* 25:2 (Spring 2001): 240–55.

Weaver, Jace. "More Light Than Heat: The Current State of Native American Studies." *American Indian Quarterly* 3:2 (Spring 2007): 233–55.

———. *That the People Might Live: Native American Literatures and Native American Community.* New York: Oxford University Press, 1997.

Weighill, Tharon. "The Two-Step Tales of Hahashka: Experiences in Corporeality and Embodiment in Aboriginal California," PhD dissertation, University of California–Riverside, 2004.

Weinberg, Marjorie. *The Real Rosebud: The Triumph of a Lakota Woman.* Lincoln: University of Nebraska Press, 2004.

White, Jerry. "Arguing with Ethnography: The Films of Bob Quinn and Pierre Perrault." *Cinema Journal* 42:2 (2003): 101–24.

White, Kevin J. *Haudenosaunee Worldviews through Iroquoian Cosmologies: The Published Narratives in Historical Context.* PhD dissertation, State University of New York, 2007.

White, Patricia. *unInvited: Classical Hollywood Cinema and Lesbian Representability.* Bloomington: Indiana University Press, 1999.

Wiget, Andrew. "Reading Against the Grain: Origin Stories and American Literary History." *American Literary History* 3:2 (Summer 1991): 209–31.

Wilkins, David E. *American Indian Sovereignty and the Supreme Court: The Masking of Justice.* Austin: University of Texas Press, 1997.

———, and K. Tsianina Lomawaima. *Uneven Ground: American Indian Sovereignty and Federal Law.* Norman: University of Oklahoma Press, 2002.

Williamson, Karla Jessen. *Inuit Postcolonial Gender Relations in Greenland.* PhD dissertation, University of Aberdeen, 2006.

Wilson, Lori Lee. "A Lady's Life in the Gold Rush," *Wild West* (August 1999).

Wilson, Pamela, and Michelle Stewart. *Global Indigenous Media: Cultures, Poetics and Politics*. Durham NC: Duke University Press, 2008.

Wilson, Raymond. *Ohiyesa: Charles Eastman, Santee Sioux*. Champaign: University of Illinois Press, 1983.

Wilson, Terry P. "Blood Quantum: Native American Mixed Bloods." In *Racially Mixed People in the United States*, edited by Maria P. P. Root. Newbury Park CA: Sage, 1992.

Womack, Craig. *Red on Red: Native American Literary Separatism*. Minneapolis: University of Minnesota Press, 1999.

Wong, Hertha Dawn Sweet. *Sending My Heart Back Across the Years: Tradition and Innovation in Native American Autobiography*. New York: Oxford University Press, 1992.

Wood, Stephanie. *Transcending Conquest: Nahua Views of Spanish Colonial Mexico*. Norman: University of Oklahoma Press, 2003.

Worth, Sol, and John Adair. *Through Navajo Eyes: An Exploration in Film Communication and Anthropology*. Bloomington: Indiana University Press, 1972.

Wunder, John R. *Native American Sovereignty*. New York: Garland, 1996.

Yamamoto, Traise. *Masking Selves, Making Subjects: Japanese American Women, Identity, and the Body*. Berkeley: University of California Press, 1999.

Yellow Bird, Michael. "What We Want to Be Called: Indigenous Peoples' Perspectives on Racial and Ethnic Labels." *American Indian Quarterly* 23:2 (1999): 1–21.

Yellow Robe, Chauncy. "The Menace of the Wild West Show." In *Legends of Our Times: Native Cowboy Life*, edited by Morgan Baillargeon and Leslie Heyman Tepper (Seattle: University of Washinton Press, 1998), 211–12.

Yellow Robe, Rosebud. *Tonweya and the Eagles and Other Lakota Tales*. New York: Dial Books for Young Readers, 1979.

Yoshino, Kenji. *Covering: The Hidden Assault on Our Civil Rights*. New York: Random House, 2007.

Index

*Page numbers in italics refer to
illustrations*

Aaron, Victor, 62
Abbott, Larry, 170
Abel, Richard, 59
Aboriginal Australians, 234
Aboriginal Peoples Television
    Network (APTN), 63
Abshire, May, 126–27
Act for the Government and
    Protection of the Indians
    (California), 230–31, 289n19
Adair, John, 156, 247n28
African Americans, 242n8; cin-
    ematic self-representation
    by, 21, 53–54; and passing,
    128–29, 272n81
Agamben, Georgio, 151
Ahhaitty, Glenda, 134
AIM. *See* American Indian
    Movement (AIM)
Alberta, Clint, 156, 281n7
Alcatraz Island, 107–8
Alcott, Louisa Mae, 263–64n85
Aleiss, Angela, 17, 248n43,
    252n65; and Iron Eyes Cody
    identity, 104, 126–27, 270n47
Alexie, Sherman, ix, xi, 18, 209
Allakariallak, 190, *192*, 195, 280n2
Allen, Chadwick, 248n36
Allmendinger, Blake, 47–48

Almanac of the Dead (Silko),
    183–85
The American Anthropologist,
    116
American Film Institute, 95
American Indian Citizenship Act
    (1924), 56, 68
American Indian Film Institute
    (AIFI), 234–35, 243n3
American Indian Movement
    (AIM), 107, 108, 161
American Indian Registry for the
    Performing Arts, 243n3
American Indians in Film and
    Television (AIF&T), 243n3
Anaana (Mary Kunuk, 2001), 157,
    203–4
Anderson, A. T., 137, 271n74
Andrade, Ron, 132
Anishinabe, 42–43, 86, 90, 141,
    181, 238, 255n16, 264n87
anthropologists, 116, 156, 187,;
    intrusion of into Indigenous
    communities, 205–6; Othering
    of non-Western world by,
    284–85n31; salvage, 63, 86,
    207, 285n37
Apess, William, 273–74n4
Aphed Elk, 56–57, 255n16
Apocalypto (Gibson, 2006), 34,
    259n45
April in Paris, 97

Arbuckle, Roscoe "Fatty," 25, 55, 74–79
Archuleta, Elizabeth, 110
Arnait Video Productions, 157, 159, 202–3, 218, 281n7, 284n26
assimilation: forced, 36, 60, 66–67, 91, 260n51; as theme in films, 65, 67–68, 79, 82; and passing, 129
Atanarjuat (The Fast Runner) (Kunuk, 2000), 209–20, 215, 219; cultural and political work of, 9, 193, 217–18, 232, 286n42; dual audience of, 193, 203, 212–13; ethnographic elements in, 9, 193, 220; humor and play in, 212–13, 220; and Inuit oral tradition, 9, 205, 209, 220; plot, 204–5; shamanistic theme in, 204, 212, 214, 215, 218; visual sovereignty in, 9, 193
Avatar (Cameron, 2009), 34, 285n40

Bailey, Mildred, 100, 266n116
Baker, Josephine, 53, 58, 95
Bakhtin, Mikhail, 228
Bald Eagle, Dave, 161, *165*
Barclay, Barry, 18–19, 247n32
Barnaby, Jeff, 275n25, 281n7
Barrett, Etta Moten, 53
Basso, Keith, 42
Baudrillard, Jean, 36, 153, 252n68
Beach, Adam, 62, 259n45
Beavers, Louise, 53
Bedard, Irene, 259n45

Behdad, Ali, 145
Benais, Wahwahtay, 238
Benally, Clayson, 235
Benally, Jeneda, 235, 236
Benally, Klee, 235, 236
Benito Cereno (Melville), 81
Benjamin, Walter, 126
Bennett, Juda, 128
Bergland, Renée, 120, 124, 125
Bergson, Henri, 44
Berlant, Lauren, 135
Bidwell, John, 263–64n85
The Birth of a Nation, 70
blackface, 70, 71, 74, 226
Blackfire, 235
boarding schools, 30, 64, 250–51n54; depiction of in film, 65, 66–67, 68; and forced assimilation, 60–61, 260n51, 282–83n14
Boas, Franz, 211, 285n37
Boles, John, 23
Boston Tea Party, 70, 139, 223
Bowman, Arlene, 155–56, 275n19
Boyarin, Jonathan, 183
Brando, Marlon, 104, 267n3
Brandon, Henry, 262n67
Brant, Molly, 176, 278n49
Broken Arrow (Daves, 1950), x, 102
Bronson, Charles, 262n67
Brotherston, Gordon, 183
Brumble, H. David, III, 116
Burdeau, George, 247n28
Burden, William Douglas, 86–87, 90, 91, 266n109
Bureau of Indian Affairs (BIA), 1, 2, 108, 268n28

Bury My Heart at Wounded Knee
(HBO, 2007), 259n45
Butler, Judith, 131

California: Act for the
Government and Protection
of the Indians in, 230–31,
289n19; Gold Rush, 85,
263–64n85; Native Americans
from, 85, 263n83. *See also*
Hollywood, colony of Native
American entertainers in
Cameron, James, 34
Camp, Margaret, 255n16
Canada, 180, 199; Indigenous
recognition in, 271n74;
Indigenous self-representation
in, 62–63, 280–81n2; Nunavut,
200–201, 263n21; outlawing of
Indigenous cultural activities
in, 90–91; residential school
system in, 64, 91, 282n14; set-
tler colonialism in, 170, 214;
territorial reserves in, 149–50
cannibalism, 49, 254n11
Carewe, Edwin, 17, 23, 71, 157,
231, 281n7; career, 23, 25,
248n43
Carmelo, Tonantzin, 162, *163*,
259n45
Carter, Forrest (Asa Carter), 143
Carver, H. P., 86, 91, 269n35
Ceremony (Silko), 138
Cesspooch, Larry, 247n28
Chandler, Jeff, 262n67
Cheechoo, Shirley, 281n7
Cheng, Anne Anlin, 111
Chestnutt, Charles, 140

Cheyenne, 78
The Chief's Daughter (1911), 67
Chorre, Gertrude, 29, 250n54,
255n16
Chorre, Joseph "Suni" Vance
(Suni War Cloud), 28, 29,
250n54
Chow, Rey, xi, 241n5
Christensen, Neil Blair, 284n30
Christian, Dorothy, 18, 157,
247n31
Christianity: compulsory, 60,
282n14; and Native American
spirituality, 186
Chude-Sokei, Louis, 73–74
Churchill, Ward, 273n90, 286n42
Clapp, Louisa Amelia Knapp
Smith, 263–64n85
Clifford, James, 285n37
Cody, Iron Eyes, *103*, *112*; career,
102; in *Ernest Goes to Camp*,
134–35; *Iron Eyes: My Life
as a Hollywood Indian*, 104,
111, 113–17; as Hollywood
Indian, 104–6, 109, 116–17,
119, 122, 124, 127, 135; in
Keep America Beautiful ads,
8, 102–4, 107, 124, 181; Native
American support for, 133–34,
135–36; outing of, 104, 126–27,
130, 131–33, 270n47; redfacing act by, 8, 109–10, 115, 119,
123, 133, 135, 136, 143–44;
support to Native American
community by, 134
Cody, Robert "Tree," 133–34, 136
Cody, William F. (Buffalo Bill),
270n47

Cohen, Paula Marantz, 46–47, 254n2
Collins, James, 4
colonization and colonialism, 125; in Canada, 170, 214, 218; and gendered violence, 101; legacies of, 158, 176; and Native American representations, 48–49, 59, 69–70, 136, 242n8, 254n8; resistance to, 39, 147, 191–92. *See also* decolonization
Columbus, Christopher, 180, 242n9, 245n17
Comanches, 78
Cooper, James Fenimore, 122, 140, 242n9
Corbey, Raymond, 245n10
Cousineau, Marie-Hélène, 203–4
Craft, William and Ellen, 129
Crazy Horse, 159
Crèvecoeur, J. Hector St. John de, 140
Crow Nation, 180
cultural memory, 138, 271–72n80
Curtis, Edward, 196, 282n13
Curtis, Tony, 262n67
Custer Died for Your Sins (Deloria), 205
Cuthand, Thirza, 156, 281n7

dance: as act of visual sovereignty, 101; modalities of time and subjectivity in, 96; in Wild West shows and silent films, 35. See also *Evening in Paris*
Daniels, Victor. *See* Thunder Cloud, Chief

Darkfeather, Princess Mona (Josephine Workman), 249n45
Davenport, Keith, 275n30
Daves, Delmer, x
Davis, Kelley, 228
Dawes (General Allotment) Act, 54, 64, 260n51
decolonization, 111; methodologies of, 188–89; Native American filmmakers and, 18; virtual reservation and, 149, 155; visual sovereignty and, xiv. *See also* colonization and colonialism
DeCorti, Espera. *See* Cody, Iron Eyes
Deep Inside Clint Star (Alberta, 1999), 156
de Lauretis, Teresa, xi
de Léry, Jean, 254n11
Deleuze, Gilles, 44, 176
Deloria, Philip J., 14–15, 24, 31, 242n8; on playing Indian, 106, 115, 139–40, 223–24
Deloria, Vine, Jr., 194, 205, 206
Del Rio, Dolores, 53
del Valle, John, 1
DeMille, Cecil B., x, 25, 249n45
DeMille Indians: exercise of visual sovereignty by, 45; petition for recognition of, 1–2, 3, 5, 244n9; tricksteresque performances of, 32. *See also* Hollywood Indians
Dench, Ernest Alfred, 37, 119–20
Devereaux, Minnie. *See* Ha Ha, Minnie
Dillon, Eddie, 74

Dix, Richard, 262n67
Dixie Chicks, 238, 239–40
Dixon, Thomas, 140
dog sacrifice, 78, 79, 262n73
Doxtater, Deborah, 172
Doxtater, Michael G., 187
Doyle, Jennifer, 216, 286–87n51
Dozier, Edward P., 20
Dr. Quinn, Medicine Woman, 114
DuBois, W. E. B., 15, 65, 105
Dunn, Carolyn, 73
DuPea, Tatzumbie, 28–29, 250n50, 255n16
Dussel, Enrique, 183

Eco, Umberto, 137, 284n31
Edison, Thomas, 35
The Education of Little True (Carter), 143
Elmer, Jonathan, 81
Empson, G. Raymond, 123
environment: Indigenous concern for, 159–60, 181–82, 200; in Indigenous world view, 172; Native Americans portrayed as stewards of, 121–22, 123–24, 126; white guilt about, 139
Ernest Goes to Camp (1987), 134–35
Escobar, Zoe, 243n3
Esquimaux Village (1901), 63
ethnic spectatorship, xi, 241n5
Evening in Paris, 93–94, 95–101, 98
Eyre, Chris, 18, 189, 195, 281n7; career, 160–61; highlights Native American spiritual-
ity, 9, 106, 182; Imprint, 108, 160–69; Smoke Signals, 209

Fairbanks, Mary, 25
Faris, James C., 219
Fatty and Minnie He-Haw (1914), 74–79
Faulkner, William, 140
Fauset, Jessie, 140
Federal Acknowledgment Project, 2, 3–4
Fidler, Leslie, 47
Fienup-Riordan, Ann, 210
film: ethnographic, 207–8, 214, 218–19, 280n1; hypervisibility of Native Americans in, x, 34–35; incorporation of social groups as spectators of, 44, 50, 253n88, 255n15; and Native American identity, 66, 157, 188; and photography, 88, 115; and racial politics, 32, 50; as shield for Native Americans, xiii, 11; temporal staging of, xiii, 172. See also Hollywood; Native American representations and stereotypes; silent era; westerns
First Americans in the Arts (FAITA), 243n3
First Nations United, 238, 290n40
Flaherty, Robert, 190–93, 280nn1–2, 281n9; ethnocentric biases of, 195, 206, 207, 210
Fleming, Kathleen, 218
Floodgates (1924), 261n56
Forrest, Edwin, 70

Fourth Cinema, 18, 19, 247n32
Friar, Natasha A. and Ralph E.,
    15–16
frontier, 46–47
Fryberg, Stephanie A., 225

Galle, Theodor de, 48–49, 254n8
Gallop, Jane, 256n18
Garroutte, Eva Marie, 141
Gaup, Nils, 18
Geiogamah, Hanay, 234
gender: equality among Inuit, 216,
    286n51; European American
    colonialism and, 50, 101;
    matrilineal culture among
    Haudenosaunee, 178–79, 188.
    See also Native American rep-
    resentations and stereotypes;
    women, Native American
General, Emily, 176, 278n49
genocide, 16, 71, 85, 183; cultural,
    16, 60; rendered as acceptable,
    46, 145, 223; visual, 156
Gettino, Octavio, 17, 203
Ghost Dance religion, 60, 90,
    258n37
ghostly Indian: about, 107; blurs
    time/space boundaries, 146,
    147, 162, 164–66, 168–69;
    history of in U.S., 120–21,
    166–67, 273–74n4; in Imprint,
    9, 108, 146, 147, 160, 162–63,
    165–66, 167, 168–69; Iron
    Eyes Cody as, 9, 105–6, 124;
    and redfacing, 104; as resis-
    tance to colonial genocide,
    145–46, 152; as technique of

removal, 124–25. See also red-
    facing; vanishing Indian trope
Gibson, Mel, 34
Ginsburg, Elaine K., 129
Ginsburg, Faye, 156, 195, 201; on
    digital technologies, 233, 236,
    259–60n47
global warming, 159–60, 200
González, Jennifer A., 155
Gordon, Avery, 145–46, 152
Grande, Sandy, 283n18
Gray, Barbara, 224
Green, Lyndsay, 196
Green, Rayna, 104, 126, 256n22;
    on playing Indian, 106, 229
Greenblatt, Stephen, 245n17
Greene, Graham, 62, 259n45
Grey Owl (Archie Belaney),
    273n90
Griffith, Alison, 218
Griffith, D. W., 69, 70
Gunsmoke, 114

Ha Ha, Minnie (Minnie
    Deveraux), 55, 81; career,
    25, 55–56; critiques Native
    American representations, 56;
    in Fatty and Minnie He-Haw,
    74–79; in Mickey, 79–86;
    nuanced redfacing roles by, 8,
    51, 53, 54, 74, 80, 101
Handsome Lake, 186
Hansen, Miriam, 44, 207, 253n88,
    255n15
Harper, Elijah, 176–78, 177,
    278n51
Harrington, M. Raymond, 118,
    268n28

Harte, Bret, 264n85
Haudenosaunee (Iroquois), 181,
    277–78n46; Confederacy of,
    181, 198–99, 277n38; and
    democracy, 22; matrilineal
    culture of, 178–79, 188; world
    view of, 170–72
Hayakawa, Sessue, 53, 262n67
Hays Code (Motion Picture
    Production Code), 10
Hearne, Joanna, 64, 261n54
The Heart of Wetona (1919), 67
Hegel, Georg Wilhelm Friedrich,
    183
Helpless Maiden Makes an "I"
    Statement (Cuthand, 2000),
    156
Hereniko, Vilisoni, 18
Highwater, Jamake (Jay Marks),
    273n90
Hoebel, E. Adamson, 78
Hollywood: alternative viewpoints
    presented by, 13, 16–17, 35,
    61, 64–65, 67–69, 80; colony of
    Native American entertainers
    in, 1–2, 3, 25, 32, 118, 243n3,
    244n5; contemporary repre-
    sentations of Native Americans
    by, 62; cowboy-and-Indian
    trope by, 244n5; and cultural
    genocide, 16, 60; depiction of
    shamans by, 164; immigrants as
    spectators of, 44, 50, 253n88,
    255n15; Indigenous filmmak-
    ers' resistance to, 160, 203;
    Native American absence/
    presence in, xii, 13, 71–72,
    racist stereotyping by, xii, 35,

36, 70, 258n41; representa-
    tional regime of, x, 53, 56–57,
    135, 229, as source of Native
    American stereotypes, ix, x, xii,
    xiv, 36, 114, 132–33; version
    of American history by, 50; as
    virtual reservation, 43–45. See
    also DeMille Indians; film;
    Native American filmmakers;
    Native American representa-
    tions; silent era; westerns
Hollywood Indians: as cultural
    shield, 11, 20; demograph-
    ics of, 27; disruption of
    Indigenous representations
    by, 20–21, 52–53, 56, 85, 93;
    establishment of virtual res-
    ervation by, 45; iconic image
    of, 34–35; Iron Eyes Cody
    playing of, 104–5, 109, 116–17,
    119,122, 127, 135; as marker
    for Native American identity,
    36, 37; preference for non-
    Indigenous actors to play, 39,
    41, 71, 73, 104, 119–20, 128,
    250n52, 262n67; and popular
    culture, 7–8, 15–16, revision of
    understanding of, 53, 93; ste-
    reotyped dress of, 27–28, 41,
    76, 109; as tricksters, 20–21,
    32, 73, 88. See also DeMille
    Indians; Native American
    actors; redfacing
Hope, Melanie Printup, 275n25
Hózhó of Native Women (Singer,
    1997), 157
Huhndorf, Shari M., 106
Humming Bird, 255n16

humor: in *Atanarjuat*, 212, 213,
220; Native Americans and,
41–42, 77, 188
hyperreality, 137

Igloolik, Nunavut, 214, 217–18,
283n21
Igloolik Isuma Inc., 203, 281n7,
284n26; as community-based
collective, 200–201, 218,
286n46; reworks ethnographic
elements, 9, 201, 204, 211, 220
illuriik (opponents/partners),
213–14, 220
Imagining Indians (Masayesva,
1992), 156
immigrants, 106, 197, 207;
Hollywood and, 44, 50,
253n88, 255n15
"imperialist nostalgia," 32, 108,
251n59
Imprint (Eyre, 2007), 160–69,
163, 165, 169, 232; ghost narrative in, 9, 108, 146, 147,
160, 162–63, 165–66, 167,
168–69; image of medicine
man in, 164–65, 168; portrayal
of women in, 161–62, 276n34;
production of, 161, 275–76n30;
prophecy in, 160, 168
Independent Indigenous Film and
Media (IIFM), 238
Indian Actors Association (IAA),
243n3
Indian Actors Workshop, 243n3
"Indian modernity," 14–15
Indigenous Action Media, 236

Indigenous Holocaust (Whiteman,
2008), 238, 239
Indigenous people. *See* Native
Americans
Internet, 9; Canadian Indigenous
communities and, 259–60n47,
284n30; and "outernet," 237–
38; as space on virtual reservation, 150, 153, 233–34
InterTribal Entertainment (ITE),
243n3
In the Land of the Headhunters
(Curtis, 1914), 196, 282n13
Into the West (2005), 259n45
Inuit: cultural practices of, 204;
and "Eskimo" term, 280–81n2;
gender equality among, 216,
286n51; impact of colonialism on, 218; and media, 203,
284n30; oral storytelling
tradition by, 9, 205, 209, 220;
portrayal of in *Nanook of the
North*, 190–91, 192–93, 195–
96, 210; shamanism among,
286n49; and visual sovereignty,
194–95, 200–3. *See also*
Igloolik Isuma Inc.
Inuit Broadcasting Corporation
(IBC), 63, 195
Inuit Tapirisat of Canada, 195
*Iron Eyes: My Life as a Hollywood
Indian* (Cody), 104, 111,
113–17
Iroquois. *See* Haudenosaunee
Isuma: Inuit Studies Reader
(2004), 211
Isuma TV, 63, 201–2, 259–60n47
It Starts with a Whisper (Niro,

1993), 9, 108, 169–81, *174*,
177, 232; ghost image in,
146, 147; prophecy in, 170,
175, 177–78, 180, 187; strong
female character in, 162; time
and space in, 177, 178, 180;
vision quest in, 170, 174

Jackson, Helen Hunt, 263–64n85
Jacoby, Karl, 226, 227
Jay, Gregory S., 70
Jefferson, Thomas, 71, 122,
269n36
Jemison, G. Peter, 199
The Jesuit Relations, 86
John & Ken Show, 225
Johnson, E. Pauline
(Tekahionwake), 13, 176, 179,
246n17, 278n49
Johnson, James Weldon, 140
Johnson, Nobel, 53, 262n67
Jolson, Al, 71, 104, 267n3
Jones, F. Richard, 79
Joss, Jonathan, 62
Just Squaw (1919), 67

Kahgegagahbowh (George
Copway), 13, 246n17
Kalen Company, 61
*Katahdin: Wigwam's Tales of the
Abnaki Tribe*, 96
Katt, Madeline, Theriault, 255n16
Keefe, Julia, 266n116
Keep America Beautiful Inc.
(KAB) ad campaign, 8, 102–4;
Native American representa-
tion in, 107, 121–22, 123, 124–
25; second version of, 125–26;

Tree on, 181–82. *See also* Cody,
Iron Eyes
Kilpatrick, Jacquelyn, 18, 247n31
King, Henry, 57
King, Martin Luther, Jr., 223
King of the Hill, 62
Kolodny, Annette, 279n64
Kunuk, Mary, 157, 203–4
Kunuk, Zacharias, 18, 211, 219;
on goal of *Atanarjuat*, 219; and
Igloolik Isuma, 201, 286n46

Lakota, 40, 159. *See also* Sioux
Lancaster, Burt, 262n67
Landzelius, Kyra, 233
Lange, Timothy, 226
Larsen, Nella, 130, 135, 140
Laughing Boy (Van Dyke, 1934),
57, 257n28
Law and Order: SVU, 62
Lear, Jonathan, 180
Lefebvre, Henri, 44, 150
Leigh, Michael, 203
lesbians and gays, 10–11
Leuthold, Steven, 18, 60, 138,
217, 247n31
Levine, Carole Quattro, 161, 162,
276n34
Lévi-Strauss, Claude, 210–11
Lewis, Sinclair, 140
Lim, Bliss Cua, 146, 147, 165–66
Limerick, Patricia Nelson, 253n1
Linn, Carolyn, 161, 275–76nn30–
31
Linn, Eric, 275 76n30
Linn, Marc, 275–76n30
Linn, Michael, 160, 161, 275–
76n30

Linn Productions, 161, 275–76n30
Lipsitz, George, 272n81
Little Chief, Tommy, 94
Little Dove's Romance (1911), 66
Little Feather, Sacheen (Maria
Louise Cruz), 273n90
Littlefield, Daniel F., 268n28
Little House on the Prairie, 114
Loeffler, Andrew, 228
Lomawaima, K. Tsianina, 197
The Lone Ranger: 1938 serial, 1;
TV program, 26, 114
Long, Sylvester. *See* Long Lance,
Chief Buffalo Child
Longboy, Zachary, 275n25, 281n7
Long Lance (Long), 142
Long Lance, Chief Buffalo Child
(Sylvester Long), 92, 94, 142–
43, 265n104
Look to the Wilderness (Burden),
86–87
Lorde, Audre, 18, 247n34
Los Angeles, Calif. 32, 244n5.
See also Hollywood, Native
American colony in
Los Angeles Times, 226
Lott, Eric, 70
Louvish, Simon, 80, 262n78
Lowell, John, 261n56
Lowell Film Production Company,
261n56
Luna, James, 155
Lyon, G. F., 211
Lyons, Scott Richard, 197–98

Mabel Normand Feature Film
Company, 79, 262n78

Making the Movies (Dench, 1915),
37
Making the White Man's Indian
(Aleiss), 17
Mala, Ray, 13, 25
Mala, Ted, 286
Malécot, André, 29
Malick, Terrence, 34
La Malinche, 49, 254n9
Many Treaties, Chief (William
Malcolm Hazlett), 26, 29
Maoris, 18–19
Mardi Gras Indians, 142,
272nn81–82
Martin, Wendy, 58
Martinelli, Elsa, 262n67
Martinez, Wilton, 284–85n31
Marubbio, M. Elise, 48, 54, 74,
80, 84,
Masayesva, Victor, Jr., 18, 247n31,
281n7; career, 156, 275n22
Matoaka-Amonute. *See*
Pocahontas
Mauryama, Joe, 284n30
Maya, Just an Indian (1913), 67
Maynor, Malinda, 131, 281n7
McBride, Bunny, 93, 95, 257n28,
257n29, 257n30, 265n90,
265n102, 265n104
McClintock, Anne, 49, 254n8,
279n64
McDaniel, Hattie, 53
McGarry, Molly, 125
McMaster, Gerald, 149–50
McNary, William (Okah Tubbee),
273n90
Means, Russell, 259n45
Medicine Woman, 78

Meek, Barbra, 88
Melville, Herman, 81, 286–87n52
Merriam Report, 68, 260n51
Metacom (King Philip), 70, 226–27, 274n4
Micheaux, Oscar, 53
Michel, Manuel, 247n32
Mickey (1918), 79–86, 262n78, 264n85
Miguel, Muriel, 92–93, 96, 101
Miles, Elaine, 62
miscegenation, 58, 266n109; portrayal in film, 36, 65–67, 75, 83, 85–86
Mita, Meralta, 18
Mithlo, Nancy Marie, 181
Moby Dick (Melville), 286–87n52
Moctezuma, 186
Moffat, Tracey, 18
Molly Spotted Elk: A Penobscot in Paris (McBride), 93
Moore, Jean Archambaud, 93
Morris, Meaghan, 36
Moses, L. G., 31, 258n40
Motion Picture World, 41, 42
Mould, Tom, 186–87
Mount Rushmore, 108
Murphy, Jacqueline Shea, 252n64
Murray, David, 87
music videos, 235–37
My People the Sioux (Standing Bear), 39

Nakamura, Lisa, 237
Nanook of the North (Flaherty, 1922), 192, 281n9; Atanarjuat and, 210, 212; as ethnographic film, 210–11, 280n1; Inuit view of, 195–96; laughing at camera in, 190–92, 280n2; portrayal of Inuit in, 190–91, 192–93, 195–96, 210
Naranjo-Morse, Nora, 153
Nash, J. Carrol, 262n67
National Congress of American Indians, 4
Native American actors: activism of, 32–34, 39, 42, 44; agency by, 5–6, 31, 32, 43, 52; as disseminators of Indigenous images, 22–23, 30–31; early history of, 245–46n17; economic opportunities for, 31, 61; Hollywood colony of, 1–2, 3, 25, 32, 118, 243n3, 244n5; Indigenous Californians as, 27–28; listing of during silent era, 25–26, 250n49; nuanced and complex history of, 3, 13, 15, 31, 53, 101; redfacing by, 11, 53, 59–60, 73, 93–94, 116; sought to deconstruct stereotypes, 2, 11, 31–32, 37, 43, 59–60, 88, 91–92; stereotyped dress of, 27–28, 41, 76, 109; as trickster figures, 20–21, 32, 43; uncredited roles by, x, 143, 208; as underpaid, 143; in Wild West shows and anthropological spectacles, 22–23, 31, 245n10, 251n58; women as, 46, 50–51, 53, 54–59, 67, 74, 80, 93–94. See also Hollywood Indians

Native American filmmakers:
    agency and empowerment by,
    32, 52; cultural parameters for,
    15, 30, 193; decolonizing work
    by, 18, 188–89; and dissemina-
    tion of Indigenous images,
    22–23, 31–32; environmental
    concerns of, 159–60, 181–82;
    ethnographic film conven-
    tions by, 208, 219; and Fourth
    Cinema, 18; ideological and
    cultural work by, 19, 30–32, 53,
    156–57, 160, 208; international
    project of, 202–3; Inuit, 194,
    203, 204; "laugh at the camera"
    tactic of, 193, 213; lists of,
    246–47n28, 275n25, 281n7;
    and Native American spiritual-
    ity, 148–49; proliferation of, 12,
    17–18; resistance to Hollywood
    by, 160, 203; visual sovereignty
    by, 19, 30, 31, 193–94, 196,
    200, 208, 240
Native American representations
    and stereotypes: in advertis-
    ing, xii, 107, 121–22, 123,
    124–25; California Indians
    and, 263nn83–84; and colonial
    fantasy, 15, 136; depicted as
    absent, 12–13, 242n8; depicted
    as bloodthirsty savages, xii, 36,
    69, 81, 84, 122; depicted as
    doomed and lifeless, x, 9, 12,
    36, 37, 47, 77, 160; depicted as
    emasculated, 36, 47; depicted
    as invisible, x, xii, 8, 61, 106,
    160, 208; depicted as lazy and
    untrustworthy, 120; depicted

as mystical and romantic, 125,
    148; depicted as noble savage,
    xiii, 36, 122, 137; depicted as
    nostalgic anachronism, 15,
    115, 173, 208; depicted as stoic
    and silent, 12, 36, 90, 119; in
    dress, 27–28, 41, 76, 109, 121,
    132; and ethnic spectatorship,
    241n5; government policy
    regulating, 59; Hollywood as
    main source for, ix, x, xii, xiv,
    36, 114, 132–33; Indigenous
    actors' deconstruction of, 2, 11,
    31–32, 37, 43, 59–60, 80, 88,
    91–92; and Indigenous self-
    representation, 19, 107, 128,
    157, 194, 197, 240; of Inuit,
    190–91, 192–93, 195–96, 210;
    and Native American identity,
    110; Native American response
    to, ix, xi, xiii, 40–41, 42–43, 61;
    negativity of, 8, 13, 16, 178;
    as sports mascots, 225, 231;
    during Thanksgiving, 221–24,
    227, 231, 287n1; of women as
    domestic servants, 29, 250n42;
    of women as drudges, 8, 36,
    54, 75, 255n13; of women as
    sexualized maidens, 8, 36,
    48–49, 54, 58, 74, 84, 94–95;
    of women as "squaws," 54,
    256n22; of women as whore-
    traitors, 49, 50, 254n9. See also
    ghostly Indian; passing and
    impostors; redfacing; vanishing
    Indian trope
Native Americans: activism of,
    107–8; agency by, 4–5, 31,

32, 43, 44, 50, 52, 191, 240;
ceremonies by, 20, 138; conceptions of time and space,
183–84, 187; concept of sovereignty among, 111, 197–98,
243–44n5; elders among, 166;
federal recognition of, 2, 3–4,
271n74; genocide against, 16,
42–43, 46, 60, 71, 85, 145, 183,
223; and humor, 41–42, 77,
188; and identity, 3, 110–11,
121, 126, 127, 128, 131, 138;
invisibility of, x, xii, 8, 61, 72,
106, 122, 160, 208; languages
of, 87–88; mixed-blood, 84,
85–86, 141, 142, 272n86; and
oral tradition, 9, 205, 206, 209,
220; as Other, xii, 50, 80, 140,
148, 214; paternalism toward,
66; population of, 242n9,
260n50; portrayed as stewards of environment, 121–22,
123–24, 126; and primitivism,
58; self-representation by, ix,
x, 19, 107, 128, 157, 194, 197,
240; and shamanism, 164, 204,
212, 214, 215, 218, 286n49;
social conditions of, 64, 68, 85,
141, 151; as transnational community, 2–3, 13, 32, 118, 153,
243n5; white guilt toward, 32,
139, 146, 166–67; world view
of, 40, 106, 148–49, 158–59,
160, 170–72, 182–83, 186–88,
256n18. See also reservations
Native American spectators, xiii,
11, 253n80; agency by, 43;
Inuit, 195–96, 212; response to

Native American representa-
tions, ix, xi, 40–41, 61
Native American Studies, 221–22;
and Indigenous identity, 110,
111; and Indigenous spiri-
tuality and knowledge, 158,
271n77; and sovereignty, 111,
196–97
Navajos, 156
Navajo Talking Picture (Bowman,
1986), 155–56, 275n19
Navajo Times, 135, 136
Nelson, Mary Alice. See Spotted
Elk, Molly
Nelson, Mildred, 57
NervousWreck Productions,
236–37
New from Indian Country, 135
The New World (Malick, 2005), 34
New York Motion Picture
Company, 61
Niagara Falls, 178–79
Nichols, Bill, 173
Nicola, Lucy (Princess Watawaso),
94
Nimura, Lisan Kay, 58
Nimura, Yeichi, 58
Ninguira/My Grandmother
(1999), 159–60
Niro, Shelley, 9, 106, 182, 189,
195, 281n7; It Starts with a
Whisper, 108, 169–81; Suite:
Indian, 181; Tree, 181–82
Nispel, Marcus, 34
Normand, Mabel, 25, 55, 55, 79,
80, 262n78
Northern Exposure (1990–1995),
62

Nova Reperta, 48
Nunatsiq News, 209
Nunavut, 200–201, 283n21

Obomsawin, Alanis, 247n28,
   281n7
Occom, Samson, 13, 245–46n17
Office of Indian Affairs, 2, 5,
   244n9. *See also* Bureau of
   Indian Affairs
Olson, Michelle, 92–93, 96–101,
   97, 98
*The Only Good Indian . . . The
   Hollywood Gospel* (Friar and
   Friar), 15–16
Orians, G. Harrison, 242n9
Osawa, Sandra, 247n28, 281n7
OutKast, 139, 272n82
Overwhelming, 236
Owens, Louis, 115, 137, 140–41

Pablo, Lizzie, 13, *14*
Paget, Debra, 262n67
Pratt, Mary Louise, 155–56,
   275n19
Parins, James W., 268n28
Parker, Arthur C., 118, 268n28
Parker, Bertha "Birdie," 117, 118
Parker, Beulah Tahamont, 255n16
Parker, Edna L., 118
Parker, Ely S., 268n28
Passing (Larsen), 130, 135
passing and racial impostors:
   African Americans and,
   128–29, 272n81; as "ethnic
   transvestites," 142; harmful
   role of, 127, 136–37, 143;
   history of in U.S., 105, 138,

140, 273n90; Iron Eyes Cody
   and, 8, 109–10, 115, 119, 123,
   130, 133, 135, 136, 143–44;
   and Native American identity,
   106–7; Native Americans pass-
   ing as whites, 129; politics of,
   129, 131. *See also* Cody, Iron
   Eyes; redfacing
Patchell, Beverly Sourjohn, 183
Pathfinder (Nispel, 2007), 34
Pease, Donald, 145
Perry, Collin, 111, 113–14, 115–16
Peter Pan (1953), 232
Petroglyphs in Motion (Luna,
   2001), *154*, 155
photography, 88, 115, 156–57
Pickford, Mary, 25
Pilgrims, 223, 226
Pine Ridge Reservation, 161,
   276n33
Pitseolak, Peter, 195
Plato, 129
playing Indian. *See* redfacing
Plenty Coups, 180, 186
Poata, Tama, 18
Pocahontas (Matoaka-Amonute),
   13, 49, 245n17, 254n9
Pond, Roscoe, 62
Popul Vuh, 186
Porter, Joy, 268n28
Pourier, Larry, 161
prophecy: and agency, 184–85;
   and environmental concerns,
   159, 181–82; ideological and
   political work of, 185, 188; in
   Imprint, 160, 168; in *It Starts
   with a Whisper*, 170, 175,
   177–78, 180, 187; and Native

American spirituality, 158, 172, 182–83, 186–88; Silko on, 184–85, 279n65; in *Tree*, 181–82; on virtual reservation, 147–48, 152, 182
Proust, Marcel, 44
"public transcripts," 22, 248n41
Pueblo, 20

Queypo, Kalani, 259n45

"racial drag," 130–31
Ramona (King, 1910), 67
Ramone, Joey, 235–36
Rasmussen, Knud, 25, 211
Real Indian (Maynor, 1996), 131
Recollet, Lena, 181
Red Elk, Lois, 133, 270n62
redfacing, 22, 32, 104; by African Americans, 272n81; in American culture, 70–71, 139, 229; and blackface, 70, 71; defined, xii, 8; government fear of, 59; historical roots of, 106, 138; Iron Eyes Cody's, 102–3, 109–10, 115, 116, 119; as means of protection, 11, 21–22; by Native American actors, 11, 21, 53, 59–60, 73, 93–94, 116; by non-Native American actors, 39, 41, 71, 73, 104, 119–20, 128, 250n52, 262n67; politics of, 129, 131, 143; as representational violence, 71, 101, 128; and trickster figure, 20, 21. *See also* ghostly Indian; passing and racial impostors

Red Love (1925), 68, 261n56
The Redman's View (Griffith, 1909), 69–70
Redroad, Randy, 275n25, 281n7
Redskin (1929), 68
Red Wing, Princess (Lillian St. Cyr), 24, 66, 255n16; career, 24–25; works to advance Native American image, 13, 35
Reineke, Yvonne, 183
"Requickening Project," 181, 279n56
reservations: deplorable social conditions on, 64, 68, 141, 151; as ghettos, 149; oppressive structure of, 56, 141; permission needed for working outside of, 60, 258n40; as site for cultural continuity, 150–51; as "vanishing Indian" sites, 43, 44, 152. *See also* virtual reservation
Retort (2007), 235
rezKast, 235
Rickard, Jolene, 194
Roach, Joseph, 141
Robinson, Amy, 129, 143
Rodríguez, Dylan, 42
Rogin, Michael, 71
Rolling Stone, 235
Rony, Fatimah Tobing, 190–91, 195, 211, 280n2
Rosaldo, Renato, 32, 108, 251n59
Roth, Lorna, 149
Rothman, William, 191
Rousseau, Jean-Jacques, 71
Ruby, Jay, 87, 195
Running Deer, 133
Russell, Evangeline, 261n56

Russell, Ron, 132, 270n47
Ryan, Marie-Laure, 152–53

Sacajewea, 49, 254n9
Salkow, Sidney, 47
Sampson, Will, 243n3
Scheckel, Susan, 152
Schellenberg, August, 259n45
Schlereth, Thomas, 261n57
Schweig, Eric, 259n45
Scott, James C., 22, 248n41
Screen Actors Guild (SAG), 2
Seattle, Chief, 123, 269n38
Sedgwick, Eve Kosofsky, 47, 254n4
Seigworth, Gregory J., 36, 44
Selwyn, Don, 18
Sen, Ivan, 18
Sennett, Mack, 55, 74, 79, 262n74
Senungetuk, Joseph E., 210
Serres, Michel, 171
Serving Rations to the Indians, No. 1 (1898), 63–64
shamanism: among Inuit, 286n49; in *Atanarjuat*, 204, 212, 214, 215, 218; in *Imprint*, 164
Shenandoah, Leon, 182, 279n59
Sheridan, Philip, 15–16, 246n23
Shibaba, Lotus Pearl (Lotus Long), 53
Shields, Rob, 179
Shively, JoEllen, 41–42
Shohat, Ella, 12–13, 47
Sieg, Katrin, 128, 129
Sierra Club, 124
[Silence] Is a Weapon (2007), 236
The Silent Enemy (1930), 56, 86–92, 89, 92, 269n35; por-

trayal of women in, 94–95; Yellow Robe prologue to, 87–90, 101
silent film era: African Americans in, 54; European immigrants and, 44, 253n88; list of Native American actors during, 25–26; nuanced portrayal of Native Americans in, 35, 61, 63–65, 67–69, 79, 252n65; privileging of frontier during, 46–47; racist portrayals during, 35, 258n41; representation of Indigenous women in, 8, 54, 74–75, 77
Silko, Leslie Marmon, 138, 183–85, 279n65
Silverheels, Jay (Harold J. Smith), 13, 27, 243n3; career, 26; on Iron Eyes Cody, 132
Silverheels, Mary, 132
Simon, Cheryl, 132
Simpson, Audra, 88
simulation, 36, 252n68
Singer, Beverly R., 16, 156, 157, 194
Sioux, 78, 262n71. *See also* Lakota
Sitting Bull (Salkow, 1954), 47
Six Nations Reserve, 277n38, 278n46
Skye, Harriet, 247n28
Skyhawk, Sonny, 243n3
Slocum, John, 186
Smith, Andrea, 247n34
Smith, Andrew Brodie, 35–36, 61
Smith, Donald B., 265n104
Smith, Linda Tuhiwai, 188–89
Smith, Paul Chaat, x, xii
Smith, Santee, 153

Smoak, Gregory Ellis, 258n37
Smohalla, 186
Smoke Signals (Eyre and Alexie, 1998), 153, 209–10
Sobchack, Vivien, 88, 172
Soja, Edward W., 150
Solanas, Fernando, 17, 203
Sollors, Werner, 142
The Souls of Black Folk (DuBois), 65, 105
sovereignty, 3, 194; cinema of, 30; cultural and intellectual, 30, 194, 251n55; European vs. Native American conception of, 198, 283n18; as key Native American concept, 111, 197–98, 243–44n5; misunderstanding of, 197; and prophecy, 184; representational, 30, 217; and "strategic essentialism," 200; visual sovereignty relation to, 193–94, 200. *See also* visual sovereignty
Spears, Michael, 259n45
Speck, Frank, 257n29
a spiritual land claim (Christian, 2006), 157
sports mascots, 225, 231
Spotted Elk, Molly (Mary Alice Nelson), 13, 92; career, 56–59, 257n29; death, 92; influence on Indigenous artists, 92–93; nuanced redfacing by, 8, 51, 53, 54, 101; portrayal of in *An Evening in Paris*, 93–94, 95–101; in *The Silent Enemy*, 86–92

The Squaw Man (DeMille, 1914), x, 25, 67, 249n45, 257n28
Stam, Robert, 12–13, 47, 178
Standing Bear, Luther, 25, 38; activism of, 13, 33, 39; autobiography, 37, 39–40, 262n71; on non-Indigenous imitators in film, 37, 39, 119, 120
Standing Horse, John, 41
stereotypes. *See* Native American representations and stereotypes
Stevens, Charles, 25
Still Alive (Thomas, 2008), 236
Storyteller (Silko), 185
Strongheart (1914), 67–68
Strongheart, Nipo T., 25, 26, 29, 249–50n48
Studi, Wes, 259n45
Sturken, Marita, 138, 271–72n80
Suite: Indian (Niro, 2005), 181
Sun Dance, 262n73
Suni War Cloud. *See* Chorre, Joseph "Suni" Vance
Suquamish, 269n38

Tahachee, Chief (Jeff Davis Tahchee Cypert), 25, 29, 243n3
Tahamont, Beulah, 118, 268n28
Tahamont, Elijah (Chief Dark Cloud), 118
Tallchief, Alexander, 253n80
Tamahori, Lee, 18
Tantaquidgeon, Gladys, 257n29
Tatu, Lee Thunderbear, 133
Taylor, Clyde R., 53–54
Taylor, Diana, 52

Tekahionwake. *See* Johnson, E.
  Pauline
television, 62, 259n45
Television Northern Canada
  (TVNC), 63
Tenskwatawa, 186
Terranova, Tiziana, 237
Thanksgiving: AIM protest on, 108;
  historical roots of, 224, 226–27,
  287–88n4; as myth, 224, 229,
  230; racial stereotyping in,
  221–24, 227, 231, 287n1
Third Cinema, 17, 203, 247n29
Thomas, Redwing (Red), 236–37
Thorpe, Jim, 250n49
Through Navajo Eyes (Worth and
  Adair), 156, 247n28
Thunderbird, Richard Davis, 29,
  33, 34
Thunder Cloud, Chief (Victor
  Daniels), 25, 29, 242–43n2;
  career, 1–2. *See also* DeMille
  Indians
Thunderface, Chief (Miguel Soto
  Holguin), 250n49
Tin Man (2007), 259n45
Tonto, ix, 1, 26, 132. *See also*
  Silverheels, Jay
Tootoosis, Gordon, 259n45
Tousey, Sheila, 259n45
The Tourists (1912), 67
Trail of Broken Treaties, 108
transnational Indigenous com-
  munity: in Southern California,
  1–2, 25, 32, 118, 243n3, 244n5;
  visual sovereignty and, 196
Travels in Hyperreality (Eco), 137
Tree (Niro, 2006), 181, *182*

tribal recognition, 2, 3–4, 271n74
Tribal Touring Program (TTP), 235
tricksters, 20, 87; Hollywood
  Indians as, 20–21, 32, 73, 88
Trujillo, Raoul, 259n45
Tsosie, Michael, 250n52
Turner, Dale, 158–59
Turner, Frederick Jackson, 46,
  253n1, 254n2
Tutelo, 173, 277–78n46
Twain, Mark, 140
Twain, Shania (Eileen Regina
  Edwards), 140, 272n84
Twohatchet, Deron, 275n25
Two Row Wampum Belt Treaty,
  198–99

Unkalunt, Atalie, 255n16
Urban Indian Relocation
  Program, 32
U.S. government Native American
  policy, 71; forced assimilation, 36, 60–61, 64, 66–67,
  91, 260n51; regulation of film
  plots, 59; tribal lands, 64; tribal
  recognition, 2, 3–4, 271n74;
  Wild West shows, 252n64,
  258n40; work permits needed
  off reservation, 60, 258n40. *See
  also* boarding schools

Valentine, Robert, 59
van der Straet, Jan, 48–50, 254n8
Van Dyke, W. S., 57
The Vanishing American (1925),
  67
The Vanishing Indian, 63
vanishing Indian trope, x, 73, 107,

148, 238; as colonial justifica-
tion, xii, 37, 242n8; cult of,
242n9; history of, 122, 269n36;
Iron Eyes Cody and, 8, 124,
127; nostalgic glorification
of, 173–74, 223; in prologue
to *The Silent Enemy*, 87, 90;
tourist interest in, 43. *See also*
ghostly Indian
Varga, Darrell, 175
Velez, Lupe, 23, 53
Vernallis, Carol, 235
Vestal, Stanley, 77
Victorianism, 71, 261n57
virtual reservation: in *Atanarjuat*,
217; communitarian impulse
on, 153, 274–75n17; as decolonizing space, 149, 155; defined,
xii; DeMille Indians and, 45;
fosters agency and empowerment, 44, 52, 240; Hollywood
as, 43–45; Internet as space
on, 150, 153, 233–34; modes
of interpreting, 152–53; music
videos and, 239; prophecy on,
147, 148, 152, 182; reinvigorat-
ing Indigenous concepts on,
152, 155–56, 182; as rereading
of time and space, 150, 153; as
site for critiquing representations and stereotypes, xiii, 9,
188; as space between material
world and imagination, 44,
152, 153; as space between
media and community, 150
visual sovereignty, xiv, 93, 175,
198–200, 233; and *Atanarjuat*,
193; and creating self-repre-

sentations, 19, 128, 157, 194,
197, 240; dance as act of,
101; defined, xii, 9; DeMille
Indians' exercise of, 45; and
ethnographic films, 208;
illuriik as form of, 213–14; and
intellectual health, 196; and
landscape, 216; "laughing at
the camera" as tactic of, 190–
93, 213; and legal sovereignty,
193–94, 200; political work of,
31, 201–2; prehistory of, 30,
194–95
Vizenor, Gerald, 252n68, 272n86;
on impostors, 136; on Native
American "survivance," 180,
241n3

Walker, George Lee, 29
Walker, Ira, 29
Wallace, Ernest, 78
Walton, Jonathan, 223
Wampanoag, 70, 224, 226, 274n4,
287n4
Wantura, Princess, 94
War Paint Club (WPC), 243n3
Warrior, Robert Allen, 194
Wayne, John, 104, 267n3
Weaver, Hilary N., 110
Weaver, Jace, 110–11, 274n17
Weinberger, Harrold, 13
Wellman, William, 28–29
Westerman, Floyd Red Crow,
205, 206
westerns: as Americans' source of
"knowledge" about Indigenous
people, 114; colonial goals of,
59; homosocial relationships

westerns (*continued*)
in, 47, 254n4; masculinist paradigm of, 46, 47–48; representation of Native Americans in, x, xiv, 35, 61, 77, 115
White, Jerry, 208
White, Patricia, 10
White Buffalo, Charlie, 161, 162, 276n36
White Fawn's Devotion (Young Deer, 1910), 65–66
Whiteman, Missy, 238
Whitman, Richard, 247n28
Wiget, Andrew, 187
Wild West shows, ix, 34, 50, 91; hyperreality in, 137; Native American dance in, 35; Native American employees of, 22–23, 31, 245n10, 251n58; U.S. government and, 252n64, 258n40
Wilkins, David E., 197
Williams, Bert, 73–74
Williamson, Karla Jessen, 286n51
Wilson, Richard A. "Dick," 161
Wilson, Terry P., 110
Wolf Lake (2001–2002), 62
Womack, Craig, 36–37
women, Native American: as absent in Hollywood films, 67, 162; and cannibal figure, 49, 254n11; and discursive agency, 22; disenfranchisement of in Canada, 91; Inuit, 216, 286n51; and land, 184, 254n8, 279n64; list of female actors, 53; Minnie Ha Ha resisting standard image of, 54, 74, 80; portrayal in *Imprint*, 161–62, 276n34; portrayal in *The Silent*

Enemy, 94–95; portrayal of as drudges, 8, 36, 54, 75, 255n13; portrayal as sexualized maidens, 8, 36, 48–49, 54, 58, 74, 84, 94–95; portrayal as squaws, 54, 256n22; portrayal as whore-traitors, 49, 50, 254n9; portrayal as domestic servants, 29, 250n42; television roles of, 62. *See also* gender
Wong, Anna May, 53
Worth, Sol, 156, 247n28
Wounded Knee, 174; 1890 massacre, 16, 60, 161, 163, 165, 197, 258n37; 1973 occupation, 108, 161
Wovoka, 186, 258n37

X-Indian Chronicles: The Book of Mausape (Yeahpau), 235

Yamamoto, Traise, 22, 130
Yeahpau, Thomas M., 235
Yellow Robe, Chauncey, 89: career, 250n49; death, 92; prologue to *The Silent Enemy* by, 87–90, 101
Yoshino, Kenji, 248n41
Young, James, 79
Young Deer, James, 17, 24, 25, 65–66, 71, 157, 281n7; career, 23–24, 248–49n43; works to advance Native American image, 13, 35–36, 231
Young Deer's Return, 24
YouTube, 9, 235, 237

Zuni, 187–88

CPSIA information can be obtained at www.ICGtesting.com
Printed in the USA
LVOW06s0139100116

469917LV00001B/66/P

9 780803 245976